1500+

MW00812396

Chalk has correctly put a finger on considers to be a critical challenge to Christians; divided loyalties between Christian and traditional beliefs put, 'syncretism'. In the 21st century church, secularism and post-modernism swell the ranks of other faiths existing alongside Christianity. We are reminded in this work that ATR continues to be the main vehicle of assimilation but never at convergence with the truth claims of our Lord and Savior Jesus Christ. Thus, life and life in abundance continues to elude the average African Christian. This is a significant work in exploring the de-syncretization of the church for Africa's emancipation and eternal salvation.

Aiah Foday-Khabenje
General Secretary/CEO
Association of Evangelicals in Africa (AEA), Nairobi, Kenya

In his book, *Making Disciples in Africa*, Dr. Chalk lays out an analysis of the African worldview that is a must read for all non-African Christians who plan on working anywhere on the continent. To understand how Christianity is viewed and received in Africa you must first know what the African worldview is. This book will answer a lot of questions and maybe save many from hours of frustration for someone trying to understand why the Africa church is miles wide but only inches deep.

Jim Dearman
Assemblies of God World Missions
Missionary to Burkina Faso, Togo and Sierra Leone

Dr Chalk's philosophical approach brings a new nuance to the issue that was not known before. I believe the book provides a useful basis, not only for a philosophical assessment, but also for a biblical examination of the problem of syncretism in the African church.

J. Boscoe Bangura, PhD.
Academic Dean
The Evangelical College of Theology, Freetown, Sierra Leone

Very few books can educate and motivate the reader to apply themselves to kingdom work as God used the words of Nehemiah, with the result that the people 'strengthened their hands for the good work' (Neh 2:18). This book can allow the intentional, kingdom-seeking reader to vividly see the need for redemption in Christ in Africa and identify essential road markers on the path that lead there. I say this from experience as one who discovered Dr. Chalk's book when it was a little known doctoral thesis. It became one of the richest gems of guidance that God used to help structure the vision for a Christian higher education institute formulated to transform Africa through the breadth of biblical worldview education across theology, the humanities and the sciences. Feast on the depth of Dr. Chalk's research which so clearly sets an African worldview in the light of a biblical worldview. As Africa is poised for a Reformation to becoming a leader of the global body of Christ, now is the time to thoroughly digest the research contained herein.

Kenneth D. Turnbull, PhD., Rev.
Executive Director
African Christian University, Lusaka, Zambia

Making Disciples in Africa

Langham
GLOBAL LIBRARY

Making Disciples in Africa

Engaging Syncretism in the African Church
Through Philosophical Analysis of Worldviews

Jack Chalk

GLOBAL LIBRARY

© 2013 by Jack Chalk

Published 2013 by Langham Global Library
an imprint of Langham Creative Projects

Langham Partnership
PO Box 296, Carlisle, Cumbria CA3 9WZ, UK
www.langham.org

ISBNs:
978-1-907713-71-2 Print
978-1-907713-70-5 Mobi
978-1-907713-69-9 ePub

Jack Chalk has asserted his right under the Copyright, Designs and Patents Act, 1988 to be identified as the Author of this work.

All rights reserved. No part of this publication may be reproduced, stored in a retrieval system or transmitted, in any form or by any means, electronic, mechanical, photocopying, recording or otherwise, without the prior written permission of the publisher or the Copyright Licensing Agency.

Scriptures taken from the Holy Bible, New International Version®, NIV®. Copyright © 1973, 1978, 1984, 2011 by Biblica, Inc.™

British Library Cataloguing in Publication Data

Chalk, Jack Pryor author.
Making disciples in Africa.
1. Christianity--Africa. 2. Christian life--Africa.
3. Christian life--Biblical teaching. 4. Christians--Africa--Attitudes.
I. Title
248'.096-dc23

ISBN-13: 9781907713712

Cover & Book Design: projectluz.com

Langham Partnership actively supports theological dialogue and a scholars right to publish but does not necessarily endorse the views and opinions set forth, and works referenced within this publication or guarantee its technical and grammatical correctness. Langham Partnership does not accept any responsibility or liability to persons or property as a consequence of the reading, use or interpretation of its published content.

Contents

Preface

At the time of this writing the church in Africa is growing faster in sheer numbers than in any other place or time in the history of Christianity. Statistically, sixty-five per cent of the population in sub-Saharan Africa is professing to be Christian. Historically, this would be considered a recent phenomenon but enough time has passed and the percentage is large enough, that by this time there should be some Christian shaping of African culture. The fact that this does not seem to be the case has been the impetus of this work.

Based upon my years of living in an African village while teaching at an African Bible college, and my considerable research on the subjects of African worldview and religion, it has been evident that the lack of Christian influence on the culture has a reason. New Christians are holding on to their African worldview while trying to assimilate new Christian doctrines into it. The result is syncretism. The purpose of this book is to present an analysis of the belief system of the worldviews behind the religions of Christianity and African Traditional Religion with a view toward helping the Christian church in Africa deal with syncretism in the religious beliefs and practices of its members. I will attempt to provide a framework for Christians in Africa to do a critical examination of their cultural worldview assumptions on a philosophical basis so that they can see where they concur and conflict with the Christian or biblical worldview.

There is a paucity of published works on worldview analysis in combating syncretism in the Christian church worldwide. Therefore, it is hoped that the method of worldview analysis put forth in this book can be used as a model to compare the biblical worldview with any other worldview, religious or secular. Areas of conflict are areas that people would need to change their views in order to believe what a Christian should believe, not just regarding salvation, but reflecting a new creation with a renewed mind.

Acknowledgements

Without the help and support of others this work would never have been completed. My profound and heartfelt gratitude is extended to the following:

- The General Secretary and staff at the Evangelical Fellowship of Sierra Leone for their sponsorship and oversight during our missionary tenure in that beautiful country.
- The Principal, staff and students at The Evangelical College of Theology in Jui, Sierra Leone for the way they, as my African colleagues, accepted me, shared their life experiences with me and helped me learn their culture.
- Prof Gerrie J A Lubbe at the University of South Africa for his kind, gentle and intellectual guidance in the thesis writing process that became the basis for this book.
- My precious wife, Ann, without whose loving support and encouragement I could do nothing.

This book is an adaptation of a thesis titled 'Genesis 1–11 and the African Worldview: Conflict or Conformity?' submitted to the University of South Africa in accordance with the requirements for the degree of Doctor of Literature and Philosophy (DLitt et Phil) in Religious Studies in 2006.

1

Introduction

Traditional religions are not primarily for the individual, but for
his community of which he is a part. Chapters of African religion
are written everywhere in the life of the community, and in traditional society there are no irreligious people. *To be human is to
belong to the whole community, and to do so involves participating
in the beliefs, ceremonies, rituals and festivities of that community.
A person cannot detach himself from the religion of his group, for to
do so is to be severed from his roots, his foundation, his context of
security, his kinships, and the entire group of those who make him
aware of his own existence.* To be without one of these corporate
elements of life, is to be out of the whole picture. Therefore, to be
without religion amounts to a self-excommunication from the
entire life of society, and African peoples do not know how to
exist without religion (Mbiti 1969:3, emphasis mine).

This book is concerned with the religions of Christianity and African
Traditional Religion (ATR) and the areas of conflict and conformity
in the worldviews behind those religions. As reflected in the above quote,
religion is an integral part of the lives of African peoples. Every book and
article on African Traditional Religion witnesses to that truth. Those from
the West will have trouble comprehending religion being such an integral
part of one's life. For most Westerners, religion is a set of beliefs loosely held
and practiced by going to a Christian church on Sunday morning. For the
traditional African, 'church' happens when the events of the day call for it.
Sickness and consultation with a herbalist or sorcerer, prayers and gifts to
ancestors, the rituals performed during rites of passage, the harvest festivals,
the avoidance of someone known to be a witch, are the ways they practice
their religion or have 'church.'

Because their religion defines who they are, to change religions, for an African, means to give up their identity and the support and security that is embodied in it. That is why missionaries of other religions find it so difficult to make converts. To whole-heartedly accept a new religion means ceasing to be African, and in the words of Mbiti above, 'amounts to a self-excommunication from the entire life of society.'

Because of the social cost of accepting a new religion to the individual African, the new religions (primarily Islam and Christianity) entering the sub-continent have had to determine how much of the traditional religion's beliefs and practices have to be forsaken before they can be accepted into the new religion. Both Islam and Christianity have holy books that define their beliefs and practices. Historically, missionaries from these two religions have looked at their holy books and looked at the religion of the African, and have defined conversion in terms of which elements of the old religion have to be abandoned and which elements of the new religion have to be adopted. The conclusions have ranged from total abandonment of the traditional religion and total adoption of the new religion, to keeping all of the traditional religion and adding certain elements of the new. The successes of Islam and Christianity in different parts of Africa can be linked to the approach their missionaries have taken in defining conversion. Religious conversion will be discussed in more detail in chapter 6.

Islam is seen to be much more inclusive than Christianity in the traditional practices and beliefs it allows its converts to hold on to. It defines its adherents in terms of what they must 'do' to be of their religion. For that reason Islam has had greater success in the rural areas of Africa where the traditional practices are more a part of everyday life than in the urban. When an African leaves his village community and goes to an urban area, he is uprooted from the sources of his identity and is forced to establish a new one. He is also removed from the daily events that require religious acts, he no longer has access to a herbalist or sorcerer, he is not present in the village for the ritual associated with rites of passage. In other words, the events that reinforce the traditional religious aspects of life are no longer there. This African is more receptive to renouncing what he no longer has and accepting a new religion, which will give him a new identity. This is a main reason Christianity is having success winning converts in urban areas of Africa. Christianity is more concerned with what a convert 'believes' than what he is required to do.

In this book I will focus on the area of religious beliefs in Africa and will investigate the belief systems of African Traditional Religion and Christianity.

These belief systems will be defined in terms of their respective worldviews. An investigation into the similarities and differences between the biblical worldview, as presented primarily in Genesis 1–11, and the African world-view will be presented. In this work 'God's worldview', 'the biblical worldview', and 'the Christian worldview' are used interchangeably as having the same conceptual meaning. The concept will be developed further in chapter 3.

The religion of Christianity is rooted in the biblical worldview based primarily on Genesis 1–11 of Christianity's holy book, the Bible. By confession, the Bible is the Christian's source of belief and practice. Where the African Christian's beliefs differ from the biblical worldview there is a failure in praxis and the Christian religion is rendered ineffectual in the lives of those who claim to be Christian. Does the typical African Christian's worldview reflect the biblical worldview or the traditional African worldview? The areas of conformity and conflict between these worldviews will be presented.

Most people are not conscious of having a worldview, but all people have one. The areas of investigation will follow along the lines of the elemental study and analysis of the fundamental realities of human existence as reflected in a worldview. The African, or anyone else for that matter, does not think in terms of the philosophical elements of reality. He lives life daily based upon assumptions about reality that he has been taught verbally from birth and by experience. However, an independent study of one's worldview can be done along those lines making it possible to compare worldviews. I will analyse the biblical worldview and the African worldview. Any paths of divergence and the resulting need for convergence will be presented.

Africa is a diverse continent and is the second largest in land mass and population of the six continents defined by the United Nations. The history, tradition, culture and thus the worldview of the people of the mostly Arab North Africa are very different from those of sub-Saharan Africa. Even though the people of North Africa are very much African and are rich in biblical history, for this work 'Africa' and 'African' will be limited to sub-Saharan Black Africa.

Relevance of Study Due to Syncretism

If the churches in Africa are not preaching and teaching the biblical worldview, accepting it as their own, and living accordingly, their members will accept the new religion of Christianity without discarding the old conflicting beliefs. That, in missiological terms, is called syncretism. According to missions author Charles Kraft (1999:390), syncretism is 'the mixing of Christian assumptions with those worldview assumptions that are incompatible with Christianity so that the result is not biblical Christianity.'

The word 'syncretism' comes from the Greek word *synkretismos* meaning a union of Cretans. It originated in the early 1600s and referred particularly to a joining together of two opposing parties on the Isle of Crete to present a united front against a common enemy. The union was not of ideals, or of hearts, but one for a specific purpose. Whether or not the purpose was accomplished, the union was not permanent. That appears to be the case in much of African Christianity.

Syncretism is certainly not new in Africa or even in the Christian Era. Some 700 years before Christ the Hebrew nation had divided into a northern kingdom of Israel and a southern kingdom of Judah, and both had succumbed to the lure of syncretism as reflected in the following verses in 2 Kings 17:

> 15: 'They followed worthless idols and themselves became worthless.'
>
> 17: 'They sacrificed their sons and daughters in the fire. They practiced divination and sorcery and sold themselves to do evil in the eyes of the Lord, provoking him to anger.'
>
> 32: 'They worshiped the Lord, but they also appointed all sorts of their own people to officiate for them as priests in the shrines at the high places.'
>
> 33: 'They worshiped the Lord, but they also served their own gods in accordance with the customs of the nations from which they had been brought.'
>
> 41: 'Even while these people were worshipping the Lord, they were serving idols. To this day their children and grandchildren continue to do as their fathers did.'

The result of the Israelites' syncretism was their rejection by God and the sacking of their land. The northern kingdom of Israel was removed from their homeland, never to return. The southern kingdom of Judah was carried away to Babylon for seventy years of captivity. Only God's promise to Abraham caused him to allow them to return to their land after they had repented of their syncretism. God did not bless syncretism in Israel nor is it blessed today in his church.

The Rev. Dr. Augustine Musopole, an African theologian from Malawi, told an audience at the Eighth Assembly of the World Council of Churches: 'While Christianity in Africa is growing in numbers and in its geographical spread, its depth is questionable. This might be the reason it is easily overcome by forces of ethnicity, patriarchy, corruption, hatred, political manipulation, racism, classism, regionalism and traditionalism.' In other words, Christianity's lack of depth in Africa is the reason it is the victim of syncretism.

Long-time missionary, Dr. Gailyn Van Rheenen, has pointed out several problems or factors contributing to the ease of syncretism entering into the Christian church. The first problem is that frequently the whole gospel is not presented in its total biblical content. God's redemption of humanity through Jesus Christ is often preached without mention of God's working in, control over and future redemption through Jesus Christ of all of creation, thus leaving rivers, forests and mountains to be the domain of lesser gods. Another factor is that Western missionaries tend to present Christianity on the cosmological level, dealing with origins and destinies, while omitting the gospel's application to the everyday issues of life. Thus, a large percentage of African Christians continue to believe that ancestral spirits control their daily lives.

The most significant factor I have seen in Africa contributing to syncretism is the lack of leadership at the denominational level. Denominations have statements of faith or doctrinal statements that define who they are as distinct from other denominations. The doctrines listed are usually biblical, but broad. They remain silent on the everyday issues of life, such as divorce and remarriage, admitting members with more than one wife, secret societies, etc. Denominations are reluctant to take a stand on these types of cultural issues, so that theological formation takes place in local churches where there is immense pressure on the pastor to accommodate the culture by relaxing biblical standards. To the local pastor, syncretism seems the best way to maintain peaceful relations in the church community. It is only by replacing the African worldview with the biblical worldview that syncretism will be seen as a bad thing rather than a good thing to Africans who profess Christianity. In his address to the World Council of Churches, Dr. Musopole concluded by saying that 'the gospel was the creation of a new humanity. To realize this, there was a need to evangelize the African worldview.'

This work will be structured upon the analysis of worldview because Africans have a worldview, and the religion of Christianity has a worldview. The African worldview is expressed in their parables, religious myths and rituals, social order, and life events. The Christian worldview is revealed in their Bible. Worldview is seen to be important because worldview determines beliefs and beliefs determine behaviour (praxis).

In analysing the biblical and African worldviews, philosophical elements involved in a worldview will be identified and compared in each. I believe that all worldviews are religious at their core. An analysis of the philosophical elements of a Christian's worldview should reflect a biblical cosmology, epistemology, ontology, etc., while the analysis of an African's worldview should reflect these same core philosophical beliefs based upon African Traditional Religion. My research has produced ample material on Genesis 1–11, Christian philosophy, and the Christian worldview. It has also produced much material on African theology, philosophy and religion. However, no work has been found that compares Christian and African worldviews using the philosophical elements that make up one's worldview. I will attempt to provide a framework for Christians in Africa to do a critical examination of their cultural worldview assumptions on a philosophical basis so that they can see where they conform and conflict with the biblical worldview.

Why Use 'Worldview'?

Analysing a people's worldview is a way of delineating the philosophical elements involved in the way people view their version of reality. Why is that important? It is important because worldview determines beliefs. Beliefs determine behaviour. Behaviour is chosen based on anticipated consequences. If belief is wrong, the consequences of behaviour cannot be accurately foreseen. Therefore, people do not get expected results and are confounded.

This work is structured upon the analysis of worldview because Africans have a worldview, and the Bible puts forth a worldview primarily revealed in Genesis 1–11. I agree with long-time missionary, Hans Weerstra (1997:1):

> Questions of origin and purpose of the universe, questions concerning who we are as human beings and what is wrong with humanity, including the remedy for the malady, cannot be answered without fundamental beliefs usually associated with religious beliefs. But we want to link religion and worldview and make the point that the dichotomy many of us see between them is false because it rests on wrong assumptions, i.e. worldview, that is founded on naturalistic and humanistic thought systems. These systems radically divide the sacred and secular, the natural and the supernatural, as well as science and religion . . . that essential dichotomy of reality is wrong because it is anti-biblical,

and also is intrinsically wrong—it contradicts and undermines reality as it objectively is.

For that reason we want to make the point that there is no essential or radical dichotomy. Worldview and religion need to be closely linked. In fact, when rightly understood on a deep belief level, they are one and the same.

As will be seen, Africans have a religious worldview. Even though their religion is not based on the Bible, do elements of their worldview conform to the biblical view of the world?

Analysis of worldview is the structure of this work. The foundation of the structure of analysis between the African worldview and the biblical worldview is the philosophical elements that make up a worldview. As with worldview and religion, philosophy and religion are closely linked. They deal with the same basic questions even though they use different terms and provide different answers. The basic questions addressed by both philosophy and religion are the three basic areas of human inquiry: metaphysics or what really exists; morals or how to know right and wrong; and epistemology, or what can we know and how can we know it for sure.

Worldview is important for a number of reasons: it determines the prosperity and development of peoples and nations; it determines the contentment and level of satisfaction of individuals; it shapes politics of nations; it determines the space-time future of individuals and nations; and it determines an individual's eternity.

As just mentioned, worldview determines the prosperity and development of peoples and nations. Let us take for example the Asian nation of Japan. According to Jason Mandryk (2011:448) Japan has a population density of 336 people per sq. km. Only 13 per cent of its land can be cultivated. It has no natural resources or oil. Yet, Japan has the world's most powerful export-oriented economy and has an enormous trade surplus with the world. The average annual income per person is $38,458. Compare that with the sub-Sahara African nation of Cameroon. Mandryk (2011:189) states that Cameroon has a population density of only 42 people per sq. km. It has an economy largely based on agriculture and oil exports and has great potential for development with ample rain and minerals. However, the average annual income per person is only $1,224 compared to Japan's $38,458. Why such a disparity between the prosperity and development in these two countries? It is not a lack of natural resources. It is not overpopulation. It is a difference in worldview. The Cameroonians view the cosmos as something they must adapt to. The Japanese view the cosmos as something that can be adapted to meet their needs.

It was also stated previously that worldview determines an individual's eternity. Every worldview contains ideas or beliefs about eternity. These beliefs can range between there being no such thing as eternity, to all humans spending eternity somewhere in some state of being. Worldview beliefs about eternity can cause anxiety within individuals and can cause wars between religions when religious worldviews clash on the national and international level. For example, the Muslim worldview says that a Muslim who voluntarily fights in a holy war and is killed, will spend eternity in paradise. On the other hand, some pacifist religions see participation in war as a sin and anyone who voluntarily fights in a war and is killed will spend eternity in hell. The Muslim believes he has nothing to lose and everything to gain by going to war for his faith. The pacifist believes just the opposite.

The Bible places this clash of worldviews on the eternal states of human beings in the context of a spiritual struggle. Philosophy professor David Naugle (2002:xvii) states:

> From the perspective of Christian theism [the Christian worldview], a clash of worldview also assumes a crucial role in the hidden, spiritual battle between the kingdom of God and the kingdom of Satan, in which the very truth of things is at stake. Between these regimes, a conflict of epic proportions rages for the minds and hearts, and thus the lives and destinies, of all men and women, all the time. Since nothing could be of greater final importance than the way human beings understand God, themselves, the cosmos, and their place in it, it is not surprising that a worldview warfare is at the heart of the conflict between the powers of good and evil.

Naugle goes on to state: 'Consequently, an in-depth look at a concept that plays such a pivotal role in human affairs seems particularly worthwhile.' This work will limit its in-depth look at the worldview concept to African and Christian, looking for areas of conflict and conformity between the two worldviews.

Value of Genesis 1–11

The value of Genesis 1–11 is first and foremost derived from the fact that it is in the Bible. The whole Bible has been esteemed by Christians and non-Christians alike to be a book of great value. *Halley's Bible Handbook* (Halley 1965:18, 19) gives us some notable sayings about the Bible by famous people in world history:

Napoleon: 'The Bible is no mere book, but a Living Creature, with a power that conquers all that oppose it.'

Queen Victoria: 'That book accounts for the supremacy of England.'

Thomas Huxley: 'The Bible has been the Magna Charta of the poor and the oppressed. The human race is not in a position to dispense with it.'

Horace Greeley: 'It is impossible to enslave mentally or socially a Bible-reading people. The principles of the Bible are the groundwork of human freedom.'

Lord Tennyson: 'Bible reading is an education in itself.'

Immanuel Kant: 'The existence of the Bible, as a book for the people, is the greatest benefit which the human race has ever experienced. Every attempt to belittle it is a crime against humanity.'

The whole Bible is known by Christians to be the very words of God to humanity. The Bible describes itself as 'given by inspiration of God and is profitable for doctrine, for reproof, for correction, for instruction in righteousness' (2 Tm 3:16 kjv). The word 'inspired' as used here, is not to be confused with the common usage of the word, as when we say Shakespeare was 'inspired' to write plays, or Handel was 'inspired' to compose great music. Inspiration in the biblical sense is unique. The Greek word translated 'inspired' actually means 'God-breathed' as translated in some of the newer versions of the Bible. It refers, not to the writers, but to the words that were written. It is the Christian belief that the Bible does not contain mere human words and ideas, but God himself has revealed in it His divine character and will, as well as His view of the world, human history and humanity itself, all by His own words that are recorded there. That is why Christians look to the Bible to get God's view of the world.

Christians look specifically to the first eleven chapters of the Bible to get God's account of the beginning of all things except himself. The Old Testament provides an answer to man's inquiry into the past. Revealed in the first eleven chapters of Genesis are the essential facts regarding the creation of man and the universe. If God had not revealed the origin of the cosmos, humanity, and all that humanity concerns itself with, that information would forever be inaccessible to man. Without knowing origins, the knowledge of meanings would also be inaccessible to man. The search for meaning in answers to life's basic questions is fruitless unless one searches Genesis 1–11. Christian philosopher Francis Schaeffer (1972a:9) states it well:

> I wish to point out the tremendous value Genesis 1–11 has for modern man. In some ways these chapters are the most important ones in the Bible, for they put man in his cosmic setting and show him his peculiar uniqueness. They explain man's wonder and yet his flaw. Without a proper understanding of these chapters, we have no answer to the problems of metaphysics, morals or epistemology, and furthermore, the work of Christ becomes one more upper-story 'religious' answer.

For Schaeffer, an upper story 'religious' answer is something that must be accepted as being true by faith only because it cannot be supported by fact or reason. The church in Africa accepts the work of Christ as fact because history records it and the Bible explains it. The Christian church in Africa must also have a worldview that corresponds to the Christian worldview of the Bible as revealed primarily in Genesis 1–11.

Value of Africans

From the Christian point of view the value of Africans is derived first and foremost from the fact that they are human beings created, according to Genesis 1:27, in the image of God. As human beings, like all human beings, they can trace their ancestry back to one of the three sons of Noah (Gn 10:1ff), and through Noah back to the first man, Adam. Africans are one in kind with, and share familial relations with, all other people on earth. Africans are part of the world (the people of the world) that God so loved (Jn 3:16).

We as human beings, created by God in His image, should value what He values. At this particular time in the history of the world, God has shown his value for the people of Africa by the supernatural building up of his church and the bringing of many African souls to salvation. The African church is growing faster than anywhere else in the world today, and south of the Sahara, Christianity is spreading faster than at anytime or place in the last 2000 years, with an estimated 1,200 new churches being started every month across Africa. Many missiologists believe that the greatest impact on the church during the twenty-first century will come from Africa and the

Africans. If God allows the Africans to impact his church to that extent, he must value them highly.

The Problem

According to the World Christian Encyclopedia (Barrett 1982:3), in the year 1900 the total population of the world was 34.4 per cent Christian, and in the year 2000 the world's Christian population had fallen to 32.3 per cent. Yet, according to Johnstone and Mandryk (2001:21), during that same century the percentage of Christians in all of Africa increased from 10 per cent to 48.4 per cent, and by the year 2000 in sub-Saharan Africa, 60 per cent of the people profess to be Christian. By 2010 that percentage had risen to 65 per cent (Mandryk 2010:33). If 65 per cent of sub-Saharan Africans are Christian, then 65 per cent of sub-Saharan Africans should have a biblical worldview and sub-Saharan Africa should have a predominately Christian culture. Since this is not the case, is there is a dichotomy between profession and practice among professing Christians in Africa? My answer is 'yes' and that is the problem.

The focus of this book is in the area of worldview with the conviction that belief determines behaviour. Unless the African Christian's beliefs are structured by a biblical worldview instead of the traditional African worldview, their behaviour will be structured more by traditional beliefs and Africa's culture will not reflect predominately Christian values. If the percentages are right, 65 per cent of the population being Christian should make a significant impact on African culture. The fact that it is not happening should be of great concern to the church in Africa.

Pathway to Recommendations

As stated earlier, this work investigates the philosophical elements involved in explaining the realities of human existence as reflected in one's worldview. These elements are examined in a biblical worldview as delineated in Genesis 1–11 and in the African traditional worldview. Areas of conformity and conflict between the two worldviews are highlighted and analysed as to their effects on the church in Africa.

Chapter 2 deals with the concept of 'worldview'. Several definitions of the term are given from the fields of anthropology and philosophy and the working definition for this work is given. An investigation is made into the history of the concept with the philological history and the history of its use in philosophy presented. The religious dimensions of worldview analysis are discussed with six dimensions being explained. The philosophical elements of worldview are delineated and explained. Finally, an analysis is made of what it takes for a worldview to accurately reflect reality with criteria given to help analyse truth claims of worldviews.

Chapter 3 presents the biblical worldview. The biblical worldview is analysed along the lines of the philosophical elements laid out in chapter 2 with the text of Genesis 1–11 being the primary source for the analysis. The philosophy of the Christian religion is introduced, followed by a discussion of the use of Genesis 1–11 in establishing the biblical worldview. The historical accuracy, or truthfulness, of the events recorded in Genesis 1–11 is dealt with and the position taken in this work is stated.

The Christian, or biblical, worldview is delineated and a basic outline referenced to Genesis 1–11 is presented. Next, the philosophical elements of the Christian worldview are discussed using a question/answer format. This is followed by an analysis of the religious dimensions of the Christian world-view. Finally, the idea of culture is introduced because worldview is lived out in culture and the beginning of human culture is recorded in Genesis 1–11.

The topic of chapter 4 is the African worldview. Africa is a huge conti-nent and diverse in tongues, tribes and nations. Given the diversity, can there be what would be called an 'African worldview' that captures the consensus of the majority of Africans? This question is investigated and answered. Next, the idea of African Traditional Religion being a worldview philosophy is presented followed by a discussion of the concept that postulates the African worldview. The African worldview is delineated much the same as the biblical worldview in chapter 3, with a basic outline being given and the philosophical elements being presented using the same philosophical questions but giving answers from the African worldview.

The religious dimensions of the African worldview are discussed fol-lowed by a presentation of the idea of culture in the African worldview. The chapter ends with a presentation of the African worldview being a worldview in transition and the forces behind that transition.

Chapter 5 presents a comparison of the biblical and traditional African worldviews in the philosophical and religious areas examined to see where the points of conflict and conformity lie. The two worldviews are compared as philosophy and the answers furnished by them to the philosophical questions asked in chapters 3 and 4 are compared. The religious dimensions of each are examined. Finally, the relationship of Christianity to African Traditional Religion is discussed.

Chapter 6 contains conclusions and recommendations. Particular attention is paid to the areas where investigation has shown that the biblical and traditional African worldviews diverge. The process of religious conversion is discussed followed by a presentation of the paths of divergence between the two worldviews. The reality of syncretism in the religious practices of Christians in Africa is presented showing the effects of Christians holding to both worldviews on the Christian church in Africa. The chapter concludes with recommendations to the Christian church on ways to combat syncretism emphasizing the importance of the convergence of the biblical and African worldviews in the belief systems of its members.

The great need for Christians in Africa today, whether they are students, pastors, or denominational leaders, is to examine their cultural assumptions to see if they run counter to Christianity and conflict with the biblical worldview. They need to critically examine them in the light of Scripture. What will be the consequences if they do not? They are more than likely to fuse and confuse their religious tradition with Christianity and maintain a culture-bound worldview. And since beliefs determine behaviour, their behaviour will be more African than Christian.

This work attempts to provide a framework for Christians in Africa to do a critical examination of their cultural assumptions so they can see if they conflict with the biblical or Christian worldview. If there are areas of conflict, they must be given special attention by teachers in theological colleges and seminaries, and by pastors in the local churches. If people do not think like Christians, they will not act like Christians.

2

Worldview

In the Western world, the shift from the modern to the postmodern era has moved the concept of worldview from the purview of philosophy departments to the warp and woof of mainstream cultural society. When a Westerner over fifty years of age reads a magazine article or watches something on television and says, 'that does not make a bit of sense', he is experiencing a conflict of worldview. The past thirty years has seen a proliferation of publications by educators, philosophers and theologians, either promoting the postmodern worldview or endeavouring to help society understand and cope with it. From a religious perspective, the shift to a postmodern cultural worldview may not be welcomed, but the mainstream cultural focus on the concept of worldview certainly is. As previously stated, I believe that all worldviews are based on core religious beliefs whether they are Islamic, Christian, African traditionalist, or atheistic belief systems. An analysis of worldviews should lead naturally to an analysis of the religious beliefs behind those worldviews. This chapter will present an analysis of the worldview concept. It will begin with some definitions of worldview and present a history of the concept. The various religious dimensions and philosophical elements that make up a worldview, and some tests to determine if a worldview reflects reality, will follow. The following two chapters will take the analysis of worldview on to a specific analysis of the religious beliefs behind the biblical, or Christian worldview, and the traditional African worldview based on African Traditional Religion.

Definitions

One's worldview is important because worldview determines beliefs and beliefs determine behaviour. A certain belief is chosen because it is believed that it will produce a certain consequence. In no area of life is this more consequential than in the practice of one's religion, for religion deals with consequences that are ultimately eternal. Behind the behaviour and beliefs of human beings as lived out in their cultures, lie certain assumptions about the way the world is constructed. These assumptions include the categories and reasoning people use in constructing their beliefs about the nature of reality. Anthropologist Paul Hiebert (1997:85) gives three sets of assumptions involved in this construction process:

> *Essential assumptions.* These provide a culture with the fundamental cognitive [mental processing] structures people use to explain reality.

> *Affective assumptions.* Affective assumptions underlie notions of beauty and style, and influence the peoples taste in music, art, dress, food and architecture as well as the ways they feel about themselves and life in general.

> *Evaluative assumptions.* These provide the standards people use to make judgements about right and wrong.

> Taken together, the cognitive, affective, and evaluative assumptions provide people with a way of looking at the world that makes sense out of it, that gives them a feeling of being at home, and that reassures them that they are right.

Worldviews are implicit (expressed indirectly) by their nature. People are usually not aware of the ways their categories, systems of logic and basic assumptions form the way they see the world. One does not think about their worldview, but worldview does direct their thinking.

Almost every worldview writer has his or her own definition of the concept. Some are short and simple. Some are long and complex, trying to be totally comprehensive in scope. Some of the shorter definitions one encounters include:

> 'Worldview' refers to a system of beliefs that are interconnected in the way the pieces of a jigsaw puzzle are interconnected. That is, a worldview is not merely a collection of separate, unrelated beliefs, but is instead an interconnected *system* of beliefs.

> A broad conceptual synthesis that forms one's perspectives on the whole of reality.

A worldview is a set of beliefs, a model that attempts to explain all, rather than some part of reality.

A worldview is a philosophical system that attempts to explain how the facts of reality relate and fit together.

A worldview furnishes the interpretive condition for understanding and explaining the facts of our experience.

The basic assumptions about reality which lie behind the beliefs and behaviour of a culture are sometimes called a worldview.

Worldview is the culturally structured set of assumptions underlying how a people perceive and respond to reality.

A worldview is a set of assumptions held consciously or unconsciously in faith about the basic makeup of the world and how the world works.

A worldview is a person's way of understanding life and the world in which he lives, including his belief about what is real and what is not real.

A worldview provides a model *of the world* which guides its adherents *in the world*.

Philosopher Diana Axelsen (1979:184), in her essay 'Philosophical Justifications for Contemporary African Social and Political Values and Strategies', gives her idea of what should be included in a worldview. According to her a worldview is a conceptual scheme that takes a position on the nature of ultimate reality (ontology); the nature of knowledge; personhood; the nature of human history; the fundamental values which individuals ought to pursue; and an identification of cultural norms.

Philosopher David Noebel (1991:8) takes the view that '*worldview* refers to any ideology, philosophy, theology, movement, or religion that provides an overarching approach to understanding God, the world, and man's relations to God and the world.'

In looking at these definitions, certain words or phrases are used, all of which describe some aspect of the concept of worldview:

fundamental cognitive structures

systems of beliefs

explains all of reality [cosmology, metaphysics]

philosophical system

assumptions about reality [conscious or unconscious, true or false]

significance of life [teleology, ontology]

culturally constructed

religion

ideologies

associated with a group or society

nature of knowledge [epistemology]

personhood [ontology]

nature of human history [philosophy of history]

fundamental values [axiology]

cultural norms [ethics]

All of these are applicable to a worldview, but the use of all of them would produce a rather lengthy and cumbersome definition. It seems that any definition of worldview should include the word 'universal' as one's worldview encompasses *all aspects* of one's world or universe. Therefore, my definition of worldview for this work will begin there:

> **Worldview**: A person's or group's universal theories (philosophical in nature, based upon religion, and lived out in relationships) which explain the appearance of truth or reality in their lives.

The structure of this work will be along the lines of the philosophical elements of African Traditional Religions and Christianity as the two religions are lived out in relationship to deities and nature and in human relationships.

History of the Worldview Concept

The term 'worldview' had its origin in Germany and experienced a rapid proliferation from Germany, to the rest of Europe and on to the English-speaking world through its usage in philosophy, the natural sciences and the social sciences.

Philological History

Prussian philosopher Immanuel Kant is almost universally credited with coining the term *Weltanchauung* (intuition of the world) in his *Critique of Judgement* first published in 1790. Kant apparently only used the term once, but the context in which he used it (the self that knows and wills and sees itself as the cognitive and moral centre of the universe) created the intellectual environment in which the concept of worldview could flourish.

The first appearance of *Weltanschauung* in English is traced to a letter written by William James in 1868 and the first usage of the English equivalent 'world-view' to J. Martineau in his book *Studies of Christianity* published in 1858. It only took sixty-eight years from Kant to Martineau for *Weltanschauung* to spread throughout Europe and into the English language, translated as 'world-view'.

It was Protestant Christianity's use of the term that gave it prominence in the English-speaking world. The works of James Orr and Abraham Kuyper putting forth a Christian worldview, were widely read in North America and Europe. They both were Calvinist in doctrine as were the vast majority of Protestant Christians in their era, so their works were readily accepted as a Protestant answer to the secular worldview challenges of the modern era.

There is a surprising phenomenon in light of the widespread use of *Weltanschauung* and worldview in philosophy in the English-speaking world. It is that little attention has been paid to the terms in English encyclopaedias and dictionaries of philosophy, with very few of them having an independent entry for either term. The ones that do have entries have very brief definitions. There seems to be more in-depth treatment of the terms in anthropological and theological reference material than in philosophical reference works.

Before leaving the area of philology, the correct English equivalent of *Weltanschauung* should be addressed. Some reference works translate it as a single word (worldview), some as a hyphenated word (world-view), and some as two separate words (world view). Following most authors, the compound English word (worldview) will be used in this work, unless reference is made to another work that uses a different English equivalent.

Philosophical History

In the nineteenth century the role of worldview in the history of European philosophy was most prominent in the thoughts of German philosophers

Georg Wilhelm Friedrich Hegel, Wilhelm Dilthey and Friedrich Nietzsche and Danish philosopher Soren Kierkegaard.

Beginning with Kierkegaard (1813–1855), a Christian philosopher, we see a connection made between one's view of the world and one's view of life. He preferred to use the term *Lebensanschauung* (lifeview) rather than *Weltanschauung,* which to him meant a deep and satisfying view of life that would enable him to become a total human self and that would embrace a truth that he could live and die for. For Kierkegaard, that deep and satisfying view of life came from Christianity. In his *Attack Upon 'Christendom',* Kierkegaard bemoans the fact that in most Christian homes children suffer from the failure of parents to impart to them a distinctively Christian lifeview.

On the European continent, Dilthey (1833–1911) had recognized the importance of worldview as a concept. His thoughts on worldview were a part of his overall attempt to formulate an objective epistemology for the human sciences. For Dilthey, the structure of worldviews reflects 'an inherent psychic order' in human beings. He held that since there are three structural aspects of the human mind (mind, emotion, will), there are therefore three structural aspects to a worldview. These three structural aspects correspond to the three sets of assumptions put forth by Herbert previously in this chapter. First, Dilthey says the structure of a worldview begins with the mind's formation of a 'cosmic picture' (Weltbild), which is a product of cognition [Essential assumptions]. Second, based upon the cosmic picture there is a formation of the 'effectual value' of life [Affective assumptions]. Finally, in the upper level of consciousness reside the highest ideals and supreme principles guiding the conduct of life [Evaluative assumptions] which give a *Weltanchauung* validity and power.

The contributions of Nietzsche (1844–1900) to the philosophical thinking on the concept of worldview were more a precursor to postmodern deconstructionism than a reflection of the prevailing views of other European philosophers of the century. Nietzsche concluded that there is no God and that nature and the ongoing historical process were the only tools humanity had for understanding the world and human life. He believed that worldviews are cultural entities which people in a given geographical location and historical context are dependent upon, subordinate to, and products of. He puts it in the form of a general law that every living thing can become healthy, strong and fruitful only within a boundary and a *Weltanschauung* provides this necessary, well-defined boundary.

Hence, he holds that worldviews are cultural entities and are specific to a geographical location and historical context and contain no 'truth' but only products of linguistic custom and habits. For Nietzsche, all worldviews are ultimately fiction. His philosophy of worldview laid the groundwork for the secular humanist worldview against which the biblical worldview and the traditional African worldview are competing today.

No philosopher of the nineteenth century has incited the ire of current African philosophers like GWF Hegel. Hegel is loathed not for his philosophical contributions to the concept of worldview, but because of his own worldview. As for his contribution to the concept of worldview, Hegel is credited with the idea of the Absolute Spirit and the existence of alternative conceptual frameworks.

Hegel saw one's worldview developing over time through a dialectical process whereby one's present conceptual framework encounters a new or slightly different conceptual framework, and by the use of reason, the superior elements of the old and the new frameworks are retained to form a synthesis, or combination, of the two (thesis→antithesis→synthesis)—a new and more accurate unfolding of the Absolute Spirit (or Mind). His use of Spirit may be indicative of his view that religion is intrinsic to human nature and that the role of philosophy is to explain the nature of the relationship between one's religion and his general theory of the universe, his *Weltanschauung*.

It is Hegel's *The Philosophy of History* that is the source of anger from the African philosophers of today. In that work he presented a grandiose picture of the universe and of human history—past, present and future. Writing from an eighteenth century ethnocentric German perspective, the soil that produced Adolph Hitler and the Holocaust, he divided the world geographically and intellectually into three regions with sub-Saharan Africa at the bottom, Asia in the middle, and Europe at the top. Reflecting the view of a number of African philosophers, Paulin J. Hountondji, professor at the National University of Benin, calls Hegel's philosophy of history a celebration of the European spirit that excludes Africa totally from the historical process. Hegel portrays Africa as the ideal and spiritual antithesis to Europe.

A preponderance of African writers have stated their beliefs that Hegel's worldview as expressed in his *The Philosophy of History* and as inherited by his Western philosophical decedents provided the justification needed by the Western world for European colonization of Africa. This is a major reason the Western world is disliked by African intellectuals and the Africans they influence. It is also a major reason why Christianity, seen as being a Western religion, is rejected by some without a hearing. The increase in interest in and publications on African Philosophy in recent years is seen as a backlash against Hegel's portrayal of Africa. African philosophers are now insisting that the African worldview has a legitimate philosophical foundation.

It is ironic that Hegel's dialectical process (thesis→antithesis→synthesis) appears to have a parallel in processes to be found in African culture. In interpersonal relationships, disagreements among individuals or groups are solved using that dialectic process. When Westerners disagree, they state their opinions, agree to disagree, shake hands, and go their separate ways. When Africans disagree (thesis→antithesis), they state their opinions, keep talking until they find common areas they agree on (→synthesis or consensus), shake hands and leave together. This reflects the African view of the harmony of the community being more important than the individual.

Religious Dimensions of Worldview Analysis

As stated in chapter 1, I believe that all philosophical worldviews are religious at their core. This work will focus on the philosophical elements involved in a worldview. Included in philosophical elements of a worldview are religious dimensions that motivate behaviour. In his book *Worldviews: Crosscultural Explorations of Human Beliefs*, Ninian Smart stresses the worldview/religion connection when he states: 'The heart of the modern study of religion is the analysis and comparison of worldviews' (1983:3). He bases that statement upon his analysis of what motivates people. People do things because they believe it will pay, or they believe something bad will happen if they don't do it, or because they believe it is the right thing to do. Their beliefs mobilize their feelings and wills.

Beliefs motivate behaviour and what people believe helps form their reality, even if what they believe is not true, with what is true being that which corresponds to or adequately expresses what is real. David Hesselgrave (1984:156) echoes this view: 'The universals [general terms that signify the nature or essence] may be true to reality or they may be ill-conceived and false, but so long as they are believed to be true, they will be of paramount importance.' People form their worldviews based upon what they believe and they behave accordingly. People's beliefs are structured upon religious dimensions. Since it is possible that what people believe may be false, it is also possible that their religion may be false. It may not put them into a proper relationship with actual reality and the religious consequences are eternal.

Different criteria for determining which worldview(s) accurately reflects reality will be presented later in this chapter.

Smart (1983:5), a professor of religious studies, says 'a main part of the modern study of religion may be called "worldview analysis"—the attempt to describe and understand human worldviews.' From the religious studies standpoint, he goes on to state: 'To see how they work, we must relate ideas to symbols and to practices, so that worldview analysis is not merely a matter of listing beliefs.' His conclusion is beliefs, consciousness and practice are bound together.

Professor Smart goes on to deal with six dimensions of religion that portray beliefs, consciousness and practice in worldview analysis. The beliefs are formed by the doctrinal, mythical and ethical dimensions, but those beliefs are experienced and practiced in the ritual, experiential and social dimensions. He begins his analysis with the experiential dimension because that is where people live.

Experiential Dimension

For many people, a religious experience, such as a dramatic encounter with the Divine, provokes a turning point in their personal history and their lives are forever changed. For others, religious experience is less dramatic but still involves certain feelings. Most religions have rituals designed to reinforce, to express or to stimulate those feelings. The magnitude of the religious experience can be measured by the magnitude of the feelings it produces.

Smart presents two strands of religious experiences. One is called the 'numinous'. The term is attributed to Rudolf Otto (1869–1937) in his work, *The Idea of the Holy*. Otto derives the word from the Latin *numen*, a powerful spirit, sensed as being holy but not seen.

For him, the numinous experience is at the heart of religion. In defining the experience Otto used *mysterium tremendum et fascinans*, meaning a fearful, awe-inspiring mystery which makes you tremble. In spite of its fearfulness it draws you toward it, like wanting to look over a steep cliff. But the sense of presence which confronts a person in the numinous experience is marvellous in power and glory.

Otto referred to this powerful spirit as the Wholly Other because it was something completely different in being than the person encountering it, and because it was mysteriously other in essence from the other things and people of the world. It is otherworldly. Otto was depicting what was for him the central experience of religion. The idea of the numinous is encountered in African Traditional Religion and in the religion of Christianity when those religions approach the Supreme Being or God.

Another type of religious experience which seems to be the opposite of the numinous is the mystical experience. The mystical experience is of something inside rather than outside the individual and is usually accomplished by attempting to purify the consciousness of the individual to such a degree that all thoughts and images are left behind and the distinction between subject and object disappears.

Some aspects of the mystical experience are found in African Traditional Religion and in some forms of Christianity. The numinous and the mystical types of religious experience are closely tied to the philosophical metaphysical views of dualism and monism. These will be addressed later in this work.

Smart deals with the truth-value of religious experiences and how truth-value is worldview dependent. The views of psychologists, such as Freud and Jung, that the human psyche constitutes its own realm of experience and that human beings are trapped within a material universe ignores the question of whether or not religious experience shows us the truth about the way things really are. If we believe that the cosmos is all there is then any experience that transcends the cosmos must have its origins within us, and the experience an illusion. Whether that experience is interpreted as the truth or as illusion depends on the worldview we start with.

Mythic Dimension

All religions have sacred narratives, called myths, which help explain why things are the way they are perceived. The concept of 'myth' has undergone changes from positive to negative, back to positive in the history of its religious usage. Smart credits the early Christian church with the idea that a myth is a false story as it attempted to discredit the Roman myths about their gods. In recent years the meaning of 'myth' has been used in religious studies in a more positive light, casting it in the frame of neutrality, giving it a divine or sacred significance without implying whether it is true or false.

My research has shown that some, but not necessarily all, African myths do express the reality of Africa, thus meeting the definition of 'myth' in current usage as a story taken to be true but not known to be true. According to this definition both African Traditional Religion and the Christian Bible contain myths. They will be examined in the course of this work.

Smart points out that myths often make use of symbols of things, beings or actions that have a meaning outside themselves. These must be understood if we are to know something of the meaning of symbols in religion and human life. Religious ideas have created many of these symbols and in turn the symbols help to communicate and strengthen religious ideas to those in the community.

The importance of religious myth in communicating a worldview is understood by those who study religion and by those who propagate a particular religion. One textbook on world religions states:

> Myths are essentially symbolic, metaphorical, or archetypical narratives that also contain supernatural or mysterious elements at their very core. Myths frequently imply an all-encompassing system of belief which explains the structure of reality and suggests how human experience should be understood. Myths need not necessarily be fictional or false. A true story may be so central to human experience that it is simultaneously mythical. . . . Even when a myth is known to be false, it may be a powerful means of encapsulating a worldview (Nielsen et al. 1988:7).

One of the most important keys available to understand a people's view of the nature of reality, the meaning of life and the foundations of value judgements that underlie their whole worldview is to understand their myths.

Religion needs to make sense of human life, where we came from, what we do today and where we are going. Myth is the tool religion uses to construct explanations that make sense.

Doctrinal Dimension

Doctrine can be defined as a body of beliefs considered authoritative and therefore worthy of acceptance by all members of the community. The religious worldview of any community is based on myths about the past and the future and stories that explain the present. Because these myths and stories change very little from generation to generation they take on a doctrinal aspect.

Smart gives five functions of the doctrinal dimension of a religious worldview. The first function is to bring order or make sense of the various myths, rituals and symbols supplied by tradition. The second function is 'to safeguard the references myths have to that which lies beyond, to that which transcends the cosmos. . . . These things are said through images and symbols in scripture, myth, and ritual; they are said more systematically in the form of doctrines' (1983:97). Another function of doctrine is to relate myths and traditions to the present day and the new knowledge that is discovered almost daily. The fourth function of doctrine is to stimulate a new vision of the world. Is it improving or degenerating? Is it permanent or transitory? The doctrines have a practical meaning, as well as a theoretical one, providing a vision or way of looking at things, which can inspire us to act or think in a certain way.

The fifth function of doctrine in a religious worldview is to define the community. This function of doctrine is very important to this work as those who belong to the community, whether traditional African or Christian, have to accept a set of doctrines in order to belong. Not accepting them warrants expulsion from the community. The affirmation of a set of beliefs about the reality of things defines the community and public affirmation expresses solidarity with the community.

The quote from John Mbiti on the first page of this book expressed the idea that for the African, traditional religions are for the community, rather than for the individuals that make up the community. Mbiti states that to give up religion (i.e., to cease believing doctrines of that religion) results in a self-excommunication from the community. The religion of Christianity also has a set of doctrines that must be believed by those wanting to be a part of the Christian community. Historically, the Christian doctrines have been summed up in creeds which are recited as public affirmations of accent to the doctrines and of identification with the Christian community. *The areas in which the doctrines of ATR and Christianity differ make up the defining choices as to which community the African belongs.*

Ethical Dimension

Smart believes that ethics cannot be studied independently of religion because every ethical system seems to raise questions about the worldview behind it and worldviews are religious at their core.

Ethics can be defined as an enquiry into how man ought to act in general, which causes confusion between the meanings of ethics and morals. The two are often used interchangeably but are technically different in application.

Ethics can be understood as a set of standards of what ought to be by which we evaluate human behaviour and judge it morally right or wrong. In other words, ethics is the law. When we go to court, the judge (or jury) decides if our actions comply with the law. If they do, we are judged innocent or moral. If not, we are judged guilty or immoral.

By what *basis* one evaluates human behaviour and judges it morally right or wrong is the concern of this work. According to Morris Inch, professor emeritus of Wheaton College, ethical inquiry can be divided into philosophical and theological. He states: 'Philosophic ethics approaches man's responsibility from what can be known by natural reason and in respect to temporal existence. Theological ethics deals with what may be gained from the alleged insight of any given religious community as to this life or that to come' (Inch 1984). Ethical behaviour is reflective of the religious beliefs defining such behaviour. An investigation into the basis of evaluating ethical behaviour in ATR and Christianity will be undertaken in chapter 5.

Ritual Dimension

The dimension of ritual is on a par with the ethical dimension in their centrality to religion and to the living out of worldviews. Talking positively about a Supreme Being as being the creator of the world and the judge of all things naturally leads to inner feelings that this Supreme Being ought to be recognized or worshipped in some outward, tangible way. There is an outward aspect to ritual that expresses a bodily reaction in the form of worship of something believed to exist even though it cannot be seen. Religious ritual is an act of communication of feelings that recognizes a relationship.

Sacrifice is one form of ritual. The victim being sacrificed, the believed transformation of the victim into something sacred, and the final destination of the victim all reflect elements of a religious worldview. Who the sacrifice is made to, and what is hoped to be gained are worldview determined. Prayer is the inner counterpart to outward sacrifice. Prayer is considered another sacrificial way of communicating with what lies beyond this world. In many cultures, including Africa, the knowledge of how to make acceptable sacrifices has given rise to religious specialists, or priests, that can be hired to perform the ritual.

Another important type of ritual is what is called rites of passage. In most all cultures important transitions in the physical and social status of an individual are marked by some sort of ritual. There is usually some ceremony to mark the transition from youth to adult, or a marriage ceremony to recognize the transition in relationship between a man and a woman. Baptism marks the transition from outside the religious community to being a full member. The difference between being a child and an adult, or married and single, makes a difference in the way people in a community treat a person and they are categories (performative categories) that define behaviour. Most societies mark the transition from one category to another through the performance of some ritual. Rituals are valued for the feelings they evoke and the visions they create, having their ultimate meaning in the experience of performing them. We shall see that both ATR and Christianity have their rituals that express their core religious beliefs and reflect their worldviews.

Social Dimension

In looking at the social dimension of religion, the size of the society determines the number of worldviews represented in it. Smaller societies usually have one dominant worldview representing a single religion. Growing societies are growing because they are attracting people from outside the society, giving rise to minority groups holding worldviews different from the norm for that society. A society comprised of individuals or sub-groups holding several different worldviews is more open to the introduction of a new religion than a small-scale society where everyone holds a common worldview. The entrance of Islam and Christianity into Africa has made it easier for each to win converts in societies where both religions are represented. Once an individual has a choice of religions, whether the choice is between two or three different religions is not that important.

The religion (singular) of a small-scale society is part and parcel of the fabric of society. People are born into and grow up in a community where a particular religion defines who they are and how they relate to the world. A religion like Islam or Christianity starts in societies as something new, from the outside. Being new implies being different from the norm, so a new religion challenges the religious assumptions of that society and provides a new, usually revolutionary way of viewing the world and of ordering society.

For Smart, the essential question regarding the social dimension of religion is this: 'To what extent is religion a reflection of what goes on in the structures of society, and to what extent does it bring these structures about?' (1983:147). As stated in chapter 1, 65 per cent of the population of sub-Saharan Africa professes to be Christian. The questions must be asked: To what extent is African Christianity a reflection of African culture; and to what extent has African culture reflected Christianity?

Philosophical Elements of Worldview

The use of philosophy to analyse religious worldviews dates all the way back to the initial use of the term. It comes from a combination of the Greek words *philos* (love of) and *sophia* (wisdom), thereby meaning 'the love of wisdom'. The term was first used by Pythagoras (570–500 BC) who stated that men could be divided into three types: those who loved pleasure, those who loved activity and those who loved wisdom. In his view, the love of wisdom (philosophy) always made one progress toward salvation in religious terms. Twenty-five hundred years later, philosophers are still dealing with religious issues such as the possibility of the certainty of the existence of God. If a God exists, what is the nature of its Being, and what is its relationship to the phenomenal world? What is the origin and nature of the phenomenal world if no God exists? These are religious questions and they tie into the seven worldview questions put forth by James Sire (1997:17) in his popular book, *The Universe Next Door*:

> What is prime reality—the really real?
>
> What is the nature of external reality, that is, the world around us?
>
> What is a human being?
>
> What happens to a person at death?
>
> Why is it possible to know anything at all?
>
> How do we know what is right and wrong?
>
> What is the meaning of human history?

The answers to these types of questions are inclusive in everyone's worldview. The right use of philosophy is to help a person form rational propositions about life's most important questions, propositions that are both justified and true. Philosophy can serve both a critical and a constructive function in analysing one's answers. Philosophy is critical because it examines assumptions from a justifiable conceptual standpoint. It is constructive because it seeks to organize all relevant facts into a rational system. This thought is echoed by Kwame Gyekye (1997:13), Professor of Philosophy at the University of Ghana: 'It is therefore, the task of philosophy to subject our lives—our ideas, beliefs, actions, values, and goals—to serious critical examination if we should be what we want to be and know what things are most worthwhile for our lives.'

In analysing the philosophical elements of two religious worldviews, one might think that the rubric under which it should be done would be philosophy of religion. However, like philosophy of science, philosophy of religion is a 'second-order' discipline, studying the concept of religion as opposed to studying specific religions. Professor John Hick (1973:2) states: 'Then we may reserve the name "philosophy of religion" for what (by analogy with philosophy of science, philosophy of art, etc.) is its proper meaning, namely, *philosophical thinking about religion*.' This work is intended to be an analysis of various philosophical elements of the worldviews of ATR and Christianity and thus will deal with standard areas of study considered to be 'first-order' parts of philosophy.

Each philosophical author has his own way of organizing the various first-order disciplines within philosophy. Professor Warren Young (1954:22) presents a philosophical tree with the traditional branches of Logic, Ethics, Aesthetics, Epistemology, Metaphysics and Value Theory. Professors Geisler and Feinburg (1980:24–34) include the first-order disciplines within philosophy as Ethics, Aesthetics, Logic, Epistemology and Metaphysics. Professor Robert Audi (1995:xxvi) gives Epistemology, Ethics, Logic and Metaphysics as basic fields of philosophy, but includes Aesthetics with the second-order disciplines of philosophy of religion and philosophy of science. This work will use the broader areas of Metaphysics, Axiology and Epistemology with Logic being considered in the following section on worldviews that reflect reality.

Metaphysics

Metaphysics is a broad area of philosophical investigation into the nature of what exists beyond matter and energy. The term *metaphysics* was first used as a title for a group of works by Aristotle (384–322 BC). One set of his writings was called the *Physics* and was generally concerned with the nature of things. Several centuries later some editors collected his writings and grouped another set into a work called 'the book after the *Physics*' (*tameta ta physica*) which became known as *metaphysics* (after the *Physics*).

The English word 'physics' comes from the Greek word for nature, *physis*. So *metaphysics* is concerned with what is beyond nature or beyond the physical. Most definitions are short and state the object of concern to be 'the nature of ultimate reality'. *The New Shorter Oxford English Dictionary*, 4th ed., gives a more comprehensive definition of metaphysics: 'The branch of philosophy that deals with the first principles of things, including such

concepts as being, substance, essence, time, space, cause and identity; theoretical philosophy as the ultimate science of being and knowing.' The range
of topics studied is very broad and philosophers have developed some widely
accepted sub-branches of metaphysics. For this work, the metaphysical elements of worldviews analysed will be categorized in the sub-branches of
ontology, cosmology and teleology.

Ontology comes from the Greek words *ontos* (being) and *logos* (knowledge), means the 'knowledge of being' and refers to the division of philosophy
directed at the study of being. The study is generally understood to apply to
all entities, including God, created or uncreated. Ontological questions addressed in this analysis of the worldviews of ATR and Christianity, include:
Is there a Supreme Being? If so, what is it like? What is the origin and nature
of man? Does man have a pre-existence? What is the nature of the external
world? Does man's existence terminate at death? What is reality? Are heaven
and hell real places?

Cosmology is from the Greek *kosmos* (world) and *logos* (knowledge or
reason concerning). Reese (1980:108) gives this definition:

> Traditionally, cosmology is considered to be that branch of
> metaphysics which concerns questions of the origin and struc-
> ture of the universe, its creation or everlastingness, vitalism, or
> mechanism, the nature of law, space, time, and causality. The task
> of cosmology can perhaps be distinguished from that of ontol-
> ogy by a difference of level, the cosmological analysis seeking to
> discover what is true for this world, and the ontological analysis
> attempting to discover relations and distinctions which would be
> valid in any world.

Cosmological questions concerning this work include: What is the origin and nature of the universe? What is God's relationship with the universe?
What is the meaning of time? Must every phenomenon have a cause?

Teleology is from the Greek *telos* (end) and *logos* (knowledge or doctrine) and is the doctrine that principles of explanation can be derived from
ends, final causes or purposes. In other words, a thing's design and purpose
can explain why the thing exists. In his *Dialogues*, Plato puts forth a doctrine
of teleology: 'everything in the universe has a purpose or proper function
within a harmonious hierarchy of purposes.' The ultimate explanation of
things is purposive rather than mechanical. 'The underlying question of
all of Plato's investigations is the "why" of an event rather than the "how"'

(Albert et al. 1988:10). Teleological questions include: Does everything in the universe serve a purpose? Why does the universe exist? Why does man exist? Does the end justify the means?

Axiology

Axiology is another broad category within philosophy. The name comes from the Greek *axios* (value) and *logos* (knowledge or theory) and can be defined as the study of, or theory of the nature of value and valuation in general. In *The Cambridge Dictionary of Philosophy*, professor Noah Lemos (1995) gives this definition:

> **value theory**, also called, axiology, the branch of philosophy concerned with the nature of value and with what kinds of things have value. Construed very broadly, value theory is concerned with all forms of value, such as the aesthetic values of beauty and ugliness, the ethical values of right, wrong, obligation, virtue, and vice, and the epistemic values of justification and lack of justification. Understood more narrowly, value theory is concerned with what is intrinsically valuable or ultimately worthwhile and desirable for its own sake and with the related concepts of instrumental, inherent, and contributive value. When construed very broadly, the study of ethics may be taken as a branch of value theory, but understood more narrowly value theory may be taken as a branch of ethics.

This work will take the broad view and include ethics/morality as a branch of value theory along with aesthetics and, following Young (1954:23), the second-order discipline of philosophy of history.

Ethics and morality are often used as synonyms, but some philosophers see the relationship between the two to be like the relationship between theory and practice, with the former denoting the theory of right conduct and the latter referring to the actual practice of right conduct. Ethics can be understood as the philosophical study of morality, which is concerned with our beliefs and judgements regarding right and wrong. Ethics comes from the Greek word *ethikos* (custom) and in ordinary usage refers to a set of rules or principles by which certain acts are permitted or prohibited. Morality comes from the Latin *moralis* (customs), and is ordinarily used to evaluate certain acts. For this work, ethics will be used in a theoretical sense as being descriptive and morality will be used in the practical sense as being more prescriptive or evaluative. Ethical/moral questions include: Who or what determines what is moral or immoral? Is right and wrong behaviour determinative by the situation? Is it wrong to lie? What justifies an action? Is infidelity ever justified?

Aesthetics is from the Greek *aisthesis* (sensation) and is usually limited to the part of the sensible world to which the term 'beauty' may apply. Aesthetics is described by professor Susan Feagin (1995) as 'the branch of philosophy that examines the nature of art and the character of our experience of art and the natural environment.' German philosopher Alexander Baumgarten (1714–1762) is credited with coining the term 'aesthetics' in his *Philosophical Meditations on Poetry* (1735). He derived it from the Greek word *aisthanomi* (to perceive) and says that it has always been intimately connected with sensory experience and the kinds of feelings it arouses. Although philosophy of art dominates the study of aesthetics, this work is more concerned with man's aesthetic relationship with the natural environment and with the aesthetic value of religious experience.

Philosophy of history is concerned with the philosophical study of human history and the attempts to record and interpret it. In everyday usage history is thought of as the progression of events that happened in the past and as the discipline of acquiring the knowledge of those events. Philosophy of history seeks to find repeated patterns or laws imbedded in the succession of historical events and to give meaning to them. The philosopher Hegel turned man's attention to the importance of history stating: 'And if the world is under the control of God then the entire process might be appropriately interpreted as the divine Reason realizing itself in history.' The concern of this work is with the analytical aspect of philosophy of history considering the views of ATR and Christianity on such things as the meaning of history, and whether or not history is cyclical or linear in progression.

Epistemology

Epistemology comes from the Greek *episteme* (knowledge) and *logos* (study of) and is defined in A.R. Lacey's *A Dictionary of Philosophy* (1986:63) as: 'Enquiry into the nature and ground of experience, belief and knowledge. "What can we know, and how do we know it?" are questions central to philosophy, and knowledge forms the main topic of epistemology, along with other cognitive notions like, belief, understanding, reason, judgement, sensation, imagination, supposing, guessing, learning, forgetting.' Epistemology is the branch of philosophy that studies the rationality and justification of what is believed. In analysing the worldviews of ATR and Christianity, we are analysing belief systems and will be investigating the rationality and justification of each.

Which Worldview(s) Reflect Reality?

In analysing worldviews from a truth claim standpoint, one would expect that the worldview that contains the most truth would best reflect reality, since by definition, truth means the quality of those propositions that accord with reality, specifying what is, in fact, the case. Philosophers use the fundamentals of logic to investigate truth-claims.

Logic

Aristotle wrote a series of essays titled, 'Logic' or 'Organon' in which he put forth principles of human reason, both valid and invalid. His goal was to establish the steps to be used in logically constructing a body of knowledge. Aristotle showed how every science begins with certain obvious truths that he referred to as *first principles*, explaining how these first principles form the foundations upon which all knowledge rests. First principles are the fundamental truths from which inferences are made and on which conclusions are based. They are self-evident, and they can be thought of as both the underlying and the governing principles of a worldview.

If Aristotle was right, then one's worldview is only as valid as the first assumptions on which it is based and the logical inferences drawn from them. Correct reasoning should enable us to determine if one's worldview is credible, and correct reasoning is established by the principles of logic. We all use logic in the form of human reason to think about the reality of our existence. The use of reason and the reality of our existence are fundamental assumptions that all people share. They are unavoidable; in order to deny them one would have to use reason to think of a basis for the denial, and one would have to exist to engage in the reasoning process. Once we begin using reason to think about our existence we have begun to philosophically construct a worldview using the principles of logic.

The first principle of logic is the principle of contradiction, also called the principle of non-contradiction, and is the principle that a statement and its negation, or opposite, cannot both be true. This principle is also called the law of noncontradiction (LNC) and asks, 'can opposite truth claims both be true?' Can the Christian claim that evil is real and the Hindu claim that evil is an illusion both be right? According to the LNC if one claim is true, the other claim must be false. The LNC is a self-evident truth and its usage is unavoidable even in its denial. To say that there is no such thing as absolute truth is to affirm a statement as being true that denies what it affirms. By invalidating the statement the LNC is automatically validated.

Two more first principles of logic are important in analysing the truth claims of a worldview. To communicate properly, we must share a mutual understanding of the meaning of the words communicated. Words are used as symbols to represent certain aspects of reality called referents. This gives rise to another law of logic called the law of identity (LID). This law states that something is what we say it is, the symbol and the referent are one and the same (A is, in fact, A). The third law of logic is called the law of the excluded middle (LEM). It states that something is either A or non-A, but it cannot be both at the same time and in the same context. These principles are absolute and form the basis of all valid thinking. Words vary from language to language, but if they refer to the same reality their meaning is universal.

These three first principles or laws of logic (LNC, LID, LEM) are necessary in analysing truth claims, but logic's function is to correct erroneous thinking and is therefore a negative test for truth. Logic by itself will not help us find truth but will only help us detect error because the true must be logical, but the logical does not necessarily have to be true. Two unicorns plus two unicorns equals four unicorns is a logical statement, but it does not mean that unicorns, of a truth, really exist. How can we discover truth in worldviews if logic, by itself, only detects errors?

The first presupposition that is required of anyone searching for truth is that truth can be found. To say that truth does not exist is to assume that view to be true which violates the LNC and is self-defeating. Truth is a symbol, or statement that matches or corresponds to its object or referent, whether it is an abstract idea or something concrete. To say that true statements can be made about reality is rationally justifiable. In the area of religion there are many conflicting statements about reality. How can we discover the correct view?

In analysing worldviews, it should be evident that some are epistemically superior to others. Many philosophers have put forth various criteria for examining the intellectual and practical validity of alternative worldview truth claims. Professor W.C. Young (1954:47–59) has given one of the more comprehensive sets of criteria which will be summarized here. He divides them into four main types, or groups, of criteria that man has historically used to determine correspondence with reality: Immediate, Social, Philosophical and Revelational, and then he describes the components of each. People that do not do a critical analysis of the sources of their beliefs are likely to use any or all of these criteria for accepting or rejecting a truth claim.

Immediate Criteria

1. *Instinct*. This is an inborn pattern of activity and response common to a specific biological group. While it may be possible to grasp certain truths instinctively, to make instinct a final judge of truth would make the lower biological nature superior to the higher reasoning capacity of man.

2. *Feeling*. Feelings can take the form of emotion as in 'it just feels right' or the form of a hunch as in 'I have a feeling that he is coming today.' As a judge of truth, feelings are usually wrong as often as they are right.

3. *Sense Experience*. A large part of what we learn comes through our senses. In fact, some philosophers claim that *all* knowledge is acquired that way. But Aristotle saw that sense data must be interpreted by the 'common sense' in the intellect before the data could be known.

4. *Intuition*. This is immediate knowledge, insight or understanding without any conscious reasoning process. Intuition has been credited for many important discoveries that seem to have been reached by 'a sudden flash of genius.' Man does seem to grasp certain things in a direct fashion, but very often the intuition of different people contradicts each other. In such cases, man's rational nature must appeal to a higher criterion to make a choice.

Social Criteria

1. *Custom*. The way people in a society are accustomed to behaving tends to become authoritative. But customs cannot be a final standard for truth because customs change and they can clash with other societies and customs.

2. *Tradition.* Customs and traditions differ in degree only. Customs that have been held for a long time become deeply rooted and become tradition. However, even traditions held for generations can, and eventually do, change. Tradition may contain truth, but does not make truth.

3. *Universal Agreement (Consensus gentium).* The fact that an idea has been universally believed is taken as evidence of its truth. One only needs to remember that at one time it was universally believed that the earth was flat to realize that universal belief does not make something true.

Philosophical Criteria

1. *Correspondence.* This is the empirical test. Truth must have a correspondence with reality. In worldview analysis the worldview should fit with reality and offer convincing explanations or interpretations of the totality of things. Distinguishing truth from error is a matter of showing just how *this* word, statement or idea corresponds with *that* reality. Correspondence is involved in every truth judgement.

2. *Pragmatism.* This is the existential test and is concerned with the practicality or workability of truth claims in a worldview. Is it liveable? A belief system should not only be practical, but it should be personally satisfactory, meeting the internal needs for a sense of peace and well-being. The major problem with this criterion of truth is that the terms practical, workable, liveable, personally satisfactory, peace and well-being are all relative. A career thief would have different meanings for these terms than would a parish priest.

3. *Coherence.* This is the rational test and implies that in order for a statement to be believed it must make sense, or be coherent, with what is already believed as part of the first truths of a worldview. It presupposes the existence of a body of truth. Coherence will not determine whether any particular worldview is based on true or false beliefs. Many supposedly coherent systems of the past, like Ptolemaic astronomy, have ceased to be. But

Young (1954:57) concludes: 'Without doubt, coherence has great value in reminding us that our world-views must hold together. It reminds us that all facts which have significance must be included in arriving at a philosophy of life. Man's mind demands an ordered and reasonable outlook.'

The non-worldview-conscious person will use the immediate and social criteria to develop their belief systems. The worldview examiner will use the philosophical criteria to determine the strengths and weaknesses of various conceptual frameworks. No one criterion is an absolute proof of truth. Taken together they may indicate a probability of truth but exception can be found for each. Therefore, these criteria may be used to show that one worldview may be epistemically superior to another, but they cannot prove any worldview accurately reflects reality in its totality. In analysing the biblical or Christian worldview another criterion of truth must be considered. The Christian worldview claims to be based upon special revelation that has been recorded in its scriptures, the Bible.

Revelation

Special revelation is the means relied upon to obtain the first truths in the Christian worldview. The Christian believes that God exists and that he has communicated some of his truth through the world of nature, but he has also revealed himself and spoken to humanity through his written Word. God has revealed divine truth, but not exhaustive truth, about the origin, nature, purpose and destiny of man and the entire cosmos. It is upon God's special revelation that the Christian bases his worldview. It is built on a supernatural basis and should be the most essential element of his philosophy of life.

In concluding this chapter, I turn to the concluding remarks of Dr. David Naugle (2002:345):

> After all, what could be more important or influential than the way an individual, a family, a community, a nation or an entire culture conceptualizes reality? Is there anything more profound or powerful than the shape and content of human consciousness and its primary interpretation of the nature of things? When it comes to the deepest questions about human life and existence, does anything surpass the final implications of the answers supplied by one's essential *Weltanschauung*? Because of the divine design of human nature, each person in a native religious quest

possesses an insatiable desire to understand the secret of life. A hunger and thirst, indeed, a burning fire rages to solve the riddle of the universe. There is a yearning in the very core of the heart to rest in some understanding of the alpha and omega of the human condition. . . . The mystery of a heart is the mystery of its *Weltanschauung*.

In the following two chapters I will examine how the philosophical elements and religious dimensions of a worldview are lived out in the biblical and traditional African worldviews. The next chapter will examine the biblical, or Christian, worldview and how it answers the questions of life. Chapter 4 will do the same for the traditional African worldview based upon African Traditional Religion.

3

Biblical Worldview

This chapter will delineate the biblical, or Christian, worldview in summary form. A worldview based on the content of the Bible, the Holy Scriptures of the Christian faith, is considered to be the Christian worldview. For the Christian, the Bible gives not only religious doctrine to be believed and religious ritual to be practiced, but it also gives a religious picture of the whole world, and all of time, that formulates into a *Weltanschauung*. This chapter is not concerned with the tenets, dogmas or doctrines of the Christian religion. It is concerned with how the Bible answers the worldview questions that we all ask, and how those answers are formulated into a Christian philosophy of life or worldview. The next chapter is concerned with how African Traditional Religion answers the same questions and how those answers are formulated into an African worldview.

Christian Religion as Philosophy

The discipline of philosophy and its relationship to the religion of Christianity has a history that follows the thesis→antithesis→synthesis pathway. Christianity began in a culture greatly influenced by Greek philosophy and the question since its beginning has been: Christianity *vs* philosophy or Christianity *as* philosophy? Tertulian (155–222), one of the earliest church Fathers, taught that philosophy has no place in religion. He reportedly said that he believed Christianity because it is absurd. Two hundred years later, Augustine (354–430), Bishop of Hippo, assimilated Platonism into his Christian theology. Anselm (1033–1109), Archbishop of Canterbury, formulated his now famous version of the ontological argument for the existence of God. Thomas Aquinas (1225–1274), a Roman Catholic philosopher, brought Aristotelian philosophy into the Christian faith believing that philosophy and religion compliment each other, with reasoning pointing us toward faith. John Wesley (1703–1791) considered philosophy to be separate from Christianity but something that ministers needed to acquire knowledge of. In his 'Address to the Clergy' delivered February 6, 1756, Wesley (1872:492) challenged the ministers to be a 'tolerable master of the sciences' by entering through the gate of logic. And he asked them to ask themselves: 'Do I understand metaphysics; if not the depths of the Schoolmen, the subtleties of Scotus or Aquinas, yet the first rudiments, the general principles, of that useful science?'

By the late nineteenth century, the concept of worldview had firmly established itself within the discipline of philosophy. James Orr (1844–1913) delivered his famous Kerr Lectures, which were published in book form, to justify the rationality of the Christian view of the world. He noted the recurrent use of *Weltanschauung* in philosophy and German theology and saw the need to expound a Christian *Weltanschauung*. However, he does not equate *Weltanschauung* and philosophy. Orr (1948:8) writes:

> Christianity, it is granted, is not a scientific system, though, if its views of the world be true, it must be reconcilable with all that is certain and established in the results of science. It is not a philosophy, though, if it be valid, its fundamental assumptions will be found to be in harmony with the conclusions at which sound reason, attaching its own problems, independently arrives. It is a religion, historical in its origin, and claiming to rest on divine Revelation. But though Christianity is neither a scientific system, nor a philosophy, it has yet a world-view of its own, to which it stands committed. . . . It has, as every religion should and must have, its own peculiar interpretation to give of the facts of existence; its own way of looking at, and accounting for, the existing natural and moral order; its own idea of a world-aim, and of that 'one far-off Divine event,' to which, through slow and painful travail, 'the whole creation moves.' As thus binding the natural and moral worlds in their highest unity, through reference to their ultimate principle, God, it involves a '*Weltanschauung*.'

Although Orr did not believe that the Christian view of the world constituted a philosophy, he used the field of philosophy to structure his work. Throughout his lectures he pits Christianity and the Christian worldview up against the philosophies and philosophers of his day and prior.

The second half of the twentieth century witnessed a synthesis of opinion among Christian theologians and educators that the religion of Christianity does contain its own worldview and it also constitutes a philosophy of life. For several decades Christian philosophers have been defending the truth of the Christian worldview with philosophically sophisticated arguments in scholarly journals. In the early 1950s two philosophy textbooks were published by professors at well-known evangelical seminaries that have been used by many Christian colleges and seminaries over the years. Edward John Carnell published *A Philosophy of the Christian Religion* and *A Christian Approach to Philosophy* was published by Warren C. Young. Carnell's book limits itself to reason reaching its perfection in faith in the person of Jesus Christ. Carnell (1952:53) states: 'Biblical Christianity outlines an epistemological and metaphysical framework which gives cosmic support to the virtue of love.' His philosophy results in a religion of love but not in a total worldview. Young's book on the other hand is an introduction to Christian philosophy for Christian colleges. It deals with the principles of philosophy and concludes with what he calls, 'The Christian realistic world-view.' Young (1954:200) writes:

> The Christian realistic faith is founded, not on human speculation, but on divine disclosure . . . if 'philosophy' be understood to mean a world-view or a way of life, as it has been used throughout this work, and as it is most generally understood today, then Christianity is a philosophy. If philosophy is . . . the attempt to see life steadily and to see it whole, or as others have suggested, to give a coherent account of all of one's experience, then certainly there is a Christian philosophy. The basic question of human experience is not philosophy *verses no* philosophy, but *good* philosophy *versus bad* philosophy. Everyone has a philosophy of life, a world-view, no matter what form it may happen to take. Our problem is not to get rid of philosophy, but to find the right philosophy, and having found it, to present it to others with a conviction that grows out of the assurance that one has found the truth.

After Young came Francis Schaeffer (1912–1984) who wrote prolifically from the late 1960s to the early 1980s. In one of his early works Schaeffer (1982:178) writes: 'The Christian system (what is taught in the whole Bible) is a unity of thought. Christianity is not just a lot of bits and pieces—there is a beginning and an end, a whole system of truth, and this system is the only system that will stand up to all the questions that are presented to us as we face the reality of existence.' If we look at a definition of 'philosophy' as given in *The New Shorter Oxford English Dictionary*, 4th ed.: 'A set or system of ideas, opinions, beliefs, or principles of behaviour based on an overall understanding of existence and the universe', then Christianity would certainly be a philosophy. Most of Schaeffer's writings use metaphysics, ethics/morality and epistemology to present the Christian system and to defend it against other philosophies.

J.P. Moreland and William Lane Craig represent a large contingent of present day Christian philosophers teaching in Christian colleges and universities. They are well educated in philosophy from prestigious universities in the U.S. and Europe and they teach Christianity as philosophy. Moreland and Craig co-wrote a mammoth textbook titled *Philosophical Foundations for a Christian Worldview* in which they present Christianity as philosophy and show how philosophy is used in constructing systematic theologies and as tools in apologetics and polemics.

From its early years in which Christianity was seen as antithesis to philosophy (the Apostle Paul wrote to the church in Colosse recorded in Colossians 2:8, 'Beware lest anyone cheat you through philosophy and empty deceit'), to Christianity and philosophy being seen as separate but friends, Christianity has now been recognized by Christian scholars as a philosophy that can compete with and conquer other philosophies. Christian philosophy is lived out in a Christian or biblical worldview which has its foundation built upon the first eleven chapters of the first book (Genesis) of the Christian holy book, the Bible.

Use of Genesis 1–11 in Establishing the Biblical Worldview

The Bible, as Francis Schaeffer stated, contains a whole unified system of thought that constitutes a biblical worldview. Converts to Christianity must look to the Bible as their rule of faith and practice and therefore, must live by and with the biblical worldview. The value of using Genesis 1–11 in establishing the biblical worldview is given by Hans Weerstra (1997d:56):

> Epistemology asks how do we know what we know, and how valid and true is what we know, and what is the source and limitations, if any, of the knowledge we have. Genesis 1–11 gives true, reasonable and reliable answers to these ultimate questions. Without God's revelation given in the first chapters of Genesis no

true reliable knowledge of ultimate reality, including the visible and invisible existence (empirical and non-empirical reality), is possible. One cannot obtain the deep answers concerning life, its origin, meaning and purpose without this fundamental basic reality as God has given it in Genesis 1–11.

Genesis as First Principles

The Book of Genesis was written in the Hebrew language and the first word of the book is *bereshith* which means 'in beginning.' The first word of a book customarily was used by the Hebrews as the title for the book. The earliest translation of the Hebrew Scriptures into Greek used the Greek word *genesis* (meaning origin, source, generation) as the title for the first book. First principles of the biblical worldview are expressed as origins. Henry Morris (1976:17) explains why:

> The Book of Genesis gives vital information concerning the origin of all things—and therefore the meaning of all things—which would otherwise be forever inaccessible to man. The future is bound up in the past. One's belief concerning his origin will inevitably determine his belief concerning his purpose and his destiny. A naturalistic, animalistic concept of beginnings specifies a naturalistic, animalistic program for the future. An origin at the hands of an omnipotent, holy, loving God, on the other hand, necessarily predicts a divine purpose in history and an assurance of the consummation of that purpose. A believing understanding of the Book of Genesis is therefore prerequisite to an understanding of God and His meaning to man.

John Philips (1980:38) has this to say about origins: 'Genesis 1 is a statement of origins, and science knows nothing of origins. Science is concerned with how things go on and has nothing to say about how they began. Science can measure the laws that now govern in the material universe, but those laws do not explain how the whole process started . . . that kind of information is not to be obtained by *reason* but by *revelation*.'

Among the first principles of the biblical worldview as given by Morris (1976:18–21) are these:

1. *Origin of the universe*—The Book of Genesis stands alone in accounting for the actual creation of the space-mass-time continuum which constitutes our physical universe.

2. *Origin of order and complexity*—Man's universal observation . . . is that orderly and complex things tend naturally to decay into disorder and simplicity. Order and complexity never arise spontaneously—they are always generated by a prior cause programmed to produce such order.

3. *Origin of the solar system*—The Book of Genesis tells that the earth, sun, moon, planets and all the stars of heaven were brought into existence by the Creator. Modern scientific cosmogonists have been notably unsuccessful in attempting to devise naturalistic theories of the origin of the universe and the solar system.

4. *Origin of life*—How living systems could have come into being from non-living chemicals is . . . a total mystery to materialistic philosophers. If the laws of thermodynamics and probability mean anything at all, the almost-infinite complexity programmed into the genetic systems of plants and animals are inexplicable except by special creation.

5. *Origin of man*—Man is the most highly organized and complex entity in the universe, so far as we know, possessing not only innumerable intricate physio-chemical structures and the marvellous capacities of life and reproduction, but also a nature which contemplates the abstract entities of beauty and love and worship, and which is capable of philosophizing about its own meaning. Man's imaginary evolutionary descent from animal ancestors is altogether illusory. The true record of his origin is given only in Genesis.

6. *Origin of marriage*—The remarkably universal and stable institution of marriage and the home, in a monogamous, patriarchal social culture, is described in Genesis as having been ordained by the Creator.

7. *Origin of evil*—The origin of physical and moral evil in the universe is explained in Genesis as a temporary intrusion into God's perfect world, allowed by him as a concession to the principle of

human freedom and responsibility, and also to manifest himself as Redeemer as well as Creator.

8. *Origin of languages and nations*—All scholars today accept the unity of the human race. Only the Book of Genesis adequately explains how distinct nations, races and languages could develop if all men were originally of one race, one language and in one location.

9. *Origin of culture*—The Book of Genesis describes the beginning of the main entities which we now associate with civilized cultures—such things as urbanization, metallurgy, music, agriculture, animal husbandry, education, navigation, textiles and ceramics.

10. *Origin of religion*—Many religions take the form of an organized system of worship and conduct. The origin of this unique characteristic of man's consciousness, as well as the origin of true worship of the true God, is given in Genesis.

This connection between origin and worldview is expressed by University of South Africa professor Petrus van Dyke (2001:156): 'all these questions pertain directly to our worldview and ultimately to our concept of origins.' Does the book of Genesis contain true history and true science as the first principles of the Christian worldview?

Genesis 1–11 and Science

The book of Genesis divides naturally into two parts. The first section (chapters 1–11) records the earliest history of the world, called primeval history. Primeval history focuses on the world as a whole and on mankind in general. The second section of Genesis (chapters 12–50) records the history of a specific family line (Abraham) and is known as patriarchal history because it tells us about the forefathers or patriarchs of the nation of Israel.

Scientists and scholars have questioned the historical accuracy, or truthfulness, of what is recorded in Genesis 1–11 for centuries. For years, scholars from the school of higher criticism questioned the factual historicity of Genesis 12–50 almost as strongly as they did of Genesis 1–11. However, because archaeological discoveries continue to prove the accuracy of what is recorded in Genesis 12–50 regarding people, places and events, its factual historicity is questioned only by the most ardent sceptics.

The factual historicity of what is recorded in Genesis 1–11 is denied by secular science and those Christians who hold to the authority of science over the authority of Scripture in the area of origins. Science, as a discipline, has become an authority unto itself. For science to recognize the factual historicity of Genesis 1–11 it must recognize the fact of God. Science will not bow its authority to God. It therefore must come up with alternative theories to explain the origin of things that are—theories that cannot be proven. They must be believed by faith.

This book does not attempt to reconcile Genesis 1–11 with science, but it does attempt to compare the biblical worldview based on what *is* recorded in Genesis 1–11 with the traditional African worldview base on ATR. David Atkinson (1990:10) in his commentary *The Message of Genesis 1–11* sums up the position taken in this work: 'the fact remains that it is this text in its canonical form which Christian people have from the beginning received as the opening chapters of their Bibles. It is this text as a whole which the writers of the New Testament had before them. It is this text through which the divine Word comes to us.' And it is this text that Christians believe.

Revelation as Postulating Christian Philosophy

Christians believe that the biblical worldview has its source in God and that God has made known to us the truths of that worldview through indirect and direct communication with mankind. The mode of that communication is in the form of revelation and it consists of two kinds. The indirect communication is called 'general' or 'natural' revelation. General revelation is not found in the Bible or in the life of Jesus Christ but in God's creation and in the conscience of man (Ps 8; Rm 1:20). Nature does not give propositional truth, but it does give data from which inferences can be reasonably drawn. While not imparting salvific truths such as the incarnation, or atonement, general revelation does impart reasonable evidence that a powerful, rational divine Being exists. Special revelation, supernatural in nature, is God's direct communication to mankind through spoken words recorded in the Bible (Gn 35:7; 1 Cor 2:10; 1 Pt 1:20) and through the incarnation of Jesus Christ, who is part of a triune God-head of one God (Jn 1:1, 14; 10:30; Col 2:9; 1 Tm 3:16). Since Jesus Christ was God in the flesh, everything he said and did was a revelation of God's mind and character.

The Christian faith is not founded on human speculation but on divine disclosure. To human confusion and sinfulness God responds with objective and concrete revelation. This supernatural revelation was given to man for his edification, so that he would know God, how to relate to God and how to relate to his fellow man. This supernatural revelation was given to man so that, if believed and practiced, his life could be all that God intended it to be when he was created, that is, a life of godliness (2 Pt 1:3), and life to the full (Jn 10:10). This is the basic postulate of Christian philosophy and the biblical worldview. All philosophical systems begin with postulates of some kind. There is no evident reason for rejecting the hypothesis that a worldview may be built on a supernatural postulate. The assumption of supernatural revelation is not something that can be validated by identification with natural categories. To prove revelation, one would have to use natural means, which would be to prove that there is no revelation after all. To *experience* revelation or the supernatural is quite another matter. The experiential dimension of revelation will be addressed later in this chapter.

Delineation of the Christian Worldview

Genesis 1–11 contains the basic propositions of the Christian worldview, either in a fully developed form (e.g. origins) or in germ or seed form (e.g. the atonement). Just like a seed contains the fruit, so the first book of the Bible contains the seed of all the themes that follow in Scripture. Genesis 1–11 and the themes that follow put forth a religious view of God called 'theism.' *Nelson's New Christian Dictionary* defines theism: 'Theological system which postulates a transcendent God who is the creator of the universe, an imminent God who sustains it, and a personal God who is able to communicate with and redeem his creation. Christian theism is also monistic or monotheistic.' Religious worldviews begin with God and the Christian worldview begins with theism. In his book *The Christian View of God and the World As Centring in the Incarnation*, James Orr outlines what he calls a 'Sketch of the Christian View' from which I have borrowed as a starting point for delineating the Christian worldview. Note: Genesis 12:1–3 is included with Genesis 1–11 because the event recorded there obviously took place chronologically prior to Genesis 11:31.

Outline of the Christian View (Orr 1948:32–34)

I.   The existence of a Personal, Ethical, Self-Revealing God: A system of Theism. [Gn 1:1, 27, 28]

II. A. The creation of the world by God. [Gn 1:1–2:1]

    B. God's imminent presence in the world. [Gn 2:8]

    C. God's transcendence over the world. [Gn 6:5, 9:17]

    D. God's holy and wise government of the world for moral ends. [Gn 11:1–8; 12:1–3]

III. A. Man's spiritual nature and dignity. [Gn 1:27; 2:7]

    B. Man's creation in the Divine image. [Gn 1:27]

    C. Man's destination to bear the image of God in a perfected relation of sonship. [Gn 3:15]

IV. A. The existence of sin and disorder in the world. [Gn 3:6, 7; 4:8; 6:5, 11; 9:20–27]

    B. Sin and disorder does not belong to the Divine idea of the world and is not inherent in the world by necessity. [Gn 1:31; 3:16–19]

    C. Sin and disorder entered the world by the voluntary turning aside of man from his allegiance to his Creator, and from the path of his moral development. [Gn 3:6]

    D. A Fall as the presupposition of its doctrine of Redemption. [Gn 3:14, 15]

V.   The historical Self-Revelation of God to the patriarchs and in the line of Israel bringing to light a gracious purpose of God for the salvation of the world, centring in Jesus Christ, His Son, and the new Head of humanity. [Gn 3:15; 6:13; 12:1]

VI. A. Jesus Christ was not mere man, but the eternal Son of God—a Divine Person. [Gn 3:15]

    B. Jesus Christ took upon himself our humanity and in him dwells the fullness of the Godhead bodily. [Gn 3:15]

    C. Therefore, Jesus Christ is to be honoured and worshipped even as God is. [Gn 3:15]

    D. The incarnation sheds new light on:

       1. The nature of God, with the work of the Spirit, reveals him as triune—Father, Son and Spirit—one God. [Gn 1:26; 3:15; 6:3]

2. The doctrine of creation—all things being created by him and for him. [Gn 1:1–26]

3. The nature of man and his capacity for union with the Divine; its possibility of perfections, and the high destinies awaiting it in the future. [Gn 1:26, 27; 2:7]

4. The purpose of God in the Creation and Redemption of man—to gather together in one all things in Christ (Eph 1:10). [Gn 3:15]

5. The permission of sin by showing the possibility of Redemption from it, Divine mercy revealing a grander discovery of the Divine Character, and far greater prospects are opened up for humanity. [Gn 2:16, 17; 3:15, 21]

VII.A. The redemption of the world through a great act of atonement. [Gn 3:15]

B. The atonement to be appropriated by faith. [Gn 3:15]

C. The atonement availing for all who do not wilfully reject its grace. [Gn 3:15]

VIII. The historic aim of Christ's work was the founding of a kingdom of God on earth which includes the spiritual salvation of individuals and a new order of society. [Gn 3:15; 7:1]

IX. A. History has a goal. [Gn 3:15]

B. The present order of things will be terminated by the appearance of the Son of Man for judgement. [Gn 3:15; 6:3a, 13]

C. The resurrection of the dead. [Gn 3:15]

D. The final separation of righteous and wicked. [Gn 3:15]

Protevangelium

Further comment needs to be made on the full content of the meaning of Genesis 3:15. The events described in Genesis 1–11 apply generally to all mankind. They are the events of primeval history of the world. The events of Genesis 11:31 to 12:4 describe the origin of the Israelites, the Jews or Hebrews, which are the descendants of Abraham. Genesis 3:15 contains the prophetic announcement of an event that would take place thousands of years in the future and which would mark the beginning of the Christian religion. The prologue to the events of Genesis 3 is recorded in Revelation 12:7–9:

> And there was war in heaven. Michael and his angels fought against the dragon, and the dragon and his angels fought back. But he was not strong enough, and they lost their place in heaven. The great dragon was hurled down—that ancient serpent called the devil, or Satan, who leads the whole world astray. He was hurled to the earth, and his angels with him.

Genesis 3 records how the serpent (identified above as Satan) tempted the first man and woman to disobey God, thus bringing sin into the world. God pronounces a curse upon the serpent, stating in Genesis 3:15:

> And I will put enmity
> Between you and the woman,
> And between your seed and her Seed;
> He shall bruise your head,
> And you shall bruise His heel. NKJV

This verse is pregnant with meaning for the Christian religion and the Christian worldview. What is partially revealed here (in germ or seed form), as words spoken by God, was further revealed as phenomenon in actual space-time history and was consummately revealed in the visions and writing of John the Apostle in the Book of Revelation, the final book of the Christian Bible. As soon as man sinned, God let it be known that the enmity (hostility) is between man and Satan, not between man and God. Satan has a seed consisting of all humanity of all time that oppose God and good and do evil (Jn 8:44; Ac 13:10; Eph 2:1, 2). The woman also has a seed consisting of those in the human family who are brought into right relationship with God through faith.

The last part of Genesis 3:15 implies that in addition to the plural and corporate meaning of the two seeds, there is another meaning as well. There is one ultimate seed of the serpent and one ultimate seed of the woman, and those two ultimate seeds will be engaged in ultimate conflict with the seed of the woman ultimately triumphant (Rv 20).

This great promise of Genesis 3:15 is called the *Protevangelium* meaning 'first gospel.' There is good New Testament authority for seeing here the *Protevangelium*, the first glimmer of the gospel which makes its debut as a sentence passed on Satan, our enemy, and not a direct promise to man. The Christian belief is that God's coming to earth in the form of His Son, Jesus

Christ (the incarnation), who was born of a virgin (Is 7:4; Mt 1:23) made him not the seed of a man but the seed of the woman (Gal 4:4). He came to establish God's kingdom on earth (Mt 4:23; 12:28; Lk 17:20, 21; Rm 14:17). That kingdom was not established without a conflict with the 'prince of this world' (Jn 12:31; 1 Jn 5:19). The final blow by the Seed of the woman to Satan was mentioned first ('He shall bruise your head') referring to his final defeat and eternal judgement (Rv 20:2, 3, 10). Satan delivered the first blow to the Seed of the woman when Jesus Christ was crucified on the cross to pay mankind's sin debt to God (the atonement)—'But He was wounded for our transgressions, He was bruised for our iniquities,' (Is 53:6). God had announced in Genesis 2:17 that disobedience would bring death (spiritual death, or separation from God, and physical death) (see also Rm 6:23) and death became an enemy of man. The bruising of Christ's heel was not a fatal blow because Christ was resurrected from the dead and became the first fruit of all who die as seed of the woman (1 Cor 15:20–23), thus destroying the enemy of death (1 Cor 15:26). The Christian gospel is that if man will acknowledge his sinfulness before God, accept by faith the death of Jesus Christ on the cross as payment of his own sin debt (substitutionary atonement), then he will only die physically and not spiritually, and that at an appointed time his body will be resurrected to newness of life. Those who die without faith in Christ's substituting atonement will be resurrected to everlasting punishment (Heb. 6:2; Jude 7; Rv 20:13–15). This is all impregnated into the *Protevangelium* in Genesis 3:15.

The Christian worldview implications of the *Protevangelium* are tremendous. The Christian sees all humanity as being of one or the other seeds. There are no other options. The Christian sees the enmity between the seeds as the source of conflicts and hostilities in the world. Moral and natural evil is explained, and the power to overcome evil and do good is revealed. The question of what happens after death is answered. The love of God for humanity is revealed (Jn 3:16). The meaning and purpose of history is explained and man's final destiny is exposed. The worldview of the Bible moves from being biblical to being specifically Christian because of the *Protevangelium* in Genesis 3:15.

Philosophical Elements of the Christian Worldview

Following the philosophical methodology of posing questions and then formulating answers to them, a question/answer format will be used in delineating the philosophical elements of the Christian worldview. Within each first-order discipline of philosophy discussed in chapter 2 some broad questions will be posed allowing for the expounding of an answer based upon the biblical or Christian view. Chapter 4 will use this format asking the same questions to be answered by the traditional African view based upon ATR.

Ontology Questions

Is there a Supreme Being, and, if so, what is it like?

This question deals with the existence and nature of God. As to the existence of God, the Christian Scriptures assume it. The Book of Genesis is the first book and it begins: 'In the beginning God . . . ' If those first four words of the Bible are believed, all else contained in the Bible becomes credible. God is, but what is God? Both philosophers and scientists seek to define their terms carefully but the biblical writers were not concerned at all with definitions. In speaking of the first verse of the Bible ('In the beginning God created the heavens and the earth') Carnell comments: 'Neither here, nor in the context, is a formal, Aristotelian definition given of any of the difficult terms which are so casually employed: "Beginning," "God," "heavens," "earth." As for God, the Being cannot be defined connotatively (how can the highest genus be subsumed under anything?) or denotatively (since there is only one specimen to which the name may be applied).' Carnell concludes: 'The biblical writers were not interested in doing the impossible, defining God, they were interested in leading people *to* God.'

God is not a term to be defined but a person to be known. A person can be known if that person's nature, character and attributes can be known by the intellect and confirmed to exist by experience. That is exactly how the Christian knows his God. From Genesis 1:1 to Revelation 22:21 the Bible is revealing the nature, character and attributes of God through his words and actions, constantly inviting the reader to a personal, experiential relationship with him.

The attributes of God are described by Professor Gordon Lewis in the *Evangelical Dictionary of Theology*:

> God is an invisible, personal and living Spirit, distinguished from all other spirits by several kinds of attributes: metaphysically God is self-existent, eternal and unchanging; intellectually God is omniscient, faithful and wise: ethically God is just, merciful and loving; emotionally God detests evil, is long-suffering and is compassionate; existentially God is free, authentic and omnipotent; relationally God is transcendent in being, immanent

universally in providential activity and immanent with his people in redemptive activity.

Lewis only mentions that God is loving and fails to mention that God is holy. These two attributes are prominent in God's self-revelation in the Bible. He is said to be 'majestic in holiness' (Ex 15:11). He states: 'I am the Lord your God; consecrate yourselves and be holy, because I am holy' (Lv 11:44). Heavenly creatures are described as worshipping God by saying: 'Holy, holy, holy is the Lord Almighty' (Is 6:3; Rv 4:8). As to his being loving, the Bible describes him as 'showing love to a thousand generations of those who love me and keep my commandments' (Ex 20:6). It also says that 'the earth is full of his unfailing love' (Ps 33:5). God's love for the world is manifest in the sacrifice of his Son, Jesus Christ, giving rise to the Christian faith (Jn 3:16), and God declares himself to be the personification of love in 1 John 4:16: 'God is love.'

In addition to the above attributes, God is revealed in the Bible and Christian philosophy as tri-personal. God's words and actions as recorded in the Bible are attributed to three different 'persons' (Father, Son and Holy Spirit) who are not three different gods or three modes of God. They are coequally and coeternally metaphysically one God. God is revealed as Father of all mankind even though they do not have a personal relationship with him, in that he is their creator. God is also revealed as a loving Father to all who are rightly related to him through faith in his Son, Jesus Christ. 'God the Son' speaks of the incarnation of Jesus Christ who is declared in Scripture to be God in the flesh. It was the death of God the Son on a cross that paid the death penalty of sin and opened the way for all humanity to know God as Father. God the Spirit is at work in the world convicting mankind of sin and indwelling those who repent of their sin and accept the atoning work of Christ by faith. The three 'persons' of God constitute a tri-unity, or Trinity, in Christian doctrine.

The Christian view of God answers man's basic question of why, besides energy, matter and form, is there personality in the universe. Man is personal, and since the personal cannot come from the impersonal, then that which is personal must have created man. Because God is personal and man is personal the possibility of feelings and communication between the two is a reality. The Christian view is of a personal and infinite God who created and sustains the universe which reflects his unity and diversity. In this sense God is a philosophic necessity. God has always been (Gn 1:1); he is the one prime existent.

What is the origin and nature of man?

The Christian view of man is that his nature is a direct result of his origin. Man's origin came about by a creative act of God and his nature came about because God created man in his own image (Gn 1:27). The mode used to put life in man was God's own breath: 'The Lord God formed the man from the dust of the ground and breathed into his nostrils the breath of life, and man became a living being' (Gn 2:7). Man is differentiated from the rest of creation, living and non-living, because only man was created in the image of God and only man has the breath or spirit of God in him. Like God, man is a tri-unity, a tri-unity of spirit, soul and body (1 Th 5:23). And, like God, man will exist in some form throughout eternity future (Da 12:2, Rm 6:23). Man is like God in image but not in essence. God is infinite; man is finite. There are no limits to the attributes of God. There are limits to the attributes of man.

Udo Middelmann (1974:15) writes that apart from the Christian view, man has only two ways to answer the question of his identity. He can seek his identity in the order of things in the cosmos, being one particular among a mass of particulars, and thus insignificant. Or he can deny that a separate identity is desirable and seek solace in a unity with all things and thus become a zero. The Christian view of the identity of man comes from outside the present external order. Man's origin is God who is not confined to this immediate existence. Man's primary relationship is to God.

Being made in the image of God who created all things, means that man has the ability to create but in a finite way. Creation requires imagination which is a mental synthesis of new ideas from elements experienced separately. Imagination is evidence of creativity. Unlike the animals, man is open to the creative restructuring of his environment. Man has the ability to act, rather than react as the animal does. Man can also enlarge his environment. Fairy tales and myths show man's creativity.

The Christian view of the nature of man is not just idealistic, it is realistic. Man as he is today does not accurately reflect the image of the God of the Bible who is absolute goodness and holiness. How can man, who was made in the image of God, be so inhuman to his fellowman? Francis Schaeffer (1972b:30) gives the Christian answer:

> at this point we must recognize . . . that man as he is now is not what he was; that man is discontinuous with what he has been, rather than continuous with what he has been. Or, to put it another way, man is now abnormal—he has changed.

Man as he now is by his own choice is not what he intrinsically was. In this case we can understand that man is now cruel, but that God is not a bad God.

There was a space-time, historic change in man. There is a discontinuity and not a continuity in man. Man, made in the image of God and not programmed, turned by choice from his proper integration point at a certain time in history. When he did this, man became something that he previously was not, and the dilemma of man becomes a true moral problem rather than merely a metaphysical one.

The space-time historic change in man came about as the result of the Fall as recorded in Genesis 3. Man wilfully chose to disobey God, his infinite reference point, and physical and spiritual separation from God was the result. Being created in the image of God, man possessed 'personality, self-transcendence, intelligence, morality, gregariousness and creativity' (Sire 1997:27). Sire (1997:33) explains what happened in each of the areas as a result of the Fall:

In *personality*, we lost our capacity to know ourselves accurately and to determine our own course of action freely in response to our intelligence.

Our self-transcendence was impaired by the alienation we experienced in relation to God, for as Adam and Eve turned from God, God let them go. Human *intelligence* also became impaired. Now we can no longer gain a fully accurate knowledge of the world around us, nor are we able to reason without constantly falling into error. *Morally*, we became less able to discern good and evil. *Socially*, we began to exploit other people. *Creatively*, our imagination became separated from reality; imagination became illusion, and artists who created gods in their own image led humanity further and further from its origin.

This being the Christian view of the present nature of man, is it any wonder that special revelation is the means relied upon to obtain the first truths in the Christian worldview. Man has changed since creation; God has not. If God has told us the truth about creation, he has told us the truth about man's present condition and what he (God) has done to provide a way of restoring his image in man (the incarnation and atonement).

What is reality, and what is ultimate reality?

The philosophical concept of reality comes from the Latin *realitas*, deriving from *res* meaning 'thing.' It was introduced into philosophy, apparently, by Duns Scotus who used the term as a synonym for 'being.' The standard philosophical definition is how things actually are, in contrast with their mere appearance. This means that appearance does not determine reality.

The Christian view of reality can be said, in philosophical terms, to encompass a form of realism embracing a form of dualism. Realism claims that we are in direct contact with a material, external world. That world exists independent of and external to our minds where ideas and sense data are processed. The Christian view accepts a spiritual realm as well as a physical realm, and in a modified moral dualism, recognizes an ongoing conflict between the seed of Satan and the seed of the woman.

Prior to the eighteenth century the Christian realistic view of reality dominated philosophy and science. Since that time the concept of reality has become highly subjective. Man desires to be autonomous, to be free from all restrictions so that he will not be bound by the external moral codes of a Supreme Being from which all other beings derive their existence. The Christian view of reality has not changed with the times.

The Christian concept of reality is based on the belief that the Bible is God's propositional revelation of truth. The Christian view is that God made an objective universe and personal beings with the ability to truly perceive that universe. God has given these personal beings the freedom to live with their perceptions and to measure them by his revealed Word (the Bible) and by the reality in which they live.

Is reality one or many or both? This metaphysical question is answered by Monism with everything as one (there is no diversity) in its very being, and by Pluralism with many beings and any unity perceived in them as not essential to their being. The Christian view is that there is a real unity and a real diversity of being in the universe. This view is based on the belief of a Trinity in the God-head. There are three persons in one God consisting of a plurality of persons and a unity of essence. Since a three-in-one God created the universe and the universe displays his glory (Ps 19:1), it is reasonable to believe that the universe reflects that same unity in diversity.

To the question of what is ultimate reality, the Christian answer is God. He is seen as the Uncaused Cause of everything that is except himself. God is the one prime existent, the one prime reality and the one source of all other reality. God is a necessary being, but his creatures are contingent.

What is truth?

At his trial, Jesus told Pilate that he came into the world to testify to the truth. Pilate responded with the question: 'What is truth?' (Jn 18:38). Pilate did not wait for an answer.

I will deal with the nature of truth here under the discipline of Ontology because of its relationship with reality. *How* the truth can be known will be covered under the discipline of Epistemology. Truth can be defined philosophically as the quality of those propositions that accord with reality, specifying what is in fact the case. Truth is an expression that matches or corresponds to its object or referent. Aristotle gave a clear and simple definition: 'To say of what is, that it is not, or of what is not, that it is, is false; while to say of what is, that it is, and of what is not, that it is not, is true.'

The biblical usage of the word encompasses the philosophical meanings with an added dimension. Noted scholar and theologian James Oliver Buswell, Jr. (1967b) states: 'The word "truth," *aletheia* in the New Testament and a variety of words, chiefly *emeth* in the Old Testament, always connotes (1) the interrelated consistency of statements and their correspondence with the facts of reality, and (2) the facts themselves. The former may be called propositional truth, and the latter, ontological truth.'

Connotation number one given above reflects the general philosophical meaning of truth. The philosophical definitions include the words 'propositions,' 'expression,' 'symbol,' 'statement,' and 'to say.' These words describe forms of communication and imply that truth is that which is communicated, *if*, that which is communicated accurately reflects facts or reality. Philosopher Thomas Hobbs stated it this way: 'True and false are attributes of speech, not of things.'

Connotation number two given by Buswell adds the idea that truth exists independent of any communication which expresses truth. The fact or reality itself is an ontological being called 'truth.' Both communication and independent existence reflects the understanding of truth in Christian philosophy and religion. God is the God of truth (Ps 31:5; Is 65:16) and God's word *is* truth (Jn 17:17). God's Son, Jesus Christ, is identified as the Word (Logos) (Jn 1:1, 14) and as the Word of God (Rv 19:13). God's Holy Spirit is called the Spirit of Truth (Jn 15:26). In Christian belief, all members of the tri-personal Godhead not only communicate truth but are truth. With the incarnation of Jesus Christ the truth became a man, the implications of which are the basis of Christian theology.

'In the beginning was the Word (Logos) and the Word was with God, and the Word was God. . . . The Word became flesh and made his dwelling among us. We have seen his glory, the glory of the Only Begotten (margin), who came from the Father, full of grace and truth' (Jn 1:1, 14). The Word (*Logos*) is a *Person* whose personal existence is identified to be with God 'In the beginning,' (Gn 1:1) before anything was created. 'The Word was God' means that not only is the Word related eternally with God but is actually identical in essence with God. It is a union (merging of two things to become one of the same), not a fusion (merging of two things to become something new). Christianity teaches that early in the first century AD this Word became a Person who not only communicated truth but ontologically was truth. That Person is Jesus Christ.

When Jesus Christ walked the earth he spoke the truth (over 70 times he is recorded in the Gospels as saying 'I tell you the truth'), he acted in truth, he lived in truth because he was the truth personified (Jn 14:6). As such he is the Christian's prime true source of special revelation about God and salvation. Jesus Christ showed the world what God is like (Jn 14:9), the God of truth. The Christian idea of truth is not only communication that accords with reality, but that reality itself is in the form of the Person of Jesus Christ. Pilate looked Truth in the face.

Cosmology Questions

What is the origin and nature of the universe?
The Christian view of the origin of the universe is that it came about by creative acts of God (Gn 1:1) in the form of words spoken by God (Gn 1:2–26). God spoke the universe into existence, not using anything but the power of his word to bring the universe into being. Philosopher Jean Paul Sartre's basic philosophical problem was that something is there rather than nothing. Philosophers and scientists through the ages have tried to come up with explanations as to how the universe came to be. The options are few. Either it all came from absolutely nothing, what Francis Schaeffer calls '*nothing* nothing' meaning no energy, mass, motion or personality (not even God) existed prior to something existing. Or it came from an impersonal beginning which may have been energy, mass or motion. It really doesn't matter. The third, and final, option is to assume that what is here came out of a personal beginning. Observation and experience relate the existence of diversity and unity in the universe as well as the existence of personal and impersonal objects in the

universe. That the universe came into existence from absolutely nothing defies all the laws of nature and science known to man and does not even enter into any widely held religious belief. Beginning with the impersonal does not explain the existence of numerous complex systems working in unity, seemingly coordinated, nor does it explain all the particulars in the universe. Some particulars have life; and one particular, man, has personality. An impersonal beginning plus time plus chance cannot adequately explain or give meaning to all that exists in the universe. Beginning with a personal being with the power and intelligence to create all that is in the universe is the only option that makes sense and is the Christian view of the origin of the universe.

The Christian view of the origin of the universe is that *'God created the cosmos ex nihilo [out of nothing] with a uniformity of cause and effect in an open system'* (Sire 1997:26). God did not make the universe out of himself or out of some chaos that existed before the universe. The universe came into being by God's spoken word. The universe is orderly and is open; it is not programmed. Certain natural laws were incorporated into the universe when God created it, but God can override the laws or operate above the laws (supernatural) as he wills. The Christian view is that God is continuously involved in the events taking place in an orderly but not determined universe.

According to the Bible, the universe reflects the power and glory of God (Ps 19:1). The Christian God is Trinitarian and what God created is trinitarian in nature. The universe is essentially made up of three elements; time, space and matter. Each of these reflects a trinitarian nature. Time is considered to be past, present and future; space has the dimensions of length, breadth and depth; matter only appears in the three forms solid, liquid and gas. As stated earlier in this chapter, man also reflects a tri-part nature of body, soul and spirit. The Christian view of the universe is that it reflects 'God's invisible qualities—his eternal power and divine nature—have been clearly seen, being understood from what has been made' (Rm 1:20).

The Christian view of the universe also includes the belief that the universe, as it presently is, is not the way God created it. God created everything good (Gn 1:31) and perfect, but because of the Fall, when sin and death entered the universe, the universe now reflects the effects of sin and the curse of sin (Gn 3:17–19). Sin has marred the image of God in man and in the universe, unleashing forces of spiritual evil ruled by Satan (Eph 2:2). The Christian view of the universe sees it as the place of a spiritual battle between the kingdom of God and the kingdom of Satan (Eph 6:12), with the kingdom of God ultimately prevailing (Gn 3:15).

What is God's relationship with the universe?

The view of Christian theism is that God is both transcendent and immanent. By transcendent is meant that God is not the universe but is beyond it. The universe is finite; God is infinite. When we look at the universe, including man, we see God's handiwork, but we do not see God. But God is not so beyond the universe that he does not relate to the universe. God is immanent or 'in' the universe as the sustaining cause of the universe.

Because God is continually and personally involved in the affairs of the universe, and because he is God and not nature, he can act *supernaturally* in the universe. Christians do not believe that natural laws are fixed, immutable and inviolable. Natural laws are descriptions of the regular way God works in His creation. They are not prescriptions of how God must work. God's special intervention in the world is called a *miracle.*

The regular and special actions of God in the universe are called *divine providence*, which is God's involvement in preserving the universe and guiding it to its intended ends. God's walking and talking with Adam and Eve in the Garden of Eden (Gn 3:8) dispels the view that God created the universe and left it to its own devices. When Jesus Christ was in the world he did not just teach about sin and righteousness. He taught much about his Father, God, who exercised providential care over all creatures to the extent that not even a sparrow could fall to the ground except it is God's will (Mt 10:29). Jesus further taught that God feeds the birds (Mt 6:26), directs the sunshine and the rain where he wants it (Mt 5:45), and knows the number of hairs on a person's head (Mt 10:30). All of this indicates God's close personal involvement in his creation. However, it does not mean that God wills positively everything that happens. God permits evil acts, but he does not will evil to exist. God's providence affects all people, but he shows special concern for those who believe in him (Rm 8:28).

What is the meaning of time?

The study of time started as a philosophical endeavour but, because of the advancement of theories of relativity, has been taken over by science. Time is a biblical concept denoting a beginning (Gn 1:1), a succession (Ec 3:1–8) and an end (Mt 28:20) to world history. However, the end of world history may not be the end of time. The Bible uses the words 'age' and 'eternity' in characterizing the biblical concept of time, dividing it between temporal events before the second coming of Christ and the future events afterward. Eternity is defined as without beginning or end. James Orr (1948:131) states: 'Eternity we may rather take to be an expression for the timeless necessity of God's existence; and time, properly speaking, begins its course only with the world.' Traditionally, the term eternity has been used by philosophy and theology to designate God's infinity in relations to time. The terms 'duration' and 'succession' do not apply, as he possesses his existence in one indivisible present.

British philosopher John McTaggart puts forth two sets of series of temporal positions. Designations of past, present and future, he called the *A series*. Designations of before, simultaneous with or after, he called the *B series*. He stated that in order to account for change, and therefore the passage of time, both series are needed.

The Christian view of time is that it is linear (or horizontal) allowing for a succession of events in chronological order and from the temporal moment can be referred to as past, present or future. In referring to multiple events they can be referred to as happening before, simultaneous with or after one or the other. The Christian view of time agrees with this philosophical view. The Christian view of time also accords with the view of science. Unlike space, time has only one dimension and an apparently irreversible direction.

Do laws and causality govern the universe absolutely?

As previously stated, the Christian view is that natural laws are descriptions of the regular way God works in the universe, but they do not prescribe how God must work. Events manifesting God's actions contrary to natural laws (supernatural) are called *miracles* (Ps 77:14). Miracles are necessary for Christianity to be believable. As to whether miracles are essential to Christianity, James Orr (1948:10) writes:

> The question is not about isolated 'miracles', but about the whole conception of Christianity—what it is, and whether the supernatural does not enter into the very essence of it? It is the general question of a supernatural or non-supernatural conception of the universe. Is there a supernatural Being—God? Is there a supernatural government of the world? Is there a supernatural relation of God and man, so that God and man may have a communion with one another? Is there a supernatural Person—Christ? Is there a supernatural work in the souls of men? Is there a supernatural Redemption? Is there a supernatural hereafter? It is these larger questions that have to be settled first, and then the question of particular miracles will fall into place.

Causality (or causation) questions whether or not every phenomenon must have a cause. Causation is usually defined as the relation between two things or events when the first is necessary and/or sufficient for the occurrence of the second. Nothing can be self-caused. A self-caused being would have to be ontologically prior to itself. The Christian theistic view is that God is not a self-caused Being. God is an uncaused Being. That being the case, the Christian view is that not everything needs a cause. Only contingent or created things need a cause.

The God of Christianity makes laws in nature but is not himself bound by them. The God of Christianity is the cause of all creation but is not himself caused by anything. The Christian view is that laws and causality do *not* govern the universe absolutely.

Teleology Questions

Why do man and the universe exist and do they have a final end?

The Christian view is that God created the universe as a free act of his will. James Orr (1948:131) states the answer to why God did it:

> A few words before leaving this part of the subject on the motive and end of creation. If we reject the idea of metaphysical necessity, and think of creation as originating in a free, intelligent act, it must, like every similar act, be conceived of as proceeding from a motive, which includes in it at the same time a rational end. And if God is free, personal Spirit, who is at the same time ethical Will, what motive is possible but goodness or love, or what end can be thought of but an ethical one? In this way it may be held that, though the universe is not the product of a logical or metaphysical necessity, it arises from the nature of God by a *moral* necessity which is one with the highest freedom, and thus the conception of creation may be secured from arbitrariness.

Thus, the creation of the universe was not an arbitrary act on God's part, but a moral necessity in order for his divine nature of love to be expressed (1 Jn 4:8, 16). All definitions of love include or imply the existence of an object. The Bible records the fact of love within the triune Godhead of God in that the Father loved the Son (Jn 17:24) and the Son loved the Father (Jn 14:31). But since this love is confined to members of the Godhead of one God it is basically self-love. The Greek word used most often in the New Testament to refer to God's love is *agapao* indicating a self-sacrificial kind of love. Vine's *An Expository Dictionary of New Testament Words* states:

'In respect of *agapao* as used of God, it expresses the deep and constant love and interest of a perfect Being towards entirely unworthy objects, producing and fostering a reverential love in them towards the Giver, and a practical love towards those who are partakers of the same, and a desire to help others to seek the Giver.' Human beings are the unworthy objects and the universe is the place love is played out.

The universe was created by God to be the dwelling place of man. Everything created was good (Gn 1:31) and had a teleological end in God's creative purpose. Man was to enjoy his home and enjoy and glorify God forever. Man only had to obey one commandment to prove his love for God (Gn 2:17; 1 Jn 5:3). Man disobeyed the command of God and the destructive consequence of sin (the Fall) was felt by man (Gn 2:17; 3:16–20) and nature (Gn 3:17–18; Rm 8:22). Therefore, neither man nor nature exists today as they were perfectly created by God.

Because man was still the object of God's love after he sinned, the universe became the place for God to glorify his Son, Jesus Christ, by sending him into the world as a man, albeit a perfect man, to redeem the world by taking the punishment of sin upon himself at Calvary (the atonement). The giving of his Son was an act of love on God's part (Jn 3:16) and his purpose was the regeneration (*palingenesia*) or re-creating of fallen human nature (Tit 3:5) and physical nature (Mt 19:28). The regeneration of man was made possible by Christ's death on the Cross, the regeneration of all creation will take place at Christ's second coming (Ac 3:21). The universe started with *genesis* and will end with *palingensia*.

However, not all of humanity will be regenerated. Man was created in the image of God (*imago Dei*) (Gn 1:7) and as such is endowed with the capacity to reason and to exercise a free will. God set obedience to his commands as proof of man's love for him (1 Jn 5:3). Since the first man, Adam, all men have wilfully sinned (Rm 3:23) and shown that they do not love God. In the biblical view sin is not only an act of wrongdoing against God, but also a state of alienation from God. The answer to the sin problem lies in what God has done for us in the gospel of Jesus Christ. The penalty for sin is death, judgment and hell, but God has chosen to pay this penalty himself in the sacrificial life and death of his Son, Jesus Christ (Jn 3:16–17; Rm 3:21–26). At the judgment those who have wilfully repented of their sins against God and believed the gospel of God's Son will receive eternal life (Jn 3:16; Rm 2:7), while those who have wilfully rejected God's act of love (Jn 3:36) will be punished with everlasting destruction (1 Th 1:9). The Christian view is that, metaphysically, the final end of man will be either eternal life with God or eternal punishment.

Does evil have a purpose?

Since God is absolute goodness, the existence of evil (both moral and natural) in the world has posed problems for theologians and philosophers for centuries. Leibniz, a German philosopher, introduced the term 'theodicy' to refer to the 'problem of evil' or attempts to explain God's reasons for allowing evil. The authors of Scripture have always viewed evil as a means by which God could bring some purpose to pass (Gn 50:20; Rm 8:28). Their faith depended on it. Their faith would be hopeless if they did not believe that God can cause all things to work for good, and that in spite of human sin, God is able, and will in His own time, bring to pass the perfection that is to come.

According to Scripture, moral evil is the cause of the existence of physical or natural evil in the world (Gn 3:16–19; Rm 8:19–22). The Christian view recognizes that God may and does use natural evil for his own ends, but it also recognizes that God did not deliberately will it for this purpose. The Bible indicates that God has allowed evil in order that his justice might be manifested in its punishment and his grace in its forgiveness (Rm 9:22, 23). Besides God's justice and grace, the Scriptures teach that God uses evil to discipline his children. That discipline can take the form of family trouble (2 Sm 12:10) or sickness (1 Cor 11:30) or natural disasters (Job 1:4) or whatever means God sees fit. God does discipline his children (Ps 39:11; Pr 22:15) and bad things are the rod he uses. However, the Christian view is that God's discipline of his children is motivated by love (Heb 12:5–11; Rv 3:19). 'My son, do not despise the Lord's discipline and do not resent his rebuke, because the Lord disciplines those he loves, as a father the son he delights in' (Pr 3:11, 12).

Ethics/Morality Questions

Who or what determines what is moral and immoral?

Ethics and morals are two words used in philosophy, general theology and Christianity sometimes to be the same and sometimes to be different in meaning. It was stated in chapter 2 that we can understand ethics as a set of standards (prescriptive of what ought to be) by which one evaluates human behaviour and judges it (descriptive) morally right or wrong. That which ethics prescribes is morals.

The Christian view is that there are moral values or standards that are objective. Some things are right or wrong whether or not anyone believes them to be right or wrong. The source of these objective moral values is God, whose nature is perfectly holy and good. God's moral nature is what Plato called the 'Good'. God's moral nature is expressed to us in the form of divine commands, which constitute our moral duties or obligations to act as he would act.

Every person being accountable to God for the moral choices he makes is also prominent in the Christian view of morality. Those who do good (by the Scriptural standard) will be eternally rewarded, while those who do evil will be troubled and distressed because they are under God's wrath (Rm 2:6–11). The moral choices made in this life have eternal significance and the sacrificing of self-interest for the sake of God and others brings not loss, but gain. Because God is holy, his moral standards are good. Because God is just, rewards and punishment for obeying his standards will be exactly as each person deserves.

Christian ethics state that when there is a conflict between God's commands and the laws of a human authority, the Christian must obey the commands of God and bear the consequences of not obeying the human authority. The Christian must obey God rather than man (Ac 4:18, 19; 5:29).

God has given the Christian everything that is needed to obey his moral commands. The 'new birth' of the Christian gives him a new nature including a new volition (will) to obey the commands of God. The indwelling Holy Spirit of God gives the Christian the power to obey. Finally, God has manifested himself in human flesh, in the Person of his Son Jesus Christ, who gives us a manifestation of perfect morality. God, himself, came to be one of us, to live among us and to show us how to live lives that please God. The Bible says that Jesus was tempted in every way a human can be, yet he was without sin (Heb 4:15). Christ is our complete human referent, a moral example. Morality is not a mere legalistic assent to a written code but a dynamic relationship to a living Person.

How do we know what is right?

Philosophers and theologians have proposed several theories that attempt to define what is right. William James suggested that something was right if it worked. Immanuel Kant put forth the idea of a 'categorical imperative' that is binding on all men: one should not do anything that he cannot will as a universal law for all men. G.E. Moore's position is that good is not definable in terms of anything other than itself, therefore it must be known only by intuition. Thomas Aquinas believed there are self-evident *first principles* for all knowledge, including the law of benevolence in ethics. Thomas Hobbes said the right can be known by appeal to some sovereign authority, such as a government or some leader. All of these theories have problems because the terms used to describe them can have different meanings to different people or they lack content altogether.

A word needs to be said about the human conscience and its function in knowing what is right. The conscience is what operates on the mind, will and emotions to apply a moral standard to thoughts, actions and feelings and then applies that standard as binding on the individual. The English word 'conscience' comes from the Latin *conscientia* combining *con* (with) and *scientia* (knowledge) indicating that the conscience operates with knowledge. The working of the conscious calls for a known objective standard of moral conduct, with reference to which, the quality of thoughts, actions and feelings may be judged as right or wrong. The knowledge that informs the conscience comes from different sources. The mores and ethics of the culture and/or religion we grow up in teach culture-specific standards of right and wrong, meaning that standards can conflict between cultures. The Bible tells us that God has placed certain knowledge in the conscience of man that is not culture-specific.

The Christian view states that God has revealed to mankind what is right using two different methods. One method is God's 'special' revelation recorded in the Christian holy book, the Bible. The intellectual discipline of Christian Apologetics deals with the Christian's justification for believing that the Bible is God's Word and the final authority for what is right and wrong. God's commandments are recorded in the Bible and they reflect his nature of absolute righteousness. The Christian accepts the Bible as his rule of conduct and faith and his conscience is governed by it.

The other method God has used to reveal what is right is available, not just to Christians, but to all men and is called 'general' revelation. Man was made in the image of God (Gn 1:27) and even though fallen and unregenerate, man has enough of God's nature in him to know right and wrong even though he does not have the will to do it. The Bible records in Romans 2:14, 15: '(Indeed when Gentiles, who do not have the law, do by nature things required by the law, they are a law for themselves, even though they do not have the law, since they show that the requirements of the law are written on their hearts, their consciences also bearing witness, and their thoughts now accusing, now even defending them.)' This natural revelation has been available since the creation of the world so that no man can be excused for not knowing that God exists and that obeying his law is the right thing to do

(Rm 1:20). According to Romans 2:15, the function of the conscience is to 'bear witness' to this.

Aesthetics Questions

What is man's relationship with the natural environment?

This question is answered under the discipline of aesthetics because by definition aesthetics includes the branch of philosophy that examines the nature and character of our experience of not only art, but of the natural environment (Feagin 1995). The Book of Genesis records that man was created in a different way (Gn 1:26; 2:7) and with a different function (Gn 1:26) than the natural environment into which he came into being. Man was created in the image of God and was given the task of ruling over the other living creatures (theologically, the vice-regent of God). Unlike animals that can only react to their environment, human beings act with or against their environment. They have imagination and the ability to engage in creative restructuring of their present environment.

In the second chapter of Genesis we read that God brought the other living creatures to man so that he could categorize his environment by the assigning of names. Genesis goes on to record that man shaped the elements of his natural environment for his own useful purposes in making musical instruments and tools (Gn 4:21, 22), making bricks and building cities and monuments to himself (Gn 4:17; 11:3, 4). Man is differentiated from the animal in that he has the possibility of being creative beyond his immediate environment and of enlarging his environment. The animal cannot do that. From man's creativity has come the industrial revolution, and great advancements in science and technology.

Man is given the ability to control his natural environment rather than being controlled by it. The Christian view is that the natural environment should not be abused or spoiled needlessly, but the natural environment was put here by God as man's dwelling place and for his benefit. Therefore, he has the right to control or change it. Termites in one's house must be dealt with or the house will be destroyed, thus causing more trees to be destroyed in order to replace the house. There must be a balance.

The Christian view is that spirits exist with, but not in, the natural environment. Rocks exist, trees exist, spirits exist, but spirits do not reside *in* the rocks or trees. Therefore, man has no need to fear the inanimate part of the natural environment or to pay any religious homage to any part of it (Ps 115:4–8).

Is there aesthetic value to religious experience?

The Book of Genesis records that an aesthetic experience led to the need for religious experiences. The first woman saw the fruit that God had commanded her husband not to eat and it was 'pleasing to the eye, . . . she took some and ate it. She also gave some to her husband, who was with her, and he ate it' (Gn 3:6). That act was the first sin (The Fall). Prior to that act God was pleased with man. Man had God's approval and direct communication with him (Gn 1:31; 2:16; 3:8, 9). There was no need for religion. Because of man's sin, he lost God's approval, but God, in his mercy, gave man a religious system of offerings and sacrifices whereby man could express his worship and regain God's approval (Gn 4:3–5). The Fall, beginning with an aesthetic experience, is the reason for religious systems.

The Christian Scriptures and the experience of Christians themselves indicate that religious experience can be, and often is, at one and the same time, an aesthetic experience. The aesthetic experience has always been intimately connected with sensory experience and the kinds of feelings aroused by that experience. Artists would contend that not all sensory experiences lead to an aesthetic experience but only that portion of sensory experiences to which the term 'beauty' may apply. The Christian's aesthetic experience of the Divine includes, but is not limited to, beauty. The writers of the Bible were human beings, and they expressed their human feelings involved in religious experience of the Divine. Verses like Exodus 15:11 are replete with aesthetic terms: 'Who among the gods is like you, O Lord? Who is like you—majestic in holiness, awesome in glory, working wonders?' 'Majestic,' 'awesome,' and 'wonders' are terms critics use to describe works of art or music. Besides these words, the writers of Scripture expressed their feelings of the Divine using other aesthetic wording: 'to gaze upon the beauty of the Lord' (Ps 27:4); 'Perfect in beauty, God shines forth' (Ps 50:2); 'O worship the Lord in the beauty of holiness' (Ps 96:9 KJV); 'I stand in awe' (Hab 3:2); 'glad with the joy of your presence.' (Ps 21:6). Even the word 'fear' (Ps 22:23, Is 59:19) as it is used in the Bible to describe a feeling toward God has aesthetic value. Rather than 'being afraid of' the word signifies a 'reverential awe' toward God. It is a reverential trust in God that makes us want to please and obey him. Christians worship God because they love and appreciate him and what he has done for them, and not because they are afraid not to. The Christian seeks religious experience because he wants to, not because he has to. Because God provides the experience, and God is good, the experience has aesthetic value.

In addition to writings, as in the Scriptures, music is used by Christians to express their aesthetic experiences. Great hymns of the faith like 'All That Thrills My Soul is Jesus', 'It is Well With My Soul', 'For the Beauty of the Earth' and 'How Great Thou Art' express aesthetic feelings toward God. More recent choruses like 'I Stand, I Stand in Awe of You' and 'Lord, You Are Beautiful' indicate that the religious experience of encountering and worshipping God does have aesthetic value to it. Whether sensing God's handiwork in a sunset or his Spirit in a sanctuary, sensing the presence of God is an aesthetic experience. But, as James Orr (1948:19) reminds us: 'For religion is more than a mere aesthetic gratification. It implies belief in the existence of a real object other than self, and includes a desire to get into some relation with this object.' The Christian's experience of the 'numinous' is an aesthetic experience.

Philosophy of History Questions

What is the meaning of history?

The philosopher Hegel regarded history as 'the locus in which the activity of the divine reason is to be observed'. Francis Schaeffer (1972a:165) gives a specific historic meaning to Genesis 1–11: 'These chapters give the history which comes before anything secular historians have been able to ascertain, and it is that pre-secular history which gives meaning to man's present history. . . . It sets in perspective all the history we now have in our secular study.' A simple definition of 'history' is a narrative or chronological record of events. The Book of Genesis and all of Scripture claims to be such a record: 'This is the account of the heavens and the earth when they were created' (Gn 2:14); 'Therefore, since I myself have carefully investigated everything from the beginning, it seemed good also to me to write an orderly account for you' (Lk 1:3). The biblical authors were writing about events that constitute history.

The Christian view of history is that the Bible records the history of God's dealings with humanity in general, first directly, then through his chosen people (Jews), then through his Son, Jesus Christ, then through the Christian church. Christians believe that God has an ultimate goal for humanity—to come to a knowledge of himself and his Son, Jesus Christ (Pr 2:15; Is 11:9; 2 Pt 1:2) and an ultimate goal for all of history—the establishment of the Kingdom of God (Lk 17:21; Rv 11:15). Both goals will be accomplished at the Second Advent, when Jesus Christ returns to earth to rule and reign (Rv

20:22). All events in all times and in all parts of the world must be seen and interpreted in light of those goals.

Is history cyclical or linear in progression?

The Jewish tradition changed the periodization of time from cycle to progression. The Bible is written using words indicative of chronological order or linear progression such as: 'then' (Gn 3:8); 'when' (Gn 6:1); and, 'Two years after the flood' (Gn 11:10). Secular historians have dated events recorded in the Bible from Abraham forward in chronological order based on archaeological evidence. The Christian view is that history is linear in progression; it had a definite beginning (Gn 1:1); and history as we know it will be consummated with the events recorded in the last book of the Bible, Revelation. Theologically, the great chronological events of human history can be summed up using four words—*creation, Fall, redemption, glorification.*

Epistemology Questions

What can we know and how can we know it?

Man knows many things. He knows there are rivers and oceans and mountains and trees. He knows that two plus two equals four and that four times four equals sixteen. He knows that there are other people besides himself and that people and things come in different shapes, sizes and colours. Man also knows that he does not know everything. Humanistic man believes that he can eventually know all that he *wants* to know. Christian man believes that he already knows all that he *needs* to know for life and godliness (2 Pt 1:3).

The Greek philosopher Plato showed great understanding of the problem of knowledge. He understood that the universe consists of individual examples or things (particulars), but we could not know what those individual things are without some way to classify them (universals). What is Fido? Fido is a dog. Without the universal 'dog' we could not know what Fido is.

Science looks at the particulars and poses universal laws to try to explain them. Christians look at the particulars and know that God has already explained them in his written word. The Christian position is that God has spoken to man about himself, the cosmos and about history. God has not spoken exhaustively on these subjects, but what he has spoken is true. God has spoken on the basis of propositional revelation concerning the particulars and what he spoke has been recorded in the Bible. God is a verbalizer (Gn 1:3) and since man was created in the image of God, man is a verbalizer in his communication to other men. There is universal agreement on that (even post-modern deconstructionists cannot deny it).

Since the same reasonable God made the knower and the thing that is known (the subject and the object) it should not be surprising that there is a correlation between them. God made the subject and he made the object, and he gave the Bible to explain, epistemologically, the correlation that exists between them. We cannot know the object exhaustively, but we can know it truly.

Another benefit of Christian epistemology based on God's revelation is that the distinction between reality and fantasy is made clear. Because man is made in the image of God man has a mind that can think creatively using imagination. Man can change the form of the universe (as an artist or an engineer) and expose the results of his imagination on the external world. At the same time, man knows he is imagining and is, therefore, not confused between his fantasy and reality.

Autonomous man is alienated from God, from others, and from himself in the area of knowing. Without the universals of the Bible he cannot explain all the particulars in the world and in his own life. There are no categories that differentiate between his internal fantasies and the objective external world. He has nothing to tell him who he is. That is not the case for the Christian.

The Christian view of what we can know and how we can know it is answered in the special revelation of God as recorded in the Bible, especially the first eleven chapters of Genesis. Epistemology asks how do we know what we know, and how valid and true is what we know. Christians believe that Genesis 1–11 gives true, reasonable and reliable answers to these ultimate questions. God's special revelation in Genesis 1–11 being true to reality is vitally important to the Christian view of the world.

What justifies a belief?

Propositional knowledge is defined by philosophers, following Plato, as justi-fied true belief. For knowledge to exist, what is known must be true, there must be evidence to support believing it, and for a person to know it, that person must believe it. Truth that is not believed is not knowledge received.

Epistemic justification involves evidence or support for holding a belief, which is referred to as the logic or structure of epistemic justification. Philosophers have put forth two alternative logics or structures, foundational-ism and coherentism. Foundationalism is the view that there is a structure of knowledge whose foundations are secure and are based on experience, reason or some combination of both. Coherentism is the view that a proposition may be known without a foundation of certainty, but by interlocking relationships. Foundationalism is seen as pyramidal in structure. Coherentism is seen as a 'web of belief.'

Christian philosophers and theologians are divided in their support of these alternative structures for epistemic justification. Aspects of both are involved in Christian belief. The core issue for Christians is proof—is there proof or evidence that confirms the beliefs that make up their worldview. The Christian worldview is based on God's special revelation in the Bible, the focal point of that revelation being Jesus Christ. If the Christian beliefs about Jesus Christ are not justified, there is no justification for the Christian worldview. For the Christian, the proof that justifies belief in Jesus Christ and what he said is his resurrection from the dead. As the Apostle Paul wrote in 1 Corinthians 15:14, 17: 'And if Christ has not been raised, our preaching is useless, and so is your faith.' 'And if Christ has not been raised, your faith is futile, you are still in your sins.' Paul goes on to state in verse 20: 'But Christ has indeed been raised from the dead.' The Scriptures go on to state that Christians in the first century had sense and expert testimony as evidence for belief in Christ's resurrection: 'After his suffering, he showed himself to these men and gave many convincing proofs that he was alive' (Ac 1:3); 'For he [God] has set a day when he will judge the world with justice by the man [Christ Jesus] he has appointed. He has given proof of this to all men by raising him from the dead' (Ac 17:31). The Bible is God's written expert testimony to succeeding generations. It is on the testimony of a God who 'cannot lie' (Titus 1:2) and is therefore utterly trustworthy.

The Christian view is that God's testimony of the virgin birth, sinless life, sacrificial death and resurrection from the dead of Jesus Christ justifies belief in all that God has said. The Christian believes that he can clearly understand what God has said and can formulate a true worldview based upon the word of God. 'We also know that the Son of God has come and has given us understanding, so that we my know him who is true. And so we are in him who is true—even in his Son Jesus Christ. He is the true God and eternal life' (1 Jn 5:20).

Religious Dimensions of the Christian Worldview

Religious beliefs are at the core of all worldviews. What one believes about God determines the direction of beliefs about absolutes and ultimates in everything else. Beliefs determine and motivate behaviour. The Christian religion, as foundational to the Christian or biblical worldview, motivates a Christian to experience an ongoing relationship to the triune God—Father, Son and Holy Spirit—and it determines how that experience is obtained. The Christian Holy Scriptures, the Bible, is the source of faith and practice and it guides how one lives out the various religious dimensions of his worldview.

Experiential Dimension

According to the Bible, a person must have an initial experience in order to become a Christian. This experience becomes a turning point in his personal history, and his life is indeed forever changed. The experience is referred to by different terms: 'being saved' (Ac 2:47), 'become a believer' (Heb 10:39), 'being born of God' (1 Jn 3:9), 'being redeemed' (1 Pt 1:18), 'renewal' ('regeneration' KJV) (Tt 3:5). Probably the term most definitive was used by Jesus when he said: 'I tell you the truth, no one can see the kingdom of God unless he is born again' (Jn 3:3). 'Born again', 'new birth', and 'regeneration' are used interchangeably to describe this initial experience. J I Packer (1984b) describes it as 'an inner re-creating of fallen human nature by the gracious sovereign action of the Holy Spirit (Jn 3:5–8).' This re-creating results in a restored relationship with God because of the redemptive work of Christ.

The new birth experience is decisive in that the regenerated man forever ceases to be the man he use to be. His old life is over and a new life has begun. He is a new creature in Christ. The Apostle Paul described the experience to the Christians at Corinth: 'Therefore, if anyone is in Christ, he is a new creation, the old has gone, the new has come' (2 Cor 5:17). In biblical theology this experience is absolutely necessary for one to become a Christian. The Bible recognizes that some will become mere adherents of the Christian faith and not true Christians and refers to them as goats (mixed in with the sheep) (Mt 25:31–33) and weeds or tares (mixed in with the wheat) (Mt 13:30). In the judgement, they will find themselves under the wrath of God (Mt 7:21–23; 25:41). The Bible does not leave the individual to wonder if he is a true Christian: 'The Spirit himself beareth witness with our spirit, that we are children of God' (Rm 8:16 KJV).

After this initial experience, the Christian enters into other kinds of religious experiences incorporating aspects of dualism and monism. Dualism is any view of reality based upon two fundamental aspects, such as matter and spirit, natural and supernatural, or good and evil. Monism is the metaphysical view that reality is fundamentally one. The Christian's experience of the 'numinous' is basically dualistic, where God is experienced as the awe-inspiring Wholly Other which involves the experience of worship (Ex 34:8; Jn 9:38). The Christian also experiences a 'oneness' with all of God's creation, sharing the same maker (Ps 8), a oneness with fellow Christians and with God himself (Jn 17:21–23; Ac 14:15; 1 Cor 6:17; 1 Jn 4:4).

The experience most precious to the Christian is the experience of God's presence in a mystical way (Ps 16:11; 51:11; 89:15; Ac 21:28; 1 Th 2:19; 2 Tm 4:1; 1 Jn 3:19; Jude 24). Because God is spirit and his Holy Spirit resides in the Christian (Ac 2:14; 1 Cor 6:19; 2 Tm 1:14) the presence of God is felt in the spirit of the Christian (1 Cor 2:14). In Christian theology Satan is also a spirit (1 Jn 4:3), a deceiving spirit (2 Cor 11:3; Rv 20:10). Therefore, the Holy Spirit has gifted the Christian to discern or distinguish between spirits (1 Cor 12:10).

Mythic Dimension

When the Bible uses the word 'myth' (Gr *Mythos*) (1 Tm 1:4; 4:7; 2 Tm 4:4; 1 Pt 1:16) it signifies the fiction of a fable as distinct from the genuineness of the truth. This work will adopt the more modern usage of the term to describe a story of divine or sacred significance used to explain the way things are and not question the truthfulness or historicity of it. However, in stating the Christian worldview, and the mythic dimension of it, notice is taken that Christians accept the epic stories of the Bible as being true and build their worldview upon them.

Perhaps the best way to treat the mythic dimension of the Christian religion is to highlight German theologian Rudolph Bultmann's attempt at the 'demythologisation' of the New Testament and his rejection of the biblical view of the world as belonging to 'the cosmology of a pre-scientific age' and as therefore quite unacceptable to modern man. Bultmann viewed the world as a closed system, governed by fixed natural laws, without the possibility of supernatural events. Therefore, he found it necessary to discard such 'obvious' mythical elements as Christ's pre-existence and virgin birth. Bultmann rejected the deity of Christ, the atonement, Christ's resurrection and his future return to earth. He rejected the existence of spirit beings, even the Holy Spirit, and the doctrine of the Trinity. He rejected all explanations of events in terms of being miracles.

All of the supernatural events and descriptions Bultmann rejected are included in, and a necessary part of, the stories that define the Christian religion. Christian ontology and cosmology are based upon the epic stories of Genesis 1–11. Christian teleology and epistemology are based upon belief in the supernatural communication of the biblical stories to man. Christian ethics is based upon the sinless life of Christ. These biblical stories are passed verbally from one generation to another in the form of 'children's stories' and in the modern era in the form of movies. In this manner, children of Christians are taught the rudiments of the faith and the story content of the Bible in hopes that they, too, will want to become Christians.

Symbols are used in the Christian religion to represent truths contained in the biblical stories. The Orthodox branch of Christianity has holy images called icons. These icons are not considered the works of men, but as manifestations of the heavenly ideals they represent. They are windows between earthly and heavenly worlds. Western Christianity does not accept a mystic nature of icons or symbols but does make use of symbols, such as a cross, as a remembrance of the act or doctrine represented by the symbol.

Doctrinal Dimension

The doctrinal dimension represents the cognitive element of religion. In his lectures of over one hundred years ago, James Orr (1948:20) made comments that are still relevant today:

> If there is a religion in the world which exalts the office of teaching, it is safe to say that it is the religion of Jesus Christ. It has been frequently remarked that in pagan religions the doctrinal element is at a minimum—the chief thing there is the performance of a ritual. But this is precisely where Christianity distinguishes itself from other religions—it does contain doctrine. It comes to men with definite, positive teaching; it claims to be the truth; it bases religion on knowledge, though a knowledge which is only attainable under moral conditions. . . . A strong, stable, religious life can be built in no other ground than that of intelligent conviction. Christianity, therefore, addresses itself to the intelligence as well as the heart.

Doctrine and teaching are fundamental to the preservation and propagation of Christianity. The Bible records in the Apostle Paul's first letter to Timothy: 'Command and teach these things. . . . Watch your life and your doctrine closely. Persevere in them, because if you do, you will save both yourself and your hearers' (1 Tm 4:11, 16), and in his letter to Titus: 'You must teach what is in accord with sound doctrine' (Tt 2:1). For the Christian, what is recorded in the Bible represents the standard for sound doctrine.

Once myths make the transition from oral to written as scriptures they take on a new and different existence. Written scripture invites interpretation and commentary which often enables us to understand the doctrinal underpinning of myth. Commentaries are an important part of the body of Christian doctrine. The original Christian Scriptures were written in Hebrew, Greek and Aramaic, which are first-languages to only a handful of Christians today. Therefore, the Scriptures have to be translated into the language of the reader and oftentimes a literal word-for-word translation loses the meaning of what was said in its original language and context. A discipline within theology called 'hermeneutics' has arisen to study and solve the problems of translating in order to reveal and express the original meaning. The need for hermeneutics has produced a large number of commentaries on the Bible, with some directed to readers at all levels of Christian knowledge.

The teaching of doctrine has been an important part of Christianity since Jesus Christ was walking the earth (Mk 6:6). He was referred to as 'Teacher' by his disciples and by the Jews (Mt 8:19; Mk 4:38). Schools were started early in Christian history and to this day are a very important part of teaching doctrine with thousands of Bible colleges and seminaries in existence worldwide. In addition to the availability of formal doctrinal education, most individual Christian churches hold classes for teaching the Bible and Christian doctrine at least once a week.

In addition to formal teachings, doctrines of Christianity have been formulated into creeds and confessions of faith, mostly because of the rise of heresies. The three most widely used creeds have been The Apostles' Creed, The Nicene Creed and The Athanasian Creed. The use of confessions of faith arose as formal statements of Christian faith written by Protestants during the Reformation. The most widely used statements of confession have been the Augsburg Confession and the Westminster Confession of Faith. Protestants do not regard confessions as absolute authorities in matters of faith and practice. Their use is in being helpful summaries of Scripture and as guides to Christian life.

Ethical Dimension

Christian ethics are based upon the commands of God and the teachings and examples of Jesus as they are recorded in the Bible. God gave rules of behaviour to follow (ex. the Law or Ten Commandments) and Jesus explained the spirit of the law, giving the only acceptable motive for obedience to them, and he set a new standard for his followers.

In explaining the spirit of the laws God gave, Jesus pointed out that sin came from the heart (Mt 5:19) and that a desire to disobey God makes one guilty as if the deed is actually done (Mt 5:28). When asked what the greatest commandment was Jesus replied: 'Love the Lord your God with all your heart, and with all your soul, and with all your mind' (Mt 22:37). He went on to give the second greatest commandment: 'Love your neighbour as yourself' (Mt 22:39). Both of these commands had been in the Jewish law since Moses received the Law on Mt. Sinai. The second commandment set the standard for ethical behaviour among God's people and Jesus reformulated it early in his ministry when he said: 'Do to others as you would have them do to you' (Lk 6:31). So the ethical standard set by God was to treat others as you want to be treated and do it because you love them as much as you love yourself. The commandment is to love and the motive for treating people right is love equal to self-love.

At the end of his ministry on earth, Jesus drew his disciples around him and gave them a new ethical standard for their behaviour toward fellow believers. After washing his disciples' feet Jesus told them that he had set an example for them to follow (Jn 13:15) and then he said: 'A new command I give you: Love one another. As I have loved you, so you must love one another.' The old standard for ethical behaviour was self-love. The new standard for Christians is the self-sacrificial love that Jesus showed for his disciples. Christ loved enough to die for them. If the Christian loves that much he will have no trouble treating people as Jesus did because his heart will be filled with love leaving no room for desire to sin. Christians believe that they are empowered by the indwelling Holy Spirit of God to help them love other people and to walk in ways that please God. The Spirit indwells them as a result of the new birth experience that gave them a new nature and a right standing before God. The Christian idea of ethics is 'Be right and you will do right.'

The Christian also believes in a righteous judgement of God as an incentive for good ethical and moral behaviour. For the Christian, the judgement is not to decide eternal life or eternal punishment. On that basis the Christian is accounted righteous because of Christ (Rm 4:22, 23). The judgement Christians will face will determine gain or loss of rewards and will be based on how they lived after becoming Christians (Rm 2:6–11; 14:12). It will include a judgement of words (Mt 12:36) and deeds (2 Cor 5:10). Christian ethics is more a matter of motive in the heart and mind than deeds done. The Bible tells the Christian that God will search his heart and mind and will repay accordingly (Rv 2:23).

Ritual Dimension

Like all major religions, Christianity has certain rituals involved in the physical practice of the faith. These rituals are designed to communicate feelings and beliefs reflective of what God has done through the Lord Jesus Christ. Many of the rituals in Christianity have carried over from its Jewish roots with some changing slightly in form or meaning.

Sacrifice is one form of ritual common to many religions and prominent in the practice of the Jewish religion. The sacrifice was to satisfy God for the sins committed against him. He had set the penalty for sin as death with the first man (Gn 2:17) and had instituted a system of delayed judgement on the sinner if the sinner offered an animal sacrifice to die in his place (Lv 1:4). The blood of the sacrifice covered the sin of the offerer for a time, but did not take the sin away (Heb 10:1–4). Jesus, God Incarnate, was born into the Jewish culture, lived a sinless life and was offered up to God as a perfect sacrifice (amoral animal for sinful man was not equal in value; perfect man for sinful man was greater in value—a true sacrifice), and a once-for-all sacrifice (Heb 10:18) for the propitiation of man's sin. God is justified in forgiving a Christian's sins because he has accepted the death of Jesus Christ in payment of the penalty sin deserves.

For the Christian, the sacrificial death of Jesus Christ has two ritual implications for worship. First, Christians are to imitate Christ and offer their bodies as living sacrifices to God (Rm 12:1). The difference between the sacrifice of Christ and the sacrifice of the Christian is that Christ's sacrifice involved his dying, while for the Christian the sacrifice involves his living. Being a living sacrifice means not living life for oneself but for God. God accepts that sacrifice as a spiritual act of worship. The ritual involves a daily sacrifice as the Christian says with Christ 'not as I will, but as you will' (Mt 26:30). The second ritual implication of the sacrificial death of Jesus Christ is the institution of an ordinance of worship called the Lord's Supper or Communion. Jesus instituted this ritual ordinance before he was crucified as he was having his last supper with his disciples. He took bread and said: 'This is my body given for you' (Lk 22:19). Then he took a cup of wine and said: 'This cup is the new covenant in my blood, which is poured out for you' (Lk

22:20). He instructed them to 'do this in remembrance of me' (Lk 22:19). The ordinance of the Lord's Supper is practiced by all branches, denominations and sects of Christianity. It is a reminder to Christians that redemption is complete and it symbolically feeds the soul.

Prayer is another sacrificial way for the Christian to communicate with God. It is a sacrifice of time and an inward acknowledgement of dependence upon God. Christians have prayer times during their worship services (Eph 6:18; 1 Th 5:17), special prayer meetings (Ac 16:13) and prayer for the sick (Ja 5:14). The Christian does not have to go to a church or even to be with other Christians in order to pray. Since it is an inward communication with God who is omnipresent, the Christian can pray anywhere and at any time. The Christian is commanded to pray continually (1 Th 5:17).

Christians celebrate certain rites of passage as rituals accompanying significant life events. The most significant rite for the Christian is the ordinance of baptism (Rm 6:3; 1 Cor 12:13) which symbolizes the death and burial of the old nature and the rising of the new nature to eternal life in the rebirth experience. Baptism is an outward sign of the transition from outside to inside the Christian community. Christians also have baby dedications (1 Sa 1:22, 28; Lk 2:22) and promotions in Sunday School classes to mark the birth and attaining of certain age levels of children. Two rites of passage invite the community of Christian friends to participate. Weddings (Jn 2:1, 2) mark the transition of two people from one relationship to another in which the two become one (Gn 2:24; Eph 5:31). Funerals mark the final transition of an individual from this life to the next. For the Christian, a funeral is the opportunity to remind the family and friends that since the deceased was a Christian he has already passed from death to life (Rm 6:13) and to bring the bereaved words of hope (1 Th 4:13) and comfort (Ps 116:15).

Social Dimension

The ramifications of the social dimension seem to cause the most problems for converts to Christianity. The Bible teaches that when people become a Christian they are born again into a new family, the family of God (1 Pt 4:17), and other Christians become their brothers and sisters (Mk 3:35; 1 Tm 5:1, 2; Ja 2:15). Jesus also told the crowds: 'If anyone comes to me and does not hate his father and mother, his wife and children, his brothers and sisters—yes, even his own life—he cannot be my disciple' (Lk 14:26). It must be noted that 'hate' is a biblical way for expressing preference. A Christian's love for Christ should be so great that love for his family would seem like hate in comparison. For the Christian, the spiritual bond with other Christians is stronger than the blood bond of one's earthly family. Spiritual relations will go on for eternity, while blood relations end at death. Therefore, the Christian is to give preference in his relations 'to those who belong to the family of believers' (Eph 6:10). In cultures where one's identity is bound to one's family or tribe, to convert to Christianity causes problems with the family. Jesus warned his followers that this would be the case in saying that he 'did not come to bring peace but a sword' and he came 'to turn a man against his father, and a daughter against her mother' (Mt 10:34–37). Therefore, Jesus warned the people to count the cost of becoming his disciple (Lk 14:28–33).

While becoming a Christian may (but not necessarily) cause problems with one's blood family, the Christian is brought into a new social community called 'the church' (1 Cor 1:2; 11:18; Phm 1:2), or the 'fellowship' (1 Cor 5:2), or the 'body of Christ' (Eph 4:12) referring to the body or totality of all believers in Christ. The Bible uses the analogy of the human body of believers (1 Cor 12:12–27). The Bible also explains that each Christian has been given a spiritual gift that is needed in the church (1 Cor 12:1–11; Rm 12:4–8). Each individual Christian is valued because of their gift and purpose in the family of believers.

The community of Christians is given specific instructions in the Bible as to how they are to conduct themselves in the social dimension. The New Testament contains many verses called 'one another' verses that define how Christians ought to relate to one another. Christians are to 'honour' (Rm 12:10), 'serve' (Gal 5:13), 'be patient' (Eph 4:2), 'be kind and compassionate' (Eph 4:32), 'admonish' (Col 3:16), 'encourage' (1 Th 5:11), 'not slander' (Ja 4:11), 'love' (Rm 13:8), and 'forgive' (Eph 4:32) one another. The Christian community should be made up of people who 'Do nothing out of selfish ambition or vain conceit, but in humility consider others better than yourselves' (Php 2:3) and who 'do everything in love' (1 Cor 16:14). This should be the goal of every Christian community.

Culture in Genesis 1–11

The Book of Genesis records that when man was created, God put him in the Garden of Eden where all of his needs were supplied and his only responsibility was to take care of the garden (Gn 2:15). Man picked the seed-bearing plants and fruit for his food and his primary relationship was with God.

When man sinned, the ground was cursed and he had to work hard for his food (Gn 3:17–19, 23) and his relationship with God was based on a system of offerings representing worship (Gn 4:3). Genesis 4 records that the first man and woman had two sons who brought offerings to the Lord, the offering of Abel being acceptable and the offering of Cain being unacceptable (Gn 4:4, 5). Cain killed his brother and was driven by God from the land, which would no longer produce food for him (Gn 4:11, 12). Cain was an ungodly man, separated from God and from his parents.

According to the Bible, Cain, being separated from God, set out in the world to develop a system in which he could have his needs met apart from God. Cain married and produced children who produced children (Gn 4:17, 18). The primary relationship of Cain and his descendants was not with God but with his fellowman, so they began to build cities to have close fellowship with each other (Gn 4:17; 11:4). Cain's family developed tools and musical instruments, raised food, developing what anthropologists call culture (Gn 4:21, 22). The Book of Genesis records that human culture came about as the ungodly line of Cain devised systems and means to get their needs met apart from God.

The cultural system started by Cain and his descendents is called the 'world' (1 Jn 2:15) in the Bible and is depicted as being under the control of the evil one, Satan (1 Jn 5:19). The Bible uses many different terms to describe the Christian's relationship with the world cultural system. They are 'in' the world, but not 'of' it (Jn 17:14–19); they are 'aliens and strangers in the world' (1 Pt 2:11); their 'citizenship is in heaven' (Php 3:20); they are instructed to 'not live by the standard of the world' (1 Cor 10:2) or to 'conform to the pattern of the world' (Rm 12:2). John R. W. Stott's (1978) commentary on The Sermon on the Mount is called *Christian's Counter-Culture* and portrays the Christian living in the world system as just that. Christians are instructed to 'not love the world' and are told that if they do love the world they 'do not love God' (1 Jn 2:15). Christians are warned to not be surprised if the world hates them (1 Jn 3:13). Jesus warned his disciples that the world would hate them because it hated him (Jn 15:18). He also told them to 'take heart! I have overcome the world' (Jn 16:33).

The Christian is to live in this world system as a missionary lives in a foreign land. The primary relationship is to be with God and, as in the Garden of Eden, God will meet all the Christian's needs (Php 4:19) as he serves God in this world. The Christian still has to work (1 Th 3:10), but God supplies the work, opening doors of opportunity (Rv 3:7). The Christian view of the world is as a temporary dwelling place, not to be loved but to be pitied, and as a place for the light of the gospel and good works to shine bringing glory to God (Mt 5:16). The world will be made right when Christ comes again.

Conclusion

This chapter has brought together the concepts of worldview, philosophy and religion. Philosopher Martin Heidegger suggested that, historically speaking, philosophy and worldview are virtually one and the same, with great philosophy culminating in a worldview. He goes on to state that the goal of philosophy is the development of a final interpretation of reality and an ideal for living. The Christian believes that his religion accomplishes that task for him.

The Christian worldview is based on the Bible. The Christian's view of the Bible is that it is the word of God and it tells man the truth—the truth about God, the truth about the world and what is wrong with it, the truth about man and what is wrong with him, the truth about what can be done about man's condition, the truth about the past, and the truth about the future. The Bible does not cover over the faults of its heroes, nor does it present an optimistic picture of humanity in its fallen condition. The Bible does present man with a way of salvation and redemption through Jesus Christ. The Christian worldview is built around this religious end and those who have obtained that end must have the Christian worldview. As stated by James Orr (1948:4):

> He who with his whole heart believes in Jesus as the Son of God is thereby committed to much else besides. He is committed to a view of God, to a view of man, to a view of sin, to a view of Redemption, to a view of the purpose of God in creation and history, to a view of human destiny, found only in Christianity. This forms a 'Weltanschauung,' or 'Christian view of the world,' which stands in marked contrast with theories wrought out from a purely philosophical or scientific standpoint.

4

African Worldview

This chapter will present a delineation of the African worldview which is based upon African Traditional Religion. In writing about the African worldview, I have the distinct disadvantage of not being African, meaning that I will mainly have to rely on research and observations for what is to follow. The danger in writing from that perspective is that one may miss the heart and intentionality behind what is read and seen. Fortunately, people born and raised in Africa have written about their experiences, views and religion, and they have provided the missing ingredients for the non-African reader. Also, many non-Africans who lived in Africa longer than my six years here have researched and observed and have written their findings. I am indebted to both types of authors.

Is There 'an' African Worldview?

Given the number of diverse tribes and languages and the geographical diversity throughout sub-Saharan Africa, the issue of any unity in that diversity must be raised. Is there *an* African religion and *an* African worldview? Fortunately, this question has been addressed by many of the works researched for this writing.

There is a plethora of authors that believe there is enough unity in the diversity found in Africa to speak of *an* African Traditional Religion and *an* African worldview. Besides the more widely-read authors like Mbiti, Magesa, King, Gehman and Lamb, some lesser-known writers have this to say on the issue:

> Imasogie (1983:53): 'However, in spite of the differences, there is a core of Africanness that runs through their cultures and

religions. In view of this, one may speak legitimately of an African world view, the local peculiarities notwithstanding.'

Sow et al. (1979:10): 'they stressed the necessity of identifying the African culture's common points, which constitute a basis for Africanism.'

Richmond and Gestrin (1998:xiii): 'Their differences notwith-standing, all Africans share many traits and traditions which visitors will encounter almost everywhere across the continent.'

Kamalu (1990:3): 'we know it makes sense to speak of African religion and philosophy universally as a single body of knowledge.'

In speaking of *an* African worldview and *an* African Traditional Religion (ATR) we are speaking of two concepts that are so intertwined that they are inseparable. The African worldview is a religious worldview based upon ATR. Ambrose Moyo is quoted in Richmond and Gestrin (1998:30): 'Religion permeates all aspects of African traditional societies. It is a way of life in which the whole community is involved, and as such, it is identical with life itself. Even antireligious persons still have to be involved in the lives of their religious communities.' Richmond and Gestrin go on to state the relationship between religion and worldview: 'Africans are very spiritual people. Life is short and difficult, and Africans, like people everywhere, need beliefs to explain and give meaning to the world they live in.' And University of South Africa professor, S A Thorpe (1991:6) writes: 'ATR is the context from which African philosophy, anthropology, soteriology and ethics have sprung. In fact, the entire African world view, which is often expressed in forms of art and dance, is rooted and grounded in an African religious approach to life.'

ATR as Philosophy

The African worldview based on ATR is equated with philosophy by Geoffrey Parrinder, John Pobee and many others. However, there is one thing that has hindered the delineation of an African philosophy based on ATR up to this time in African history. Unlike the Christian religion, ATR has no written scriptures. In this work the Christian worldview is based primarily on the first eleven chapters of the first book (Genesis) of the Christian holy book, the Bible. There are no such written historical expositions of African traditional beliefs and practices which form the basis of ATR and African philosophy.

A look at the development of Hindu religion and philosophy minimizes the importance of the lack of historical literature. The hymns of the Vedas and the dialogues of the Upanishads, while containing much philosophy, were not written down until well into the Christian era. From inception, they were passed down verbally by priests of the Brahmin castes. In spite of a long history of having no written scriptures, Hindu religion and philosophy are recognized by scholars as being as legitimate as any others studied today. Likewise, the lack of scriptures for ATR should not diminish its legitimacy as a major belief system incorporating religion and philosophy.

Probably the most widely read and often quoted author writing on African religion is the Kenyan, John Mbiti. In the introduction to his book *African Religions and Philosophy*, Mbiti (1969:1) talks about religion being the strongest element in a traditional background and exerting probably the greatest influence upon the thinking and living of the people concerned. Philosophy is behind the thoughts and actions of all people and Mbiti believes that a study of traditional religion is the best route to discern the philosophy of Africans.

Philosophical systems of African peoples have not, as yet, been formulated but, as will be pointed out later, efforts are under way to do so. In this work I will not try to formulate an African philosophy as a whole, but will answer the philosophical questions asked based upon the African worldview as influenced by ATR. Because traditional religions permeate all the areas of life, there is no formal distinction between the sacred and the secular or between the spiritual and the material realms of life. It is clear that any attempt to speak of African philosophy must incorporate African traditional religious beliefs.

In reviewing the literature on African philosophy that has been published in the last three or four decades, and especially the most recent publications, it is surprising that the religious dimension of African life, which permeates all other dimensions, is all but completely ignored. Only one of the works (Kamalu 1990) on African philosophy consulted for this research (see Bibliography) gives any positive reflection on religion as it affects one's philosophy or worldview. Modern philosophers take the position that modern Africa and modern philosophy must be secular. Karp and Masolo and Kwame Gyekye are African writers educated in the West and their approach to African philosophy reflects the Western mindset of scientific materialism. For them, religious thought and science are mutually exclusive models of knowledge. The observed trend in African philosophy is that philosophy is following science in trying to be prescriptive instead of descriptive. It is the opinion of this writer that African philosophy wedded to science is an adulterous relationship and will produce illegitimate offspring because African philosophy is already inextricably wedded to African Traditional Religion.

Vital Force as Postulating the African Worldview

Africans are very aware of an unseen world of spirits, powers and forces. In anthropology, philosophy and theology this view is commonly referred to as 'animism' even though the definitions vary from discipline to discipline. Philosophy sees it as: 'A perspective on the world that sees spiritual powers or forces as residing in and controlling all of the natural world' (Evans 2002:10). Theology sees it as: 'The worship of physical objects in the belief that spiritual forces are present within them' (Erickson 2001). Most African theologians and philosophers today would reject the idea of Africans worshipping physical objects even though they might see them as possessing a power or force and therefore, treating them with reverence.

The Contribution of Tempels

One of the first attempts to delineate an African philosophy was done by Belgian Catholic missionary/priest, Placide Tempels, whose work *Bantu Philosophy* about the Baluba people (a sub-group of the Bantu) in the Belgian Congo was published in French in 1945. Tempels wrote of the Bantu's belief in a kind of psychic power that he calls 'vital force.' Tempels' main contention is that the ontology of the Bantu Africans is different from the ontology he held as one having a Western worldview. Tempels (1959:50) states: 'We can conceive the transcended notion of "being" by separating it from its attribute, "force," but the Bantu cannot. "Force" in his thought is a necessary element in "being," and the concept "force" is inseparable from the definition of "being." There is no idea of "being" divorced from the idea of "force."' The theory put forth by Tempels in *Bantu Philosophy* has been defended and attacked by subsequent African theologians and philosophers

Those African theologians and philosophers that cannot see past the colonial period reject anything Western and most all Africans reject the negative connotations of words like primitives, natives and savages used by Tempels throughout his book. One notable detractor of Tempels is John Mbiti (1969:14) who claims the theory of 'vital force' cannot be applied to other African peoples besides the Bantu with whose life and ideas he is familiar. However, in the same book, *African Religions and Philosophy*, Mbiti (1969:113) writes about spirits that animate trees, rivers, animals, charms, etc. Would it not take a 'vital force' to animate non-living objects just as Tempels wrote about?

Another detractor to Tempels' work is K A Opoku of the University of Ghana. In his book *West African Traditional Religion*, Opoku (1978:7) takes the position of Mbiti that the concept of 'vital force' may apply to the Bantu, but its application to other African peoples is bound to be erroneous.

Contrary to this opinion is Parrinder (1974:21) who writes about the West African word *nyama*, which is translated by European writers as energy, power or vital force. Variants of the word are found in the Western Sudan down to the Guinea coast. *Nyama* is found in people, animals, nature and objects.

Tempels was a Catholic missionary and his ultimate purpose for living with and studying the Baluba was religious, attempting to establish a relation of identity between Bantu philosophy and Christian theology. Tempels' concept of vital force is important for understanding African Traditional Religion as well as for understanding African ontology and the African worldview.

Proponents of the Vital Force Concept

The concept of vital force as the prime presupposition for the African Traditional Religion, ontology and, thus, worldview is accepted as valid by many who study religion and worldview. A sample of published words includes:

> Nyamiti (2006): In his survey of African traditional worldview he states as a main heading, 'Dynamism and vitalism, comprising an existential, concrete and affective way of approach. Reality is seen and judged especially from its dynamic aspects closely related to life. The farther a being is from these elements, the more unreal and valueless it is conceived to be. Hence, the emphasis on fecundity and life, and the identification between being and power or vital force. Indeed, the ideal of the African culture is coexistence with and the strengthening of vital force or vital relationship in the world and universe.'

> Thorpe (1991:88): 'The goal of Yoruba life is to achieve holistic unity in the midst of the multiplicity of forces that shape people's circumstances. . . . It is a person's lot to accept the myriad forces

that influence human lives and destinies. In themselves these forces are neither good nor bad. They simply exist. One should not try to overcome them but should simply accommodate oneself to them. . . . Thus unity and spiritual harmony or composure . . . are the main goals of life. . . . Their concept of the Supreme Being, for example, seems to be that of a pulsating life force, present in all people and permeating the entire universe. This vital force is evident in the Yoruba's ways of self-expression.'

Kamalu (1990:87): 'We start from the African premise that everything has its own level of consciousness or vital force and thus its own level of response to external action from other objects. There is a hierarchy of forces descending from human beings through to the animals, the plants and finally reaching stones and rocks at the lower end. But nothing is dead.'

Even such an unrelated organization as The International Observatory on End of Life Care acknowledges vital force as being prominent in African thinking. In an article posted on their website titled 'Ethical Issues in Uganda', they write: 'We may note that what has been named *The Vital Force Principle* within African thinking has a profound religious meaning in that "this vital force is hierarchical, descending from God through ancestors and elders to the individual," and that "whatever increases life or vital force is good; whatever decreases it is bad"' (The International Observatory on End of Life Care 2006).

Authors such as Richard Gehman, Lamin Sanneh and Gailyn Van Rheenen are also proponents. But perhaps the most ardent proponent of Tempels' concept of vital force is Laurenti Magesa. His book *African Religion: The Moral Traditions of Abundant Life* is centred on that concept. His contention is that the human person is central in the universal order and that religious practices are intended to enhance the life force of humans. The interaction of vital forces in the universe must be for the benefit of humanity in order that universal order can be maintained.

Delineation of the African Worldview

The delineation of the African worldview based upon ATR becomes a subjective endeavour because of the lack of objective writings in the form of scriptures or any other accumulated body of knowledge. Raymond Ogunade (2003) writing for the Metanexus Institute states:

> African Religion is therefore, the indigenous Religion of the Africans. . . . This is a religion that has no written scripture, yet it is 'written everywhere for those who care to see and read. Its scripture is what I call the 'Book of Universe.' It is largely written in the people's myths and folktales, in their songs and dances, in their environment, in Nature, in their liturgies and shrines, in their proverbs and pithy sayings. . . . It is religion whose historical founder is neither known nor glorified.

The African's worldview is shaped according to African religion. There is no distinction or separation between religion and other areas of human existence because life is religion and religion is life. Peter Addo (2002) states: 'There are no creeds written down because through the traditions of the elders all creeds and functions are carved on the individual's heart. Each individual by his very nature and life style is a living creed from the time one rises until one returns at night.' Ogunade (2003) concludes: 'It is not a fossil religion but a religion that millions of Africans today have made theirs by living it and practicing it.' For the African, religion is a matter of doing and practice rather than doctrine and principles.

Because African religion is lived rather than written, the delineation of the African worldview based on African Traditional Religion must be initially based on observation rather than research. Beginning early in the last century anthropologists and Christian missionaries began living among the African people so that they could observe their lives and write about what they observed. In the past few decades many African scholars have read what was written earlier, critiqued it and added their own observations from either being African or living in Africa, and have produced quite a few works on ATR. Only a few have tried to quantify an African Traditional Religion worldview either in the form of cultural presuppositions or common elements of all African cultures. Some of these works and my own observations have contributed to my delineation of the African worldview. I am grateful to Gehman (2005), Magesa (1997), Mbiti (1969, 2006), Nyamiti (2006), O'Donovan (1996) and Van Rheenan (1996) for their efforts in formulating a view of ATR. Their works and my observations have been my guides in writing this brief outline of the African worldview.

Outline of the African Worldview

I.   The existence of one Supreme Being or God, that is higher than all other divinities.

II.   A. The creation of an ordered cosmos by God.

B. Creation included the physical and spiritual worlds.

C. The cosmos is imbued with a vital force flowing from God through everything he created.

D. The vital force is there to sustain life in all of its dimensions.

III.   A. The nature and dignity of man.

B. Man is God's highest created being.

C. The cosmos was created for man.

D. Man finds his personal identity in his community.

IV.   A. Community is defined in terms of common participation in life, history and destiny.

B. Community includes the living and the dead.

V.   A. A holistic view of life.

B. Life is made up of events rather than time.

C. Fatalistic view of life.

D. Total cosmic harmony motivates actions.

VI.   A. The past holds the future.

B. One's destiny is to join those who make up the history of the community.

Philosophical Elements of the African Worldview

Following the scheme used for the biblical or Christian worldview in chapter 3, a question/answer format will be used to answer the same worldview questions asked in chapter 3.

Ontology Questions

Is there a Supreme Being, and if so, what is it like?

All African people believe in a Supreme Being called God. It is at the centre of African religion, but it is not known how this ancient belief in God originated. In a recent work John Mbiti (2006) claims to have never found a single African people without a word or name for God. ATR is often thought to be polytheistic, that is, believing in and having many gods. In truth, ATR is closer to being henotheistic, believing in one Supreme God, while not denying the existence of other deities. Opoku (1978:5) concurs by stating:

> In classical polytheism, the gods in the pantheon were all independent of one another. One of the gods might be regarded as the chief, but he was never regarded as the creator of the other gods.
>
> In African Traditional Religion, however, the picture is quite different. God, or the Supreme Being, is outside the pantheon of gods. He is the eternal creator of all the gods, and of men and the universe. This makes him absolutely unique, and He is differentiated from the other gods in having a special name. This name is always in the singular, and is not a generic name, like *Obosom* (Akan) or *Orisha* (Yoruba). All the other divinities have a generic name in addition to their specific names.

This is the African's way of showing the uniqueness of God. Peter Addo (2002) echoes this when he writes: 'Traditional African religion is centred on the existence of one Supreme High God. . . . The traditional African belief is that the Great One brought the divinities into being.' In the African view, things that appear to have divine powers are only exhibiting the vital force emanating from the Supreme Being, God.

The nature of God in African belief can be gathered from the qualities attributed to him. These attributes of God are not self-revealed as in some religions. The major source of the African beliefs regarding the attributes of God is their ancient myths. African myths express many beliefs about God in graphic form using picture language. Other sources for an understanding of God's character in African Traditional Religion are found in prayers, songs, proverbs, riddles and even some rituals.

No area has produced more writings or more contradictory opinions than African beliefs about the Supreme Being. A book that should have been most helpful is Mbiti's *Concepts of God in Africa*. However, he is writing as a Christian with an ecumenical presupposition and used Christian theological and biblical terms as chapter titles and sub-headings throughout the book. A reader might think that ATR and Christianity were almost the same religion. Those writing from an anthropological or philosophical view (including some non-African Christian missionaries) present ATR as a distinct religion unique to Africa. In this work I have endeavoured to rely on the writings of those authors in which was detected the least bias and whose writings closely harmonize with my own observations and interviews. One such work is *God: Ancestor or Creator?* by Harry Sawyerr. Sawyerr was born in Sierra Leone, my country of residence, and was a Professor of Theology at Fourah Bay College, University of Sierra Leone. This book is the result of his study of the concept of God among three West African peoples—the Akan of Ghana, the Yoruba of Nigeria and the Mende of Sierra Leone.

Among the attributes of God in ATR the one that is foundational is that God is real, with no African people lacking a name for the Supreme Being. The one glue that seems to hold all the other ATR beliefs together is the belief that God is there, above all things, the source of all things and the reason for all things, giving everything a reason for being. Sawyerr (1970:10) writes that God is not just a philosophical concept but a reality, even though he may not be manifest directly. However, the cultic and nature spirits are understood to be concrete manifestations of the power of God. God is considered to be all-powerful. The power of lightening, thunder and wind come from God. The power of witchcraft and sorcery come from God. However, the evil use of power is not God's will.

God is spirit. He has no physical body; but is invisible. Like the wind he cannot be seen, but he can be known by its effects. The Akan say: 'If you want to speak to God tell it to the wind.'

Besides being all-powerful, God is all-knowing. The Yoruba say he is 'The One who sees both the inside and outside of men.' God can be all-knowing because he is present everywhere. He is spirit and his spirit fills the cosmos. There is no other being like God. He is unique. No one can draw an image of God for God cannot be comprehended. Unlike the creatures, God has no limitations, and unlike creation, God had no beginning. God is beyond our ability to comprehend. In his power, knowledge and uniqueness, God is seen as good and merciful. Sun and rain producing crops, one's health and the birth of children are seen as proofs of God's mercy.

The question arises as to whether or not the God of ATR is personal or impersonal. No doubt he is often referred to using personal pronouns, but is he someone the traditional African has a personal relationship with, or is he only a concept that the traditional African has a knowledge of? The mysterious nature of God combined with other factors may suggest an impersonal, transcendent power rather than a personal being. Scholars have taken different interpretations on the subject. Jomo Kenyatta (1965:224) after describing the God of his people (the Gikuyu) writes: 'The Being thus cannot be seen by ordinary mortal eyes. He is a distant Being and takes but little interest in individuals in their daily walk of life. Yet at the crises of their lives he is invariably called upon.' Anthony Gittins (1987:46) makes these comments:

> A somewhat dismissive statement by a Christian Mende man, provides a useful focus for our enquiry. He said, 'The Mende has an idea and some knowledge of a Supreme Being. But who is he? Where is he? They don't know this. Natural objects and the spirits of the dead—that is their firm belief.' Who then is the Supreme Being?

Gittins (1987:47) goes on to give what he believes to be the traditional Mende belief that the Supreme Being is 'up' looking after them. He states: 'The vagueness of this statement seems to me to capture well the attitude of the majority of Mende people uninfluenced by one of the world religions.' And he concludes with the comment that the Supreme Being he has been describing seems a remote figure, hardly a personality. And Sawyerr (1970:5) states that in West Africa, God is believed to be remotely situated from the everyday events of human life.' Although many Christian writers say the Supreme Being of ATR is a personal Being, the majority of writers portray the Supreme Being as distant and approachable only through intermediaries.

What is the origin and nature of man?

Without having a common scripture or a single founder to put forth what Africans should believe concerning the origin of man, they have relied on myths to explain what is not obvious. The general belief in ATR is that man was created by God, or a Supreme Being. This explanation affords man the highest dignity and satisfactorily fits in with the other African ontological and cosmological beliefs. The mythical explanations about the origin of human beings vary as to where they were created (on earth or in the sky or heaven) and how they were created (moulded from clay, they fell like fruit from a tree, etc.). Regardless of the details, some general beliefs are the same in ATR: man was created by God; male and female were created; man was created after all other things were created.

As to the nature of man, ATR asserts that the human being is a bipartite or, in some tribes, a tripartite being. The general African belief concerning man is that he is made up of material (biological) and immaterial (spiritual) substances, resulting in the unity of the personality of man. It is the material part of man that dies while the spiritual continues to live.

The spiritual part of man is identified by various terms: soul, life, breath, shadow or doubt and the spirit and soul are considered to be different parts by some. For instance, the Nuer regard man as tripartite beings. They believe that the life or breath comes from God and returns to him at death. The flesh is buried in the ground, and the soul becomes a ghost and goes to be with God. Other Africans consider the spirit to be the personality of man giving individuality and the soul being the vital force that animates the body. Still, others would reverse the role of spirit and soul. But the general concept of the nature of man is the same.

ATR and African philosophy is basically anthropocentric. The African sees humanity as the centre of the universe and the reason for creation. There is a clear distinction between man and animals.

The moral nature of man is believed to be more or less neutral, not being inherently good or evil. A person acts in ways which are 'good' when they conform to the customs and regulations of his community or 'bad' (evil) when they do not. Africans recognize that some event in history separated God and humanity, but it did not turn persons into 'fallen' creatures, making them evil (sinful) before God. The story of the event serves to explain the ontological separation between God and man. Man may commit evil acts but that does not make him evil by nature.

What is reality and what is ultimate reality?

In his book *Foundations of African Thought* Chukwunyere Kamalu (1990:24) uses as one of his themes 'Being and Becoming' in which the world is seen as being two in one, a duality of the void and matter, the spiritual and the physical. The spiritual is not manifest in itself, but through its opposite, the physical. The physical and the spiritual are but two dimensions of one and the same universe.

John Mbiti (1969:20) gives five categories of African ontology as God, spirits, man, animals and plants, and phenomena and objects without biological life. It is an anthropocentric ontology in that everything is seen in terms of its relation to man. God is the Originator and Sustainer of man. The spirits hold the destiny of man. The animals, plants and natural phenomena and objects constitute the environment in which man lives, providing a means of existence.

In addition to the five categories of ontology, there seems to be a force or power permeating the whole universe. God is the source and ultimate controller of this force. The spirits have access to some levels of it, as do a few human beings who have the knowledge and ability to manipulate and use it. These would include the medicine men, witches, priests and rainmakers. Some use the power for the good and others for the ill of their communities.

The Africans are capable of abstract thought, and they believe in a latent energy in things, which is not visible outwardly, but can be seen in the effects produced by their use. This latent energy is understood as power, and power is associated with spirits. Animals and plants have spiritual forces akin to those of men, but generally they are of lesser power than man's. The spirits are the ancestors and the forces of nature: the powers behind storm, rain, rivers, hills, rocks. They are spiritual powers capable of manifesting themselves in many different places.

For those interested in doing further reading in this area, Janheinz Jahn, in his work *Muntu: African Culture and the Western World*, takes a more philosophical approach to the African ontological understanding of reality. Jahn, in building on the works of Tempels and Kagame, proposes four categories of reality: Muntu—human being; Kintu—thing; Hantu—place and time; and Kuntu—modality. For Jahn, these four categories must be conceived of, not as substance, but as force. Man (Muntu), dog (Kintu), home and today (Hantu), beauty and laughter (Kuntu) are forces and as such are all related to one another. The relationship of these forces is expressed in their names, for if we remove the determinative, the stem 'ntu' is the same for all the categories. These categories are drawn from the Bantu language and are couched with a philosophical bent but are descriptive of the basic traditional understanding of reality throughout Africa.

For the traditional African, reality is being and being is force. Therefore, ultimate reality is the Supreme Being or Divine force. Mbiti gives an ontological hierarchy of God/spirits/humans/animals and plants/phenomena and objects without biological life. So the 'life' or 'force' that resides in a stone is ontologically lower than that of a plant, and plants life lower than animals, and animals life lower than humans. At the top of the hierarchy of the universe is the Divine Force, which is both the primary and the ultimate life giving Power, God the Creator and Sustainer of the universe.

Jahn's NTU, Magesa's Divine Force, and Mbiti's God are references to the same ultimate reality in ATR. Basic to the African worldview that penetrates all religious traditions in Africa is the belief that God, the creator of the universe, is the first cause, the Prime Mover and that he is the Ultimate Cause of the natural phenomena, which manifest many different forms.

What is truth?

In researching the concept of truth in ATR it has been surprising that for the most part, it is not addressed. Books on ATR, even by Christian authors, lack entries for truth in the subject index. Where truth is mentioned in the text it is never defined. Books on African philosophy do deal with the concept of truth, but only from a philosophical and not a religious standpoint. Religion puts presuppositions on philosophy that philosophy does not want. A few articles posted on the Internet have been helpful in delineating the traditional African view of truth.

There are three philosophical theories of truth: correspondence theory—a truth equals fact; coherence theory—a truth coheres with our system of beliefs; and pragmatism—a truth works or has practical value. From a philosophical perspective a combination of the correspondence and pragmatic theories of truth would best describe the traditional African view of truth.

H K Dzobo (2006) did a study of the concept of truth among the Ewe and Akan of West Africa. He states, 'The normative truth-statement [*Nyadzodzoe*] is therefore what is generally known by the society, represented by the elders, to be true in speech as well as in deed. The truth of a statement is therefore in its identity with what has been known to be the case in such matters.' That would be the correspondence theory of truth. The most interesting of his findings is what he calls 'the creativity or *Nyano* theory of Truth.' Dzobo (2006) states: 'This can be said to be unique to the indigenous concept of truth. It is different from the pragmatic theory of truth in that it is not only the workability of an idea that makes it true, but its power to bring about a better human situation and continuously to improve the conditions of life. The defining characteristic of the creativity theory is its emphases on the ameliorative [able to make better] nature of truth.' He concludes: 'Finally, truth, like knowledge and wisdom, is the statement that has the power to create new and better situations in life.'

It has been the observation of me and others that what is creating better situations in the traditional African view includes avoiding negative consequences by telling a lie. Much of knowledge that informs everyday cultural practice is the result of theoretical deliberations and negotiations between the producers of traditional knowledge whom are called sages. The sages are considered to be the keepers of traditional beliefs. In an entry he wrote for *The Stanford Encyclopedia of Philosophy* Masolo (2006) quotes a sage's answer to the question, 'Why would people tell lies?' His answer was 'So that they may eat.' The positive benefit of telling a lie created a better circumstance and therefore met the criteria for truth.

In Western cultures truth and lies are opposites with the former being good and the latter evil. That is not necessarily the case in Africa where truth is not good in itself, nor is lie always evil. Lies are objected to when they are socially inconvenient. Not only is it expected that a man will lie to get out of difficulties but there are cases in which lying is called for. In order to avoid giving offence, Africans will often say 'yes' when they really mean 'no'. The avoidance of offence is considered the true thing to do and therefore, the false statement is considered to be the truth. Truth is not absolute, nor is right and wrong. In traditional African cultures there can be many versions of truth and many extenuating circumstances. Truth in the traditional African view does not have an ontological correspondent but it has great utility value.

Cosmology Questions

What is the origin and nature of the universe?

It was stated earlier that the African ontology is a religious ontology. Likewise, the African cosmology is a religious cosmology so that African ontology and cosmology are closely aligned. Africans generally believe that the universe was created by God, but there is no agreement on how the creation of the universe took place. It is also a widespread view that God continues to create. It is an ongoing process which will probably never end.

Many Africans hold the view that nothing existed before God. That means that God created *ex nihilo* in the original act of creation, but subsequently he can be using existing material to continue his creative acts. It is also believed that in addition to creating the material universe, God also endowed it with natural laws and is also the source of some human customs.

As previously stated, Africans believe the nature of the universe to be made up of visible and invisible, or material and spiritual realities. These divisions are seen as being linked together. Some African peoples believe the physical universe to be of two spheres (the heavens and the earth) and others believe it to be a three-tier creation made up of the heavens, the earth and the underworld, which is below the earth. Regardless of the number of levels believed to be in the universe, man is considered to be the centre of the universe.

Africans believe that there is an inherent order to the universe. The philosophical explanation of this order is much less convincing than the religious ones. Most Africans cannot understand the philosophical explanation, but the religious explanations are a reality to them. Order in the universe is seen as operating at various levels. There is order in the laws of nature which provide a sense of stability in the universe. There is a moral order working among the people providing peace and harmony with one another. There is a mystical order governing the created things in the universe, consisting of mysterious power that is available to spirits and spiritualists. Finally, there is a religious order to the universe with God as the focal point of interpreting life experiences. Whether or not God is pleased affects order at the other levels.

Many authors identify the concept of power in the universe in terms of force, a life force in the universe that is the basic understanding of the nature of the universe in Africa. It is believed that every creature has been endowed by God with its own force of life, and because of the common divine origins of this power, all creatures are seen to be connected with each other so that each one influences the other for good or for bad. The life force of the older creatures is perceived to be the stronger and is understood to claim the allegiance of the younger. Therefore, God has given the ancestors a quantitatively more powerful life force than their descendants have. African's relationship to their ancestors will be dealt with in chapter 6.

What is God's relationship with the universe?

In ATR God is believed to be not only the creator of the universe, but also the continuing sustainer of the universe. God is the One who provides food, sunshine, rain, children, health and protection from harm. As Supreme Ruler over the earth, his will is absolute and he rules with power.

This view of God's relationship with the universe is confirmed by most writers on ATR. Parrinder (1969:41) writes: 'Not only did he make the world, but he established the laws of society and the existence of justice depends upon obedience to him. Creation is not only in the past; the divine work is continued in sustaining the universe.' Opoku (1978:9) attributes these duties to God: 'He rewards men and also punishes them when they do wrong. He may be likened to the Overlord of society for He is the Final Authority in all matters.'

God's divine involvement in the ongoing activities of the universe is attributed to God's personality consisting of will which governs the universe and the life of mankind. It is an immutable will, and man generally has to seek it or accept it in situations that man cannot change.

God's involvement also includes a concern for the universe. He cares for it and keeps it so that it does not come apart. God provides for what he has created. He provides life and everything needed to sustain life including food and the sunshine and rain needed to grow it. God is also actively involved in ruling the universe as King and Judge. In the African view, God's relationship with the universe is very much pro-active and beneficent.

What is the meaning of time?

Kenyan John Mbiti is credited with expounding an African view of time that is widely accepted (though there are some detractors) and often quoted. He first expressed the findings of his research in his doctoral dissertation at Cambridge University dealing with New Testament eschatology in the African perspective. Mbiti's research found that the question of time and its meaning is of little concern to the traditional African. For them, time is made up of a composite of events that have already occurred, are occurring now, and those which will likely occur immediately. Beyond that, what is certain to occur in the future, or what falls within the rhythm of natural phenomena is in the category of *potential* time. This traditional view makes time two-dimensional, with a long past, a present, and virtually no future. The future is absent because whatever events will happen there have not taken place, and therefore, cannot be a part of time. Time is being, or has already been, experienced. The result of this concept of time is that, for the African, time moves 'backward' rather than 'forward.' The focus of attention is on what has already taken place, rather than on what is going to take place, unless the anticipated event falls within the rhythm of natural phenomena. The rhythm of natural phenomena is measured in rains or new moons, not in months or years.

Mbiti divides the African concept of time into two dimensions and uses Swahili words based upon an analysis of the verb tenses available to identify them. The *Sasa* covers the 'now-period' and is the immediate concern for Africans because that is 'where' or 'when' they exist and experience time. Events in the *Sasa* must either be about to occur, occurring or just occurred. The 'future' has to be brief because any meaningful event in the future must be so immediate and certain that people have almost experienced it.

Zamani covers all past time and overlaps with *Sasa* to include the events occurring or just occurred. *Sasa* feeds into *Zamani*. Events 'move' backward from *Sasa* into *Zamani*. It is the final storehouse for all phenomena and events which constitutes history. *Sasa* functions to bind individuals and their immediate environment together. It is the period of current conscious living. On the other hand, *Zamani* is the period of myth, giving a sense of foundation or security to the *Sasa* period, binding together all people and events.

Mbiti's position that there is virtually no future in the African concept of time has probably brought the most detractors. Byang Kato in his work *Theological Pitfalls in Africa* analysed Mbiti's position and took the opposite position that the African does live a life which demonstrates an awareness of the future. For example, every traditional African male anticipating his initiation to manhood does have a definite future outlook. Also, the financial planning necessary for the payment of a bride-price before marriage requires a look to a future event. However, it has been my observation in six years of living among Africans that virtually nothing is done to prepare for the costs of initiations or weddings until the event is eminent (*Sasa* period), and then they scurry to raise the necessary funds. It is also evident in my students who did not begin term assignments until a few days before they were due or not studying for exams until the night before. Africans have learned from experience to be present-oriented, preferring to focus on the present and deal with the uncertain future events as they come along.

For traditional Africans, time really has no meaning. It is like a vehicle that carries them through the cycle of known and repeated events, such as planting season, rains and harvest followed by the dry season. There is a rhythmic succession of events for the individual made up of birth, initiation, marriage, having children, eldership, death and ancestorship. These events are measured by time moving in a circle as it moves backward.

Do laws and causality govern the universe absolutely?

The existence of natural laws and the search for causation when those laws are violated are important elements in the traditional African worldview. As stated previously, order in the universe is seen as operating on several levels. First, there is order in the laws of nature. These function everywhere, and give a sense of security and certainty to the universe. However, Africans do not believe that the natural laws govern absolutely. When the natural laws are violated the principle of causality does govern absolutely and the cause must be found. Africans see the connection between cause (considered to be supernatural) and effect as being immediate; secondary causes are not considered.

The Oxford Dictionary of Philosophy (Blackburn 1994) gives this definition of causation: 'Causation is the relation between two events that holds when, given that one occurs, it produces, or brings forth, or determines, or necessitates the second.' An event that brings good fortune is considered to be ultimately caused by God and an event that brings bad fortune is considered to be caused by a spiritual force and ultimately allowed by God. Seeking the causes of bad events is the reason for much of the religious activity of the Africans.

Life forces of different beings on earth can directly reinforce or diminish the life forces of other beings under what some call the 'general laws of vital causality.' This relationship between and among created vital forces—just as that existing between God and creation—is also causal. Thus, causation flows in all directions to maintain life in the universe. Therefore, every event is seen to have a cause. Fundamental to African causal theory is the conception of an orderly universe in which all events are caused and potentially explicable.

The laws of nature are general and considered to be beneficent since they were put there by God. But, as stated previously, these laws do not rule absolutely and can be controlled by spiritual forces. Some traditional Africans see physical objects that once belonged to an ancestor as having power to control nature and thus giving the ancestors control over the physical world. The causes of events bringing bad or evil results are sought after with the most diligence. The true cause of some events may only be determined upon consultation with one who is qualified to look into such matters by virtue of the possession of powers of divination. Punishment by the ancestral spirits, deities and personalized talismans; the operation of witchcraft and sorcery; and the unfolding of a person's destiny are the most frequently cited causes explaining serious cases of misfortune and illness and to account for death.

Natural causes of misfortune are rarely recognized. The root cause is usually moral or spiritual. It is the African view that when natural or religious explanations fail to satisfy, the social explanation—witchcraft—is certain to be involved.

Teleology Questions

Why do man and the universe exist and do they have a final end?

In the African view the universe exists for man and man exists to provide continuation and harmony in the life forces in the universe. Because man thinks of himself as being at the centre of the universe, he looks for what the world can do for man, and how man can use the world for his own good.

Man's function as the centre of the universe is a priestly function, linking the universe with God its creator. Man speaks to the universe and he listens to it, as he tries to create a harmony with it. As indications that man considers it to be a religious universe, he turns some parts of it into sacred objects and uses other parts of it for sacrifices and offerings.

In the African worldview based upon ATR both man and the universe will never cease to be. Events come and go in the form of major and minor rhythms. These rhythms of time suggest that the universe will never come to an end of itself. It will keep on going as it always has.

Man has a final destiny but his spirit never ceases to exist according to ATR. The human race will continue to exist as individual humans sustain the vital life force through procreation. Each individual human is moving to a final end in the world of spirits. John Mbiti (1969:31–33) explains the human progression toward its final state. It is a gradual progression from the *Sasa* period to the *Zamani*. After physical death, a person continues to exist in the *Sasa* period as long as friends and relatives remember him *by name*. This could last several generations. When the last person who knew the deceased by name dies, then the deceased passes from the *Sasa* into the *Zamani* period. The changing of periods is quite significant for the living and the deceased. As long as the deceased is in the *Sasa* period he has all the rights and powers of an ancestor (what Mbiti calls the *living-dead*) and is in a state of *personal immortality*. When the deceased passes from the *Sasa* period it completes the dying process but he does not cease to exist. He now enters into the state of the 'spirits' who are no longer formal members of the human families. In African ontology this is the final destiny of man.

Does evil have a purpose?

In the African view evil does not have an ontological existence. It is seen in terms of negative or harmful effects or consequences of an act. Acts are considered bad or evil if they bring bad or evil consequences. A person is not good or evil but he acts in ways which are considered good or evil. The acts that act against the life force or harmony of a person or the community are considered to be an evil act.

The question of culpability must be raised. Does evil reside in the act or in the person that commits the act? Unfortunately, there is a scarcity of writing on the nature of evil in ATR. Most Africans would agree that evil resides in forces or spirits that influence people to do evil acts. Africans see evil as a punishment for some act that disrupts the harmony of the life forces in the universe. My research revealed no stated purpose that evil serves in the world. If the position that evil is in the act is accepted, then the punishment that attends the act should serve as a deterrent to commit such acts. If the position that the person that commits the act is evil, then the punishment that attends the act should serve to reveal who the evil people are. When bad things happen to an African, the first assumption is that he did something to deserve it.

Ethics/Morality Questions

Who or what determines what is moral and immoral?

In African religion the conception of morality in the universe is the understanding of the good that sustains life and the bad that destroys it. Laurenti Magesa's book *African Religion: The Moral Tradition of Abundant Life* is centred around this concept of moral acts sustaining life and immoral acts destroying life, indicating both the physical and social life of the individual and the community. Magesa states that God is the source of moral values or laws, and that the ancestors are the depository and policemen of morals. Moral rules or laws were given by God, which provides an unchallenged authority for morality. The ancestor spirits keep watch over people making sure they observe the moral laws and punishing them when they violate the moral laws.

Morality operates on two dimensions. Personal morality has to do with the life and conduct of the individual. Social morality has to do with the life of the larger society. Since Africans view the individual as existing only for the community, African morality is more concerned with social behaviour, that is, the effects of one's behaviour on the peace and harmony of the community.

African religion's concept of morality is steeped in tradition. The moral agents (God, the ancestors and the spirits) are all powers that impinge on human life in one way or another, policing moral behaviour. The way they act in policing morality has been determined by the ancestors and is 'stored' in the traditions of the people. Therefore, tradition determines what the people must do to live morally in the community.

That is why Africans hold fast to their traditional religion. It is seen as a religious act to honour traditions because the moral laws of their society are embedded in the traditions and to violate them would bring the wrath of the ancestors. The wrath of the ancestors is seen as the manifestation of the wrath of God, who is the source of moral values in their traditions.

How do we know what is right?

The African individual sees his existence within the framework of the African community, therefore, whatever happens to the individual happens to the whole group, and whatever happens to the whole group happens to the individual. The maintenance of social harmony and relationships in daily living by the individual and the community is the central moral and ethical imperative of African Religion.

Since the maintenance of peace and harmony in the community is the moral imperative, anything that does not do that is considered to be immoral or not right. Right conduct is oriented not from any absolute standards of honesty or truth, but from the social good in each situation.

Aesthetics Questions

What is man's relationship with the natural environment?
As stated previously, man thinks of himself as being the centre of his universe and believes that the universe exists for him. That being the case he seeks to use the part of the universe he occupies (his natural environment) to his best interest. It has also been previously stated that man has a priestly function in his natural environment linking it with God its creator. Since Africans believe that spirits reside in natural phenomena such as trees, rocks, rivers and lakes, the natural environment is seen as animate rather than inanimate. This guides man's relationship to his natural environment.

Africans divide the things in their environment into the specific uses they make of them. Some things have physical uses (food, tools); some have religious uses (as symbols or in rituals); and some are used for medicinal or magical purposes. This gives people the opportunity to religiously manipulate the objects. If a lake contains spirits, a sacrifice to those spirits should help catch fish in that lake. It makes them feel like they are in harmony with the lake and the spirits and still get what they want. The idea of living in harmony with the universe—obeying the laws of natural, moral and mystical order—is of utmost importance. If these are upset, it is man who suffers.

It has been my observation that Africans take a passive attitude toward their natural environment, not changing anything in it unless absolutely necessary. In the traditional village setting they will not move a rock out of the road or hush a barking dog or crying baby. They know that there is something there that they do not see and they respect it.

Is there aesthetic value to religious experience?
As stated previously, the 'aesthetic' has always been intimately connected with sensory experience and the kinds of feelings it arouses. From that standpoint, the African's religious experience does have aesthetic value. Since religion is an integral part of African life, any aesthetic experience is seen as a religious

experience. Most religions offer their religious experiences during worship services or at sacred buildings, temples or shrines. But, in Africa, there is little ordered worship of God and few places where rituals are performed for him. The worship is done and experiences obtained from ordinary events of the African's life.

Religious experience is found in the rituals, ceremonies and festivals of the people, and through their observation religious ideas are perpetuated and passed on to the next generations. Much of African music and songs deals with religious ideas and practices. The religious rituals, ceremonies and festivals are always accompanied by music, singing and sometimes dancing giving an outlet to the emotional expression of religious beliefs.

Sacred objects and symbols have religious meaning and also evoke religious feelings, as do prayers. Prayers help serve to remove personal and communal anxieties, fears, frustrations and worries. With that result, praying would certainly be an aesthetic experience for the African or anyone else.

With Africans living close to nature and seeing all nature as possessing spirits or forces, observing nature can be an aesthetic experience. The sky contains God and men lift up their eyes to the sky and regard its spirit as transcendent and mighty.

Philosophy of History Questions

What is the meaning of history?

Africa has a long history, most of which is unknown. The fact that much of African history is unknown is a concern only to current scholars who are trying to construct such a history. The traditional African does not have a sense of history beyond a few generations of ancestors. My research revealed very little written about history in books on ATR. John Mbiti was the most helpful author and his books spoke of God working in current events as his working in history. For example, in *Concepts of God in Africa,* Mbiti (1970:247) wrote: 'It is to be remembered that, for many African peoples, God's active part in human history is seen in terms of his supplying them with rain, good harvest, health, children, and cattle; his healing them when sick or barren; his helping them in times of difficulties; and making his presence felt through natural phenomena.'

The African's answer to the meaning of history is closely aligned with the previous question of the meaning of time. It was pointed out there that time is viewed as moving from the *Sasa* to a much longer *Zamani* period. But the latter period only lasts for a few generations. For the African, life is like a play acted out on a stage. The actors perform for a while and then are replaced by new actors who may have a slightly different script. The former actors are remembered for a while and then are forgotten. But the play continues on *ad infinitum*.

Is history cyclical or linear in progression?

Each African tribe has its own history. This history moves backward from the moment of current experience to the period beyond which nothing can go. The idea of being linear in progression connotes moving forward in a straight line toward a stated goal or destination. In traditional African thought, there is no concept of history moving forward towards future climax or towards an end of the world. Since the future does not exist beyond a short period, the future cannot be expected to usher in a golden age that is a radically different state of affairs from what is happening or has already happened. John Mbiti says the African looks forward to being part of the past.

For the traditional African, time moves in the cycle of known and re-peated events, in a rhythmic succession which is measured by time moving in a circle. In the life of the individual the future is thought of in terms of the life cycle of birth, initiation, marriage, children, eldership, death and ancestor-ship. Death moves the African backward in history so that some of his human features or characteristics can be 'reborn' in future generations.

Epistemology Questions

What can we know and how can we know it?

Of all the works consulted on African culture and ATR, none written from an anthropological or theological perspective dealt with the area of knowledge. Only those writing from the philosophic perspective attempted to extract an African epistemology. N K Dzobo did a study of the epistemic conceptions found in the everyday language and oral literature of the Ewe and Akan of Ghana. He gives four main categories of knowledge in Ewe: traditional, deduc-tive, formal education, and knowledge resulting from gaining an understand-ing of things in terms of their fundamental principles. Dzobo did a strictly philosophical study based on what has come to be known in the Western tradition as ordinary language philosophy. Of the categories of knowledge he expounded, only the category of traditional knowledge is apropos to this study. Dzobo describes traditional knowledge as 'that which is passed down (by word of mouth) from one person or from one generation to another.' That which is passed down is the lessons of wisdom as stored by the elders in the proverbs and other wise sayings of their indigenous culture.

In Africa, traditional knowledge is propositional knowledge which is associated with information in oral propositional form that is supposed to be knowledge and therefore true but which the individual recipient cannot test or verify. It therefore has to be *accepted as true* because it agrees with common sense or because it corresponds with the limited amount of information that people are able to test and confirm in a firsthand or direct manner. This results in a weak evidential basis of much of the information that Africans are conditioned to regard as knowledge, or truth. However, this is not a problem for the traditional African holding the traditional African worldview based upon African Traditional Religion. He trusts his *source* of knowledge.

Knowledge in the traditional African culture is embedded in the ethics and morals, values, customs, traditional laws and taboos which are passed on through songs, myths, proverbs and sayings. As stated previously in this chapter, God is considered to be the source of all traditions and morality, which he passed on to their ancestors who are the depositories of knowledge. The African can know all things about the traditional way of life and about his traditional religion by consulting the depositories of that knowledge. These include the ancestors, who pass on to the chiefs and elders, the medicine men and sorcerers. The knowledge residing in each of these is a received knowledge passed to them from a previous depository.

In *The Prayers of African Religion* John Mbiti lists the things that Africans pray for. He names things like children, healing, health, rain, harvest, success in hunting, security, happiness and peace. It is interesting that there are no prayers to receive knowledge. It is as if they expect (or want) God to act but not to speak. It shows the reliance Africans have on the knowledge gained through the traditional human sources. Africans can know how to live life in harmony with the life forces in the universe, and they can know how to correct it when there is disharmony because they can consult the traditional sources of their knowledge and believe what they say.

What justifies a belief?

In the last chapter, it was stated that propositional knowledge is defined by philosophers as justified true belief. It was also stated that two logics or structures have been put forth to justify holding a belief: foundationalism and coherentism. For the African, their traditional beliefs are foundational and coherent. The foundation of their traditional beliefs is the tradition of the ancestors and every belief is coherent and justified because it is shared with all others in the people group.

Religious Dimensions of the African Worldview

Religious beliefs are at the core of the African worldview. The Africans' beliefs about God and their delegation of knowledge and duties motivate them to revere and obey the elders of the community, both living and dead. They have no scriptures, so they rely on the teachings of the elders as their source of faith and practice. Those teachings guide them as they live out the religious dimensions of their traditional worldview.

Experiential Dimension

For the traditional African all of life is religion and as life is experienced religion is experienced. ATR is not primarily belief, but is best understood in the way African's practice their traditional worldview. There is no conversion experience in ATR as in some other religions. You are born into it.

Religious experience begins a few days after birth at the naming ceremony. During the festivities prayers of thanksgiving are offered and the announcing of the name given to the child links it to at least one of its ancestors. From that point on the individual has his own ceremonies commemorating the various rites of passage he passes through and also sharing in the ceremonies of others in the community. Every event is a community event and every event has religious connotations. ATR is a lived religion with man at the centre of his religiosity.

Like Christianity, ATR contains religious experiences incorporating aspects of dualism and monism. God's transcendence is recognized and he is believed to be separate and distinct from creation, dwelling far away in the sky, or in some important remote places such as mountains. Even though God is seen as 'completely other', transcendent and separate, he is also believed to be imminent and near. In many acts of worship Africans acknowledge God to be near and approachable. Such acts include sacrifice, offerings, prayers and invocations. The transcendence of God and the immanence of God in ATR make God the Supreme Being, because no other being can be both. His distinctness makes him worthy of worship, and his nearness, watching over his people everyday, inspires acknowledgement of him. As life is lived, God is honoured.

Mythic Dimension

In traditional Africa, myth is the road ATR rides on and the car it drives. Myths are the foundation of traditional beliefs and the vehicle by which they are transported from one generation to the next. For Africans, myth, together with ritual, form a symbolic language that expresses the truths of human existence in a way that rational language cannot. Some myths are more meaningful than others and some have longer histories. The nature of African myths allows them to evolve over time to accommodate societal changes.

The origin and nature of the universe is the theme of more African myths than any other thing. Though there is really only one basic cosmology in ATR, it occurs in many varied mythical forms about the creation and nature of the universe, the creation of man, the separation of God from man, the loss of original paradise, and how life came to be as it is now.

Life has meaning because there is a myth to explain each part of it. ATR must be seen as a whole system with a coherence of its own. Myths represent the forefather's effort to explain the universe and the place of man in it in their own way.

Symbols are used in ATR to represent the beliefs incorporated into the myths. However, there are no images or physical representations of God by African peoples, but they do make religious images. Myths are not only oral. Some myths are carved on wood, clay, ivory and stone; some are represented in arts and crafts; and others are retained in rituals and ceremonies. The mythic dimension of African religious experience is all-pervasive.

Doctrinal Dimension

There are two main difficulties in studying ancient traditional religious beliefs of Africa. One is the great variety and multiplicity of peoples. The other is the complete lack of written documents from within the religion. There are no written summaries of doctrines in ATR and no written exposition of spiritual experience. There is nothing written to tell what it was like to be a believer in the traditional religion. ATR, including the worldview it provides, is entirely a lived religion, not a doctrinal one.

Not only is there a lack of specific doctrines of teachings in ATR, there is also a lack of any formal creeds. The creeds are written on the heart of the individual African, and each one is himself a living creed of his own religion.

As previously stated, ATR is a lived religion. To study it one must study the religious journey of the African from birth to death. A study of ATR and the African worldview cannot be limited to research. The lives of Africans must be observed. That is why nothing has been included in this chapter on the African worldview that does not concur with my observations from living in an African village for six years.

Ethical Dimension

Ethical requirements in ATR are not based on written commands but on an established principle: the system of ethics revolves around the purpose or goal of preserving human life and its 'power' or 'force.' Doing the good that sustains life and avoiding the bad that destroys it is the foundation of the ethical dimension of ATR. It does not mean just physical life, but all of life. Thus, anything that breaks the peace and harmony in society is unethical. Individual acts are considered ethical or unethical based on the consequences of the act.

Traditionally, the most grievous violations of the ethical dimension are acts motivated by greed. Sharing and hospitality are the societal norms. It is the African view that the earth and its resources belong to all human beings equally. It does not matter whose farm it is on, or whose house it is in, or what use it is put aside for, failure to share it is an inhospitable act, an act of greed and is unethical. Failure to share would bring a breach in relations and disharmony to the forces of life. The ethical consequence of such actions is that we must repair every breach of harmony as soon as possible.

Ritual Dimension

The ritual dimension of religious experience for the African is the most public and the most prescribed of the acts of worship. The purpose of these acts of worship is to promote the well-being of the person or community concerned.

Reverencing God, honouring the ancestors, and appeasing the spirits are directly relevant to human needs and wants. Since ATR is anthropocentric, the rituals practiced in ATR centre on the individual, the family and the community. Rituals are performed as each of these progresses through the cycles of life.

From a psychological perspective, rituals provide many personal benefits to the African psyche. They generate a sense of certainty and familiarity, providing continuity and unity among those who perform or attend them. In participating in rituals together, people find a degree of identity through this common observance and experience. For example, groups of youth who go through the rite of circumcision at the same time are bound together into a unity, and each finds his own identity within the unity of that group.

There are many rituals and ceremonies involved in ATR. There are personal rituals drawing attention to the uniqueness of the individual which are performed at various times in the life of that individual. They begin at birth and include naming, initiation to adulthood, engagement, marriage, childbearing, eldership, old age and death. After a period beyond death a ritual is performed by the living commemorating the passing to living-dead status. Each step along life's way brings the individual new status and new responsibilities. There are agricultural rituals which include rain-making, dedicating new fields, planting, first fruits and harvest. Health rituals are used to find the cause of sickness, the cure of sickness and protection from harm to health. Homestead rituals are performed at times of building a new house or barn, moving to a different house and welcoming guests.

Occasionally, festivals enhance the experience of both personal and communal rituals. Festivals provide entertainment and a release of tension in the community bringing people together as a group strengthening their unity. These festivals give opportunity for religious and social values to be repeated and renewed.

Sacrifice and offerings are other elements that are sometimes included in a ritual. These are done when the restoring or maintaining of the power of life is an issue. The distinction between sacrifices and offerings is important. Sacrifices involve the shedding of the blood of human beings, animals or birds, while offerings do not involve blood. Offerings consist of giving foodstuffs or even money. A blood sacrifice is very serious in ATR and is only performed when the lives or well being of many people are in danger. The life of one is given to save the lives of many. Some tribes, such as the Massai, sacrifice only to God. Others sacrifice to other spirits or deities as well as to the Supreme Being.

Offerings are generally not destroyed as a sacrifice is, but are 'separated by dedication' to God or spirits. The offering is symbolic and the item offered may remain in the household of the one making the offering.

Sacrifices and offerings are accompanied by prayers. The prayers declare the purpose of the sacrifice or offering and include requests for what may be gained from them.

Social Dimension

As stated throughout this chapter, life for the African is lived in community. His existence is tied up in his relationship to his community. Traditional religions are for the benefit of the community rather than the individual. As far as his religion is concerned, he believes what the others in his community believe. And this religion is utilitarian, not purely spiritual; it is practical and not mystical. That practical faith is lived out as the individual abstains from doing anything to harm relationship with others and with the natural order of things.

In ATR there are no private prayers, no private rituals and no desire to draw away from other people in order to commune with God. For the traditional African, his religion is fused with life, and life is fused with his community.

African Worldview and Culture

The traditional African does not see himself as living in one particular culture as opposed to a different culture. If culture is thought of as the beliefs, values, behaviour and material objects shared by a particular group of people, then culture has nonmaterial and material dimensions. The nonmaterial culture would include the beliefs, values and ideas of the group; and the material culture would consist of the tangible products used by the group. Culture does not refer to what people actually do, but to the ideas they share about what they do and the material objects they use while doing it. For the African, culture and society are the same, and beliefs, values, behaviour and possessions define who they are in African. When an African looks at his culture he sees himself.

The African traditional worldview is 'holistic' because ATR affects the whole of life from birth to death. There is no division between the sacred and the secular. African religion and culture can be understood as self-contained systems that are internally coherent without reference to metanarratives, but includes all of everyday life.

For the traditional African, his culture, worldview and religion are all logically consistent and coherent. They define life, explain life and provide the script for life. Culture is the stage on which religion, and therefore life, is acted out. African religion is a religion that promises well being and wholeness here and now. It is a religion that affirms life and celebrates African culture in its fullness. The African culture is where Africans live. They love their culture because it fits them like a glove.

A Worldview in Transition

A chapter on the traditional African worldview cannot end without saying something, even lamenting, about the current changes taking place in that worldview and the forces behind those changes. The changes are a result of colonialism and globalization which have opened the gateways to Africans and their culture. Over a half a century ago, African writers recognized that profound changes were taking place. In 1954 Daryll Forde (1954:xvii) wrote: 'It has not been possible in this book to attempt the complex task of describing and analysing the multifarious social changes and the transformation of beliefs and morals that are so marked a feature of Africa today.' Eight years later Colin Turnbull published *The Lonely African* in which he studied the dilemma of Africans trapped in the lonely void created by the transition from traditional to modern ways of living. The transition brought dissatisfaction. Turnbull (1962:58) writes: 'The traditionalist also points to a lack of any effective system of values, and the consequent moral instability. It can hardly be called immorality, they say, because there no longer are morals, there is only law. . . . In all these aspects of life they find that the traditional way was sounder because there was an overall unity achieved by a respect for a far greater power than that of the modern police force.'

Probably the most graphic exposition of the pain caused by the changes being experienced by traditional Africans was incorporated into a novel titled *Things Fall Apart* by Chinua Achebe, published in 1958. In the section from which the novel gets its title, Achebe (1958:124) pens:

> Does the white man understand our customs about land? How can he when he does not even speak our tongue? But he says that our customs are bad; and our brothers who have taken up his religion also say that our customs are bad. How do you think we can fight when our brothers have turned against us? The white man is very cleaver. He came quietly and peaceably with his religion. We were amused at his foolishness and allowed him to stay. Now he has won our brothers, and our clan can no longer act like one. He has put a knife on the things that held us together and we have fallen apart.

In a chapter titled 'Changing Man and His Problems' Mbiti (1969:282–98) points to Christianity as the cause of the rapid changes in Africa, stating that it came carrying Western culture (politics, science, technology, medicine, schools) as well as the gospel. He says it is a total change affecting all spheres of life. The biggest aspects of change he sees were the importation of the awareness of a future dimension of time and a dichotomy between religious and secular life. The problems caused by the changes taking place are delineated by Mbiti with much of the same feeling we saw in Achebe.

To Christianity must be added the religions of Islam and secularism as causes for the rapid changes in African society. Islam has been less of a force in change from traditional ways than has secularism (called by Comte the 'religion of humanity'). The construction by African intellectuals of a modern African worldview is being done on the basis of secular humanism, totally ignoring the religious basis of the traditional African worldview. The past thirty years has seen many intelligent Africans go to some part of the Western world to earn post-graduate degrees and then turn their attention to constructing African history and African philosophy. Unfortunately, most have had to stay in the West in order to earn a living from their trade. The efforts to construct African history and philosophy have produced a concept called 'Afrocentrism.'

Afrocentrism is a backlash to colonialism and to what is seen by some African scholars as an accompanying narrow-minded 'Eurocentrism.' Afrocentrism challenges the Eurocentric view, and exalts Africa as the pinnacle of civilization. The goal of Afrocentrism is the restitution of the genesis of modern civilizations to its rightful claimants by writing the 'correct' histories. What postulates this movement? In *The Invention of Africa* Mudimbe (1988:18) writes: 'One is the postulation that history reflects or should translate the dynamics of human needs through time.'

Africa has no written history prior to the colonial period, and it does need one. The history that is being developed does not account for the way things were in Africa at the beginning of the colonial period or the way things are in African today beyond 'blame it on the colonial powers' (see Hountondji 1996:135; Gyekye 1997:26; or any issue of *New Africa* magazine). Diop (1974), Kamalu (1990), Hountoudji (1996) and many others are propounding an illustrious pre-history for sub-Saharan Africa claiming it to be the source of the people and technology of the ancient Egyptian empire, that ancient black Africans sailed to the Americas about 10,000 BC (Barton 2004:38), and even that Great Britian's Queen Elizabeth has black African blood 'coursing through her veins' (Zamani 2004:35). The traditional African living in a mud hut trying to cross a rain-swollen river in his dugout canoe must wonder how they could have fallen so far if what they are being taught is true.

This kind of historical construction does have its detractors. E G Parrinder, for one, puts forth correct knowledge as being more important than history. For the current African historians, meeting the need for a history overshadows correct knowledge. In reading the cited works, no sources for their claims are quoted as there are no written records from the pre-colonial period in Africa. Therefore, supposition is stated as fact.

Another element in the African history being constructed has to do with the origin of Africans and of the whole human race. The discovery by Richard Leakey in East Africa of some fossilized bone fragments from a creature believed to be the first pre-human, has crowned Africa as the cradle of humanity. Basil Davidson (1991:11) states: 'Even if *Proconsul*, as Leakey named this creature, was not a man, it was quite probably an ancestor of man.' The 'probability' aspect has been erased in the minds of most African historians. Diop (1974:xv) makes this claim: 'The triumph of the monogenetic thesis of humanity (Leakey) even at the stage of "Homo sapiens-sapiens," compels one to admit that all races descended from the Black race, according to a filiation process that science will one day explain.' The works of Diop and others have greatly influenced the African philosophers and historians who in turn influence public opinion. In a magazine read throughout Africa, Nick Hordern (2004:57) writes:

> It is Africa which has given the world's greatest gift to humanity—life itself. And it is Africa where a common ancestor sired not only the line that resulted in today's chimpanzee but human beings—7.5 million years ago in East Africa, one group of apes, in a desperate bid for survival, began walking on two legs to reach food in a steadily shrinking forest. This group's descendants eventually evolved into humans, who today proliferate the planet to such an extent that they threaten its destruction. Meanwhile, our four-legged closest cousins, who stayed behind, cling on to life as an embattled species.

Even leading African Christian theologian, John Mbiti, is now of this historical evolutionary persuasion and has questioned whether or not it includes the evolution of religion. In a recent article Mbiti (2006) states: 'If according to palaeontologists, the history and evolution of human beings began in eastern

Africa and made its way to the rest of the world, what did persons take with them from this place of their origin? . . . One of these commonalities is the religious constituent that is found everywhere, with particular variation. . . . Can it be established that Africa has contributed not only physical but also spiritual genes to modern persons?'

From a religious studies standpoint, what are the effects of these cultural changes brought about by foreign religions on the African worldview which is based upon African Traditional Religion? What does the individual African think when he is told that Africans used to be the most technically advanced and prosperous people in the world, and all he sees is poverty? What does he think when his religion tells him he was created by God, and his village school teacher says he descended from primates which to him is 'sweet meat' to eat? When he looks at the developed world and then looks at his world does he feel like his 'four-legged cousin' that got left behind? Not only is his origin in question, but so are his loyalties. The governmental state left behind by the colonial powers has, to a great extent, replaced tribe, clan, and in some ways even family, as the group with ultimate power over people's affections and loyalties. Tradition tells him loyalty to his family, clan and tribe defines who he is. Confusion as to identity and desire to enter the global technological age but lacking the resources to do so, brings great frustration.

The result of all this is that the African and his worldview are in a state of schizophrenia (the presence of mutually contradictory qualities or parts). He is looking at the modern scientific world and its desire for things and with a future orientation. At the same time he is looking at the traditional world he came from with its security being in human relationships and with eyes looking 'toward' joining his ancestors. In uncertain times such as these, he turns to his religion.

Throughout Africa traditional customs are changing. Some change is driven by new technology; some by new religion. Yet, during times of crisis, and especially when there is death to deal with, the traditional African, even those professing to be Christians, revert to tradition. Outward custom may change, but the deep core beliefs are very persistent. That has been my experience in six years of teaching in an African Christian college. It is not unusual to find fetishes in the dorms and it is almost impossible to convince students of the Christian belief that there is a heaven and a hell. In Africa, the advent of Christianity, Islam and secularism has moved the bedrock of African Traditional Religion but very little.

5

Two Worldviews: Conflict or Conformity?

The biblical worldview (BWV) of Christianity and the traditional African worldview (AWV) based on African Traditional Religion have been delineated in the last two chapters. In this chapter these two worldviews will be compared in the areas examined to see where the points of conflict and conformity lie.

The Two Worldviews as Philosophy

Both the BWV and the AWV are lived out on a philosophical level that remains subconscious for most adherents to each. Life is understood and events are interpreted based upon the paradigms learned, consciously and subconsciously, as one grows and experiences new things on a daily basis. The teachers of paradigm are usually hidden within cultures and therefore go unnoticed. The African is born into and raised in the African philosophical worldview making it the normal and correct worldview for him. Likewise, a Christian that was born into a Christian family was raised with a Christian philosophical worldview making it the normal and correct worldview for him. However, someone born into a secular culture or into a family that embraces another religion, who converts to Christianity finds that their original philosophical worldview now conflicts with how they are to understand and relate to the world they live in. The conversion is brought about by a change in beliefs which will result in a change of behaviour.

The change of beliefs required for religious conversion requires a change in philosophical views because philosophical worldviews are religious at their core (the view about God affects the views about absolutes and ultimates in all areas). On an academic level, world religions are defined by their philosophical worldview beliefs so that conversion from one religion to another requires a change in philosophical worldviews. By analysing the philosophical elements of the Christian and traditional African worldviews, the areas of conflict and conformity can be noted and the areas where change in worldview beliefs required for conversion can be identified.

Basic Postulates of the Two Worldviews

Chapters 3 and 4 put forth the idea of God's general revelation (in nature) and special revelation (the Bible) to mankind as postulating the biblical world-view, and the concept of vital force as postulating the African worldview. The postulates of both worldviews reflect a supernatural character. The BWV is supernatural in historical origin and ontology and the AWV is supernatural in ontology with its historical origin being unknown. Christians believe God's special revelation was communicated to mankind supernaturally in written form. A study of Christian apologetics would reveal the evidences Christians have for believing the Bible to be a supernatural communication from God. Africans have no written sources for their beliefs in vital force but have just as much faith in the trustworthiness of the myths passed down from the ancestors as Christians do in the myths recorded in the Bible. The Christian would ask the African: 'Where are the facts supporting your beliefs?' The African would answer: 'If by facts you mean that which is actual or real I show you the river. Can you deny there is a vital force there?'

The postulates of both worldviews would share the same judgement when put before the science of today. The world has elevated science to be the final authority of what is true. Since science denies the supernatural, science pronounces the postulates of the Christian and African worldviews to be false, thus giving them a commonality in public opinion they did not share two centuries ago.

Philosophical Elements Compared

The answers presented to the various philosophical questions based on each worldview will be compared in this section. Some of the questions are two-part questions with the worldview answers conforming on one part and conflicting on the other. Some questions are broad requiring broad answers incorporating several aspects of belief. A comparison of the two worldview answers will show conformity in some aspects of belief and conflict in other aspects of belief in answering the same question. A compendium of those worldview beliefs deemed important in converting from ATR to Christianity will be presented in chapter 6.

Ontology Questions

Is there a Supreme Being, and, if so, what is it like?

Both the biblical worldview and the African worldview assume the eternal existence of a Supreme Being. This Being is called 'God' and by various Hebrew names in Christianity, and 'God' and by various tribal names in ATR. There is conformity of belief in a Supreme Being.

As to the nature of this God there are some areas of conflict. In his book *Biblical Christianity in African Perspective* Wilbur O'Donovan (1996:42) states:

> The physical creation does indeed reveal the existence of God and African Traditional Religions confirm this. However, based on what we can see or hear or touch, we can know very little about what God is like. We know that he exists because we can see the evidence of his great power and wisdom in the world around us. We also see the evidence of his care for the things he has made, so we have an idea of his character. It is like finding the tracks of an animal in the bush. We may never see the animal, but from its tracks we know it had passed that way. From the size and shape of the tracks we may even get an idea about the size of the animal.
>
> Who is this invisible God and what is he like? We can get a limited idea of what God is like by looking at nature. . . . From the care he shows for his creation, such as providing rain, crops, and food, and by providing each kind of animal with a mate, we can see that God has a will, and emotions, and that he cares for the creatures he has made.

What can be known of God from looking at nature is called natural revelation and forms the limit of what Africans know about God. In the AWV many attributes are attributed to God by default. He cannot be seen so he must be spirit. He created and sustains the earth so he must be all-powerful. He punishes when an evil act is performed so he must be all-knowing. In the BWV the attributes of God are self-revealed, being communicated verbally to the writers of the Bible and being confirmed by what is observed in nature.

Two attributes of God are central to the BWV and almost totally absent in the AWV. They are the attributes of love and holiness. Africans do not talk about the love of God, nor do they typically talk about loving each other. Africans show their love through acts rather than expressing it with words. Likewise, they assume God loves them because he created them and he provides for them. God's love is an abstract quality at best in the AWV. However, in the BWV God's love is something that can be experienced (2 Cor 13:14) and is revealed to be the motivation of his self-sacrificial and salvific dealing with mankind (Jn 3:16). The BWV holds God to be the personification of love (1 Jn 4:16).

As to the holiness of God in the AWV, one does not find any direct references to the holiness of God. If the concept is present among African peoples, it is arrived at by inference, both in the sense that he is separate from his creatures and he is separate from wrongdoing. In traditional African beliefs, there is usually an unspoken awareness of the sinless perfection or holiness of God. But in the BWV God declares himself to be holy (Lv 11:44) and is declared by his worshippers to be holy (Is 6:3, Rv 4:8). The biblical view of God's holiness has to do with his character. He is perfect, faultless, pure, and free from all defilement by sin. The prophet Habakkuk said about God, 'Your eyes are too pure to look on evil; you cannot tolerate wrong' (Hab 1:13).

The AWV assumes God to be holy because he is set apart and he commits no sin. The idea that he cannot even look upon sin is absent. In the African view an evil act is not sin until it is made public in the community. The fact that God saw the act and still sees the perpetrator is not an issue in the concept of God's holiness nor is it seen as an offence against God himself. In the BWV an evil act is an abomination in God's eyes and causes spiritual separation between God and the perpetrator, regardless of who knows about it.

Another problem area between the two worldviews comes to light in the ontological nature of God's being. The BWV presents God as a tripersonal being revealed as Father, Son and Holy Spirit in his dealings with mankind but co-equally and co-eternally metaphysically one God. Because God is personal he is directly approachable on the personal level through verbal communication. The basic AWV presents God as a transcendent spirit who is distant and approachable only through intermediaries.

What is the origin and nature of man?

The BWV and the AWV see humanity coming into existence by a creative act of God. Both agree that man's body was created out of materials already existing and that God gave life to the material body by adding spirit or breath. There is conformity in the area of the origin of man.

Just as there is conflict in certain areas regarding the nature of the God who created man, there is also conflict in certain areas regarding the nature of man as a creature. The BWV gives man a history of transition in nature while the AWV sees man today being as he was when first created. The BWV is that man was created in the image of God as perfect, but finite, in his attributes as opposed to God's being infinite. In the BWV the first man chose to disobey God and caused sin to enter into the nature of mankind and the universe, resulting in every man that has been born the natural way being born with a nature bent toward sinning. The AWV sees man's nature as being morally neutral, not being bent toward doing good or evil. In the AWV man may commit acts that are deemed to be sinful, but that does not make him sinful by nature.

In the BWV man has a personality that continues to exist apart from the body for all eternity. In the AWV man has a personality that continues to exist only as long as there is someone alive that remembers him personally. After that he ceases to be a personality and joins the world of nameless spirits.

What is reality and what is ultimate reality?
The BWV holds that God created an objective universe that can be perceived by personal beings. That objective universe consists of physical and spiritual realms displaying a unity of purpose and diversity in existence. Man's perception of the universe can be measured by what is revealed by God in the Bible and by what is experienced. In the BWV reality exists whether or not man is there to perceive it. The BWV sees physical objects as being animate and inanimate with spirits being able to inhabit only animate objects.

The AWV is that while there is an objective part to the universe consisting of physical and spiritual realms, there is also a part consisting of forces that permeate the universe. The existence of this vital force animates all objects in the AWV, and all objects are beings, and therefore all beings are interrelated because the same force permeates all. In the AWV spirits can act benevolently or harmfully depending on the circumstances and spirits can inhabit both animate and inanimate objects. There are areas of conflict between the two worldview's views of reality in that the BWV does not hold to a vital force permeating and interrelating the entire universe. It also does not hold the view that spirits can inhabit inanimate objects.

In the BWV God is the Uncaused Cause. He *is* being and everything else in the universe *has* being. In the AWV reality is being and being is force.

Therefore, ultimate reality is the Supreme Being or Divine Force. The two worldviews are in conformity regarding their views of ultimate reality.

What is truth?

This question reveals an area of conflict between the two worldviews. In the BWV truth has an ontological correspondent in reality. It holds to propositional truth based on the interrelated consistency of statements and their correspondence with the facts of reality. It also holds that truth is the facts of reality themselves—ontological truth. Stated simply, truth is the communication of facts and it is also the facts communicated. This view of truth gives rise to the belief in Jesus Christ being the communication of truth (Logos) and also the personification of truth (Jn 14:6).

The AWV does not hold to a propositional or ontological view of truth. Its view of truth is stated as what is already known or believed or what brings about a better human situation. Truth is relative to the situation. In the AWV truth is not absolute which conflicts with the BWV of truth being absolute.

Cosmology Questions

What is the origin and nature of the universe?

As to the origin of the universe there is complete conformity between the BWV and AWV with both holding the view that God created the universe out of nothing. The BWV adds the detail that God spoke everything into existence in its final form while the AWV holds that God first created matter and then formed the matter into the various forms found in the universe.

Beliefs regarding the nature of the universe show areas of conformity and conflict between the two worldviews. Both worldviews hold that there is order built into the universe in the form of natural laws with the AWV adding the belief that some human customs were also built into the universe by God. Both worldviews hold that the universe consists of three levels or areas where beings can exist. The BWV calls them heaven, earth and hell. The AWV calls them heaven (or sky), earth and the underworld. There is conformity in these areas.

The BWV says that the present state of the universe, with earthquakes, typhoons, floods, drought, disease and famine, is not the way the universe was created. Everything was created perfect and the natural evils that exist today came about only when the first man sinned. The curse of sin affected man and his environment, the universe. The AWV holds that the present state of the universe is the way it was created. The natural evils that happen are caused by God as punishment or by some malevolent spirit. The AWV does not recognize the effects of sin in the universe. There is conflict between the two worldviews in this area.

Another area of conflict between the two worldviews involves beliefs about the spiritual realm of the universe. The BWV holds that the universe is the place of a spiritual battle between the kingdom of God and the kingdom of Satan. The kingdom of God consists of the good angels and the born-again people on earth (Jn 3:3). The kingdom of Satan consists of the fallen angels and the rest of the people on earth. The two kingdoms have a conflict of values and destiny and are at war with each other. The AWV recognizes no such kingdoms and no such war. In the AWV every creature, whether spiritual, human, animal, plant or mineral, has a life force and because of the common divine origin of that force shared by all, all are connected in a metaphysical way. In the AWV there is not war in the universe but harmony when everything is as it should be.

What is God's relationship with the universe?

Both the BWV and AWV hold the view that God is transcendent and immanent in the universe. God is continuously and personally involved in the affairs of the universe as its Sustainer. Natural laws are descriptions of the regular way God works in his creation, but God can work contrary to natural laws if he so chooses. God is never the cause of evil in the universe but he does allow it to happen. God rules the universe as King and Judge. These views are shared by both worldviews and are in conformity.

The BWV holds that God exercises special providential care over these human beings that believe in him and are called his children. The AWV recognizes God's providential care as being equally provided to all human beings. There is also conflict in the views of God's role as Judge. The BWV is that there will be a final judgement of all humanity at the end of time while the African view is that God rewards and punishes people temporally as life is lived.

What is the meaning of time?

The meaning of time is an area of conflict between the two worldviews. The BWV sees time as a chronological succession of events. Time had a point of beginning in the past when the first part of the universe was created and in the BWV is unidirectional, flowing irreversible to a future of indeterminable length and to events that have not yet happened in time. The AWV sees time as a composition of events that have occurred or are about to occur in a very near future. Everything moves backward toward the past. The hope of the traditional African is that, in time, he will join the ancestors who live in the past. In the BWV time moves like an arrow shot forward. In the AWV time moves in a circle that is rolling backward.

Do laws and causality govern the universe absolutely?

In the BWV natural laws reflect a cause/effect relationship and are descriptive of the regular way God works in the universe. God is not bound by natural laws. When God sets aside natural laws to accomplish something it is described as a miracle. Only God can set aside natural laws. In the BWV there are natural causes to bad events (recently in Freetown a strong wind blew over a big cotton tree with rotten roots and killed 27 people).

In the AWV natural laws can be set aside by God and by forces and powers in the universe. When natural laws are violated the principle of causality does govern absolutely and the cause must be found (in the above Freetown incident the survivors said: 'Sure the tree had rotten roots but why did the tree fall at this particular time and fall on these particular people. The cause must be found.' For some time after the incident that tree was the scene of much religious activity as the real cause of the tragedy was sought).

Both worldviews agree that natural laws do not govern absolutely. Both also agree that God is the Uncaused Cause and everything else is governed by the principle of causality. There is conformity in these areas. The two worldviews conflict in their views on natural causes.

Teleology Questions

Why do man and the universe exist and do they have a final end?

This is really a four-part question—Why does man exist? Why does the universe exist? What is man's final end? What is the universe's final end? It is only on the second question that the two worldviews are in conformity. Both the BWV and the AWV see the universe as existing to give man a place to exist. That was the purpose for which God created it.

The two worldviews are in conflict in their beliefs about why man exists. In the BWV man was created to be the object of God's love and a source of love for God. Human life is to be centred on God. In the AWV man exists to provide continuation of and harmony between the life forces in the universe. Human life is centred on the physical and spiritual world he lives in.

The final end of man is another area of conflict between these two worldviews. In the BWV the final end of man is not fixed. The relationship of each individual to God is determinative. As stated in the previous paragraph, man was created to be the object of God's love and a source of love for God. The BWV holds that man's response to God's love (as shown by the Gospel) will determine his final end. Those who choose to love God and show that love by obeying his commands will retain their personalities and spend eternity with God. Those who choose to reject God's love and disregard him in their lives will retain their personalities and spend eternity in a place of eternal torment. This view of man's final end is held to be universal in that it applies to all humans that have ever lived. In the AWV man's final end is fixed from the beginning. Man dies and his spirit retains his personality as it joins the ancestors, the living-dead. Man's personality survives as long as there is someone alive that remembers him personally. After several generations, when there is no one alive that remembers the deceased, he becomes a spirit without personal identity living in the spirit world. In the AWV this view does not have universal applications but applies only to those born into ATR.

There is also conflict in how the two worldviews understand the final end of the universe. The BWV holds that at some point in the future Jesus Christ will return to earth and all creation will be regenerated, or restored to the condition of original creation. This regenerated earth will be the dwelling place of man for a time certain. In contrast to that view, the AWV holds that there will be no divine intervention to regenerate the earth and that the universe will remain the same as it is now throughout all eternity.

Does evil have a purpose?

In the BWV man's sin nature is the reason he commits evil acts and the curse of sin brought disruption to the perfect order of the universe resulting in natural disaster (earthquakes, floods, etc.) or what is called natural evil. Evil is a given in a fallen world. Because it is a fallen world innocent people suffer. The BWV holds that God can use natural evil as a means by which he can bring some purpose to pass, but God does not will evil to happen for that purpose. The AWV does not see evil as a given in a fallen world. It does not recognize a sin nature in individuals or the curse of sin on the world. In the AWV natural evil is seen as punishment for some act or acts, by individuals or groups, that disrupt the harmony of the life forces in the universe.

Moral evil is that which is committed intentionally by man. Again, in the BWV God can use moral evil to serve a purpose even though he did not will it or want it to happen. God is a God of justice and his justice is manifested when evil acts are punished. God is also a God of mercy and his mercy is made manifest when evil acts are forgiven. Moral evil in the

BWV is disobedience to God's commandments regardless of the immediate consequences. Moral evil in the AWV is understood in terms of harmful or negative effects or consequences resulting from an otherwise neutral act. Acts are considered evil only if they bring bad consequences. Those acts will be punished by God or some other being. Therefore, when bad things happen to some person or group it is assumed that it was deserved. In the AWV evil does not fall on innocent people. These two worldviews conflict in the area of natural and moral evil.

Ethics/Morality Questions

Who or what determines what is moral and immoral?

The BWV holds that there are objective moral values and standards which apply to all men everywhere. God's word, the Bible, is the source of those objective moral values. Every person is accountable to God for the moral choices he makes. Because God is just, rewards and punishment for obeying or disobeying his standards will be exactly as each person deserves. When there is a conflict between the laws of human authority and God's commands as recorded in the Bible, God's commands are to be obeyed.

In the AWV God is considered to be the source of moral values on the assumption that he has communicated them to the ancestors. Moral values are embedded in the traditions received from the ancestors. Moral values have a personal and a social dimension. When an individual commits an act that is harmful to society he has committed an immoral act. What is good for society determines what is moral. Ancestors are the moral policemen meting out reward and punishment for acts committed. Tradition supplies the moral code and determines what the people must do to live ethically.

This question about morals reveals several areas of conflict between the two worldviews. As to the source of moral values the BWV looks to the Bible while the AWV looks to the tradition of the elders. As the standard of what is moral the BWV looks to the Bible while the AWV looks to what is good for society. Where there is conflict between civil laws and the worldview's source of moral values the BWV calls for obedience to the Bible while the AWV calls for obeying the dictates of tradition.

How do we know what is right?

The BWV holds that man can know what is right because God has revealed it to him by two different methods. The first is by his special revelation recorded in the Bible. For those who do not read or believe the Bible, God has put a general revelation of what is right into man's nature. As a result of being made in the image of God, man, even though fallen and unregenerate, has enough of God's nature in him to know right and wrong even though he does not have the will to do what is right. Man has a conscience to inform him when he has done wrong.

In the AWV anything that disrupts the peace and harmony in the community is considered not right. Anything that does not disrupt the peace and harmony in the community is considered right. Right is determined by consequences. An act is right until it produces anti-social consequences. Even an act of adultery is not considered 'evil' if it is not made known to the society which forbids it. That is in direct conflict with the BWV that believes in an absolute objective standard of right and wrong based on God's commands recorded in the Bible. The BWV holds that to sleep with someone else's wife is not right regardless of who knows about it. What is right is not determined by consequences in the BWV. This question reveals an area of conflict between the two worldviews.

Aesthetics Questions

What is man's relationship with the natural environment?

Man's relationship with the natural environment reveals another area of conflict between the two worldviews. The BWV holds that God gave man the task of ruling over the other living creatures and the ability to creatively reconstruct his environment for his own useful purposes. Man was created in a different mode from the rest of creation, and being created in the image of God, is the highest in the order of creation. Man can control his natural environment rather than be controlled by it. In the BWV spirits exist as part of man's environment, but they do not reside in inanimate natural objects.

In the AWV spirits or vital force resides in all natural phenomena from humans to rocks. Therefore, everything is considered of equal status. Not only are deities the objects of rituals and sacrifices but so are rivers and forests and mountains. Whereas one holding the BWV would think he could outsmart fish with bait and hook, one holding the AWV would sacrifice to the lake trying to entice the lake to give up fish in exchange for the sacrifice received. One holding the AWV sees the natural environment in terms of himself and seeks to live in harmony with it.

Is there aesthetic value to religious experience?

Experiencing God is considered to be a beautiful experience in the BWV. God is expressed as having beauty and as creating beautiful things. The terms man uses to express his experience of God (majestic, awesome, wonder, beautiful) are terms used to describe other objects of aesthetic value. One holding the BWV seeks religious experience because he wants to, not because he has to. He wants to because of its aesthetic value. Music is used to express the aesthetic value of God. God's handiwork can be seen in the beauty of nature and the awesomeness of a high mountain, a deep valley or a colourful sunset and invokes aesthetic feelings. There is aesthetic value to religious experience for those holding the BWV.

Likewise, religious experience and aesthetic experience are joined together for those holding the AWV. Since religion is an integral part of African life any aesthetic experience is seen as a religious experience. Rituals, ceremonies and festivals have religious meaning and are accompanied by the aesthetically pleasing experience of music, singing and dancing. There is definitely aesthetic value to religious experience for those holding the AWV making this an area of conformity with the BWV.

Philosophy of History Questions

What is the meaning of history?

In the BWV the Bible is a history book recording the history of God's dealing with humanity. It begins with the record of God dealing with humanity in general, then through his chosen people, the Jews, and finally through the church. History is a record of cosmic and human events happening within God's eternal plan. In the BWV history has an ultimate goal—the establishment of the Kingdom of God. This was spiritually accomplished as an historic space-time event with the first coming of Jesus Christ and will be physically accomplished in history with his second coming.

In the AWV history involves the compilation of people and events of the present, and a past consisting of a few generations. God's working in history does not involve any sort of long-term plan but is seen only as God's working in the present to send rain, harvest, health, children, etc. In the AWV history is the stage on which life is acted out with no real meaning or goal. The meaning of history is an area of conflict between the BWV and the AWV.

Is history cyclical or linear in progression?

The BWV holds that history is linear in progression moving forward and not backward. History had a definite beginning at an unknown time in the past. In the BWV history, as humans know it today, will be consummated with the events recorded in the last book of the Bible, Revelation. The progression of human history follows the path of creation→fall→redemption→glorification.

In the AWV there is no concept of history moving forward toward a future climax. History moves backward from the moment of intense experience (the present) to the period beyond which nothing can go. Since the future does not exist beyond a few months, things cannot be radically different in the future than they are now. History is made up of a cycle of known and repeated events in people's lives consisting of birth, initiation, marriage, bearing children, eldership, death and ancestorship. These two worldviews conflict in how they understand history.

Epistemology Questions

What can we know, and how can we know it?

According to the BWV man cannot know everything because of his finite mind, but he can know all that he needs to know to live a life of godliness. We see particulars, and universals are formulated by man to give the particulars meaning. Science poses universal laws trying to explain the particulars. In the BWV God has already explained the particulars in the Bible. God has informed man about himself and about history and the cosmos—not exhaustively, but truly—on the basis of propositional revelation. The BWV holds that the special revelation given in the Bible answers what we can know and how we can know it.

In the AWV traditional knowledge is passed down from generation to generation by word of mouth using myths, proverbs and wise sayings. Knowledge itself is embedded in the ethics and morals, values, customs, traditional laws and taboos which make up tribal tradition. Knowledge is deposited with the ancestors, chiefs, elders, medicine men and sorcerers. What can be known is what they know and it can be known by listening to them. What can be known and how it can be known is an area of conflict between the BWV and the AWV.

What justifies a belief?

God's special revelation in the Bible justifies the beliefs making up the BWV for those who hold it. Jesus Christ is the focal point of God's special revelation and there is sufficient evidence to prove that what the Bible says about Jesus Christ is true. In the BWV God's testimony of the supernatural events concerning Jesus Christ justifies belief in all that God has said.

In the AWV the foundation of belief is the traditions of the ancestors. A belief is justified if it is shared by all others in the same traditional group. This again is another area of conflict between the two worldviews.

Religious Dimensions Compared

The religious dimensions of the biblical and African worldviews are vital to each as each is a worldview based upon religion. The biblical worldview is based on Christianity and the African worldview is based on African Traditional Religion. The religious dimensions of the two worldviews, using the religions behind the worldviews, will be compared in this section.

Experiential Dimension

Becoming a Christian requires an initial experience of transformation that represents a turning point in one's personal history. As part of that initial experience God's Holy Spirit comes to reside inside the Christian. One function of the indwelling Holy Spirit is to guide the Christian into an understanding of the truth of Scripture (Jn 16:13; 1 Cor 2:14) so that he can appropriate the beliefs necessary for a biblical worldview. Without this experience one cannot be a Christian or comprehend the full extent of the biblical worldview. The Christian experiences God as the awe-inspiring Wholly Other spiritually and physically through the senses. The common beliefs and the common initial experience allow the Christian to experience a oneness with fellow Christians that is not possible with non-Christians.

There is no conversion experience in ATR. The African is born into it and assimilates it as he grows. ATR is more practice than belief and since religion permeates African life, religion is experienced as life is lived. Africans associate God with many natural objects and phenomena but not with themselves. The experience of God is external and everywhere. In the AWV as life is lived, God is honoured.

The experiential dimensions of the religions behind the two worldviews are in conformity in their experience of God everywhere but conflict in the areas of initial experience required and the indwelling of God's Holy Spirit in the individual.

Mythic Dimension

Christians accept the mythic stories in the Bible and build their worldview upon them. Christian ontology and cosmology are based upon the epic stories of Genesis 1–11. Christian teleology and epistemology are based upon the belief in the supernatural communication of the biblical stories to man. Christian ethics are based upon the biblical account of the sinless life of Christ. The biblical or Christian worldview is based on the stories in the Bible making the mythic dimension foundational.

Likewise, myths are the foundation of African traditional beliefs incorporated into ATR and the African worldview. Myths are used to transmit traditional beliefs from one generation to the next. In the AWV myths do not have to be taken literally as their purpose is to provide a working explanation for something. For the African, life has meaning because there is a myth to explain each part of it.

Although the myths are different, there is conformity in the use of myths in both worldviews. There is also conformity in the use of symbols to represent beliefs incorporated into their myths.

Doctrinal Dimension

Doctrine and teaching are fundamental to the preservation and propagation of the BWV. What is recorded in the Bible represents the standard for sound doctrine. The recording of myths in written form has given rise to interpretation and commentary on what is recorded in the Bible. The teaching of doctrine has been an important part of Christianity with a great many Christian schools teaching the biblical worldview around the globe. Christian doctrine has been formulated into creeds and confessions expounding the BWV.

There is conflict in the use of doctrine by the religions behind the two worldviews. In ATR there are no summaries of doctrines or written expositions of spiritual experience. There are no formal creeds or confessions. ATR is a lived religion, not a doctrinal one.

Ethical Dimension

Christian ethics is based upon the commands of God and the teachings and example of Jesus as they are recorded in the Bible. The Bible teaches that ethics is a matter of the heart intent so that just the desire to commit an unethical act makes one guilty as if the act was actually committed. Every act of the

Christian is to be motivated by love. In the BWV a coming righteous judgement of God provides incentive for good, ethical and moral behaviour. Every unethical act is viewed as a sin against God.

In ATR ethics is based upon outcome. All principles of morality and ethics are sought within the context of preserving human life and its power or force. Doing the acts that sustain life and avoiding the acts that destroy or diminish life are the foundations of the ethical dimension of ATR. Anything that breaks the peace and harmony in society is unethical.

The religions behind these two worldviews are in conflict in their ethical dimensions. In Christianity unethical behaviour toward your neighbour is a sin against God. In ATR unethical behaviour toward your neighbour is a sin against society.

Ritual Dimension

In Christianity rituals are designed to communicate feelings and beliefs reflective of what God has done for humanity through Jesus Christ. Sacrifice is recognized as a ritual in most religions and the sacrifice of Christ has two ritual dimensions for the Christian. Christians are to emulate Christ by offering their lives to God as living sacrifices, and Christians are to partake of Communion or the Lord's Supper as a remembrance of Christ's sacrifice. Prayer is another ritual act acknowledging dependence upon God. Rites of passage are celebrated in Christianity as ritual acts.

The most public and most prescribed of the acts of worship in ATR are the rituals. Since man is the centre of the universe, the rituals occur within the context of human needs, wants, anxieties, etc. Therefore, the primary purpose of ritual acts of worship is not God but the well being of the person or community. Religious rituals are performed as individuals, families and communities pass through the cycles of life. Rituals provide familiarity, continuity and unity among those who perform or attend them. Sacrifice, offerings and prayers are a usual part of ritual observance in ATR.

Though the religions behind both of these worldviews have a ritual dimension, they are in conflict in the area of the purpose behind the rituals. In Christianity the purpose is remembrance of God, dedication to God and submission to God. In ATR the purpose is to foster the well being of the individual or community.

Social Dimension

Converts to Christianity encounter more problems in the social dimension than any other areas of their lives. Christianity redefines family. Love for Christ should be so strong that love for earthly family would seem like hate. The spiritual bond with other Christians is stronger than the blood bond of earthly families. The Christian is to give preference to those of the family of God over one's blood family or tribe. Accepting Christianity puts one in a new family whose members all have the same Heavenly Father, God.

ATR is defined by its social group. It is not primarily for the individual but for the community which demands absolute loyalty. ATR is lived out as the individual abstains from doing anything to harm social relationship or relationships with the natural order of things. To change religions is to lose your identity. To cease practicing ATR is to cease being an African.

The two religions have a conflict of beliefs regarding the social dimension. Christianity binds the individual to Christ, redefines the social group and gives a new identity in a new family. ATR binds the individual to the social group of family and clan with blood relations being of the highest order.

Relationship of Christianity to ATR

The fundamental beliefs of the biblical worldview and the African worldview have been compared in this chapter along with the religious elements involved with those worldviews. The focus of this work is those who have moved from ATR to Christianity with a concern that many have accepted a new religion without discarding old beliefs resulting in less than true conversion. The worldviews of the two religions conform in sufficient areas to make the transition from ATR to Christianity relatively easy if some basic beliefs of ATR can be merged with Christianity. The extent that this can be done without resulting in syncretism will be addressed in the next chapter. The remainder of this chapter will offer three categories of relationship historically taken by Christianity toward ATR.

I am indebted to Dr. Richard Gehman and the epilogue to his book *African Traditional Religion in Biblical Perspective, Revised Edition* for much of the outline of this section. The three categories or approaches taken by Christianity in relating to ATR are given by Dr. Gehman (2005:396-399) as continuity, discontinuity, and continuity/discontinuity.

Continuity

'By *continuity* we mean the belief that all religions contain divine revelation and are a means of salvation, though Christianity may be recognized as "final" and "superior". The relationship between ATR and Christianity is that of imperfect-perfect, ordinary-extraordinary, preparation-fulfilment' (Gehman 2005:396). The idea here is that seeds of salvific beliefs can begin in ATR and can continue to develop into the full fruit of biblical salvation in Christianity. This approach to other religions did not come into prominence until the Age of Reason (circa eighteenth century) which corresponded to the approximate time Christian missionaries came in force to Africa. Philosophers began teaching an evolutionary development of religion beginning with animism, to polytheism and then to monotheism. Liberal theologians gave up the biblical teaching of the uniqueness of Christ and began teaching that all religions contained a measure of truth giving all religions an underlying unity. This attitude has been adopted by a number of prominent African theologians. Gehman (2005:37) quotes Emmanuel Twesigye, Karl Rahner, Bolaji Idowu, John Mbiti and J N K Mugambi to name a few. Of Mugambi, Gehman (2005:398) writes:

> J N K Mugambi, professor in the University of Nairobi, laments the 'superiority' of Christian missionaries who preach that salvation is found only in Jesus Christ. The solution to conflict between ATR and Christianity is 'the abandoning of this attitude of superiority. People of all cultures and all religions ought to be willing to accept that they do not have a monopoly of truth.'

Gehman points out that the problem with these viewpoints, from the Christian perspective, is that they are not faithful to the Scripture. These African theologians are letting the cultural situation dictate the reading of Scripture and their assessment of it instead of letting Scripture judge culture.

Discontinuity

'By *discontinuity* we refer to the belief that a near total disconnect prevails between ATR and Christianity; that salvation cannot be found in ATR, but only through Jesus Christ' (Gehman 2005:398). Karl Barth was a modern exponent of discontinuity. In *Christianity and Other Religions*, edited by John Hicks and Brian Hebbelthwaite, Barth contributed an essay titled 'The Revelation of God as the Abolition of Religion' in which he denounced all religions as worthless.

He saw religion as man seeking God which was unnecessary because God, in his grace, has revealed himself in Jesus Christ. This was the approach taken by many early Western-trained missionaries. Referring to Kwame Bediako, Gehman (2005:399) writes: 'Bediako echoes the consensus of many scholars today: "Western missionaries failed to see 'much continuity in relationship' between Africa's pre-Christian traditional religious heritage and Christianity. They did not see it as 'preparation of the Gospel', but instead, emphasized *discontinuity*."' The writings of Bediako deserve a closer look.

The issue of continuity or discontinuity is of vital importance for the future of Christianity in Africa. Probably no African writer at the turn of the twenty-first century was more passionate to state a case for the continuity of ATR into Christianity than Kwame Bediako, an eminent scholar and theologian.

The Contribution of Bediako

Manasseh Kwame Dakwa Bediako (1945-2008) was the founder and director of the Akrofi-Christaller Institute of Theology, Mission and Culture in Akropong, Ghana. He held doctorates from The University of Bordeaux, France and The University of Aberdeen, Scotland. His writings are more scholarly and lucid than I have encountered in any other African writer and more than many well-published writers from the West. His works are well researched and well presented. The two that touch most on the issue of *continuity* are *Theology and Identity: The Impact of Culture upon Christian Thought in the Second Century and Modern Africa*, first published in 1992, with a new edition in 1999, and *Christianity in Africa: The Renewal of a Non-Western Religion,* published in 1995.

Becoming a Christian in the African context necessarily involves a measure of conflict with the pre-Christian past. The source of the conflict is perceived to be more acute if it is felt that missionaries bringing the gospel are also bringing and imposing their own culture as part of that gospel. In his book, *Theology and Identity*, Dr. Bediako traces the conflict between Christianity and culture back to the Graeco-Roman culture of the second century and its permeation with Greek philosophy and then brings the conflict forward to modern African culture and its permeation with its traditional religion and worldview.

Bediako analysed the writings of four writers from the early church theologians and then four modern African theological scholars. Of the early writers, he saw Justin Martyr and Clement of Alexander as promoting substantial continuity between the Greek philosophical tradition based on Socrates and his disciples and Tatian (who had a reputation for heresy [1992:64]) and Tertullian (who for a time identified with the heretical Montanist but was orthodox enough to be the first to use the term 'Trinity' to refer to the Godhead of Father, Son and Holy Spirit) as promoting discontinuity between Christianity and the Graeco-Roman culture. Of the four modern African writers, he chooses the writings of Bolaji Idowu of Nigeria, John Mbiti of Kenya and Mulago gwa Cikala Musharhamina, a francophone Catholic theologian, to argue for religious and cultural continuity, and Byang Kato to represent discontinuity.

The basic position of this book by Kwame Bediako is that just as the Old Testament prepared the Jews for the coming of Jesus Christ, and the Greek philosophers Socrates and Plato, along the lines of the Old Testament prophets, prepared the Greek culture for the coming of Jesus Christ, so too, African Traditional Religion prepared the Africans for the coming of Jesus Christ. In other words, he believes that anywhere Christianity has taken hold in a culture there is something of Christianity rooted in that pre-Christian culture. In striving for significant continuity between the pre-Christian and Christian experience of African Christians he has to understand conversion in terms of completion (just as Jewish Christians are sometimes called 'completed Jews') rather than transformation from one condition to a radically opposite condition (i.e. darkness to light).

Christianity in Africa: The Renewal of a Non-Western Religion originated as the Duff Lectures Bediako gave at New College, University of Edinburgh between 1989 and 1992. Part 1 of the book deals with his concerns for Christianity in Africa as expressed in his Ghanaian context. The concern that Christianity came to Africa through European missionaries who thought the only way to Christianize Africa was to Westernize Africa is seen as the problem. His answer is (1995:15):

> On the other hand, if the Christian way of life is to stay in Africa, the African Christianity should be brought to bear on the fundamental questions of African existence in such a way as to achieve a unified world-view which finally resolves the dilemma of an African uncertain of its identity, poised between the impact of the West and the pull of its indigenous tradition.

The content of the book is Bediako's way forward in protecting Africa's self-identity. Of particular importance to the work is what he considers to be 'a unified world-view', which for him means giving a Christian interpretation to the traditional African worldview.

In part 1 he deals with the writings of Edward Blyden who was born in the nineteenth century in the West Indies and became a citizen of Liberia. Blyden sought to liberate the Negro race from the European stereotype of the day. Since Christianity was considered to be a European religion, Blyden was 'troubled by a lingering sense that Christianity has an alienating effect on African life' (1995:14). Bediako goes on to say that the 'cultural nationalists' like Blyden have concluded that traditional religion is the 'authentic repository of the African personality'.

Part 1 goes on to deal with a movement in Ghana that rejected Christianity and Islam as African religions and proposed a 'new synthesis' as a reconstruction of the traditional religion. The movement was started by an ex-Roman Catholic priest named Osofo Okomfo Kwabena Damuah. Damuah called the movement 'Afrikania' representing and manifesting the religious beliefs and practices of pre-Christian and pre-Islamic times. It is included in the book to illustrate that late into the twentieth century, Africa's Christian century, African writers were still dealing with the Christianity and identity issue.

In moving on to a chapter on Christianity as Africa's religion, Bediako states that the single most important element for postulating an indigenous Christian tradition is the Scriptures in the vernacular language of the people, and he attributes the massive presence of Christianity on the African continent to the availability of Scriptures in many African languages. He states: 'Thus, the existence of vernacular Bibles not only facilitates access to the particular communities speaking those languages, but also creates the likelihood that the hearers of the Word in their own languages will make their own responses to it and on their own terms' (1995:62).

In speaking of the failures of churches of missionary origin, Bediako (1995:68) states:

> The state of the churches in their relation to the traditional world-view presents a rather paradoxical picture: the churches which have a longer historical connection with the society, and a profound vernacular heritage, appear to be less effective in meeting the spiritual and psychological needs of their members for

most of whom the traditional world-view continues as a potent element in their understanding of reality.

Of course, what he sees as a problem with the churches of missionary origin in that they do not accommodate the traditional worldview, others see as a problem with African Christianity. If the worldview does not change then beliefs have not changed; and if beliefs have not changed, conversion has not taken place.

In a chapter titled 'Primal Imagination and a New Theological Idiom' Bediako presented Harold Turner's six-feature analysis of the nature of the primal worldview, which for Bediako means the pre-Christian African world-view (1995:93):

First, a sense of kinship with nature, in which animals and plants, no less than human beings, had 'their own spiritual existence and place in the universe' as interdependent parts of a whole.

Second, a deep sense that man is finite, weak and impure or sinful, and stands in need of a power not his own.

Third, the connection that man is not alone in the universe, for there is a spiritual world of powers or beings more powerful and more ultimate than himself.

Fourth, the belief that man can enter into relationship with the benevolent spirit-world and so share in its powers and blessings and receive protection from evil forces by their transcendent helpers.

Fifth, the acute sense of the reality of the afterlife, a conviction which explains the important place of ancestors or the 'living dead' which remain in affection and in mutual obligations with the 'living living'.

Sixth, the conviction that man lives in a sacramental universe where there is no sharp dichotomy between the physical and the spiritual so that . . . one set of powers, principles and patterns runs through all things on earth and in the heavens and welds them into a unified cosmic system.

I presented this six-feature analysis because it basically sets forth the traditional African worldview and Bediako (1995:96) affirmed it and states: 'it seems important to state that it is the sixth and final feature, conveying the primal conception of the universe as a unified cosmic system, essentially spiritual, which provides the key to the entire structure.' From this his conclusion is:

> the existence of 'affinities' between the primal and Christian traditions could have far-reaching significance for our understanding of the nature of the Christian faith itself. If there is only a minimal 'paradigm-shift' as we pass from the spiritual universe of primal religions into the spiritual environment of the Christian faith . . . then one would want to pursue the matter by asking how the primal imagination might bring its own peculiar gifts to the shaping of Christian affirmation.

Dr. Bediako's notion, that passing from primal religion to Christianity involves only a 'minimal paradigm-shift', is a novel approach to the continuity/discontinuity issue.

It is the nature of God, spirits and the spirit-world that Bediako sees as a vital link between African Traditional Religion and Christianity; one that has not been fully developed. He writes (1995:97):

> By stressing the centrality and uniqueness of God in African tradition, African theology has, however, left the wider spirit world of African primal religions—divinities, ancestors, natural forces—unaccounted for. In other words, it has answered to only part of what has been described as the 'unity and multiplicity of Divinity' in African primal religion, which I prefer to call the unity and multiplicity of the Transcendent.

In a succeeding chapter Dr. Bediako deals with the place of ancestors in his African Theology. 'The thesis of this chapter is that the place and significance of ancestors in the African primal world-view actually offers opportunities for "filling out" some dimensions of spiritual experience and historical consciousness which are inherent in the Christian religion.' (1995:212). He goes on to state:

> Rather, a theology of ancestors is about the interpretation of the past in a way which shows that the present experience and knowledge of the grace of God in the Gospel of Jesus Christ have been truly anticipated and prefigured in the quest and responses to the Transcendent in former times, as these have been reflected in the lives of African people.

A theology of ancestors becomes, therefore, the corollary and unavoidable by-product of the continuity of God in African experience. (1995:224)

In these two books, Bediako has put forth his well-presented case for an *Africanisation* of Christianity (1995:4) in Africa. He has made his points and now some comments and counter-points. He has argued for almost total continuity in conversion from African Traditional Religion to Christianity, but it seems like he is proposing a discontinuity between the Christianity of the Bible and the Christianity of Africa.

A Response to Bediako

Three points of Dr. Bediako's position need to be addressed:

(1) The relationship of Christianity to pre-Christian Jewish, Graeco-Roman, and African culture.

(2) The adaptation (redemption) of African Traditional Religion

(3) The re-defining of terms.

As to the first point, *Theology and Identity* is a study in comparative historical theology and not in biblical theology. Any attempt to write history, especially of the early history of one's present religion, is always going to be influenced by the author's use of history to present a case for or against a present desired practice of that religion. In this case, Bediako used the early Christian history in the Jewish religious tradition and the Graeco-Roman philosophical tradition as a model for Christianity in the African religious tradition of today. He states his position clearly (1999:160):

What is particularly interesting in this universalising of 'salvation-history' is that it involves Christianising not only of Hellenistic tradition, but the Jewish also; 'holy pagans' and Jewish saints became 'Christians before Christ' on the same terms; and the Old Testament, by virtue of Christ foreshadowed therein, becomes a Christian book.

Christ being foreshadowed in the Old Testament, including over three hundred prophecies about the coming of the Jewish Messiah that were fulfilled in the birth, life and death of Jesus Christ does, in fact, make the Old Testament a Christian book. However, Bediako fails to point out no other religion or philosophical tradition points toward a specific person, who was God and Man, who did in fact come, live a perfect life, perform miracles, die on a cross for our sins, rise from the dead and ascend back to heaven. That is the Christian gospel that defines Christianity. It is found in the Jewish religious tradition and nowhere else.

Dr. Bediako's sole attempt to support his idea of the Christianising of the Hellenistic (Graeco-Roman) tradition from the Bible was the use of Paul's preaching to Greek philosophers in Athens as recorded in Acts 17. He states (1999:245):

> It is interesting that Luke's presentation of Paul's encounter with Greeks on Mars Hill in Athens has been interpreted as 'the symbolic summit of the Apostle's mission'. It can rightly be said therefore, that the apostle who grasped most firmly the significance of Christ for the entire universe, and who strenuously preached Jesus to Jews as the fulfilment of the promises of the Old Testament, proclaimed with equal conviction that Jesus was to Gentiles also the fulfiller of their deepest religious and spiritual aspirations.

Farther along in *Theology and Identity*, Bediako (1999:354) writes of Mulago, the Catholic theologian:

> It is understandable, therefore, that, for Mulago, the speech of St. Paul—'the perfect type of Gospel herald and missionary theologian'—to the Athenians on Mars Hill, provides the most eloquent demonstration of what, in his view, the proclamation of the Christian Gospel is meant to achieve: to reveal to people their own treasures, whilst also bringing to them that fullness which is found only in the Gospel itself. For, in the final analysis, those treasures are intrinsic to the universal Gospel entrusted to the church whose mission it is to set forth 'the divine treasure of which she (the church) is the sole trustee.'

Bediako goes on to state that 'adaptation' is the missionary activity of the church and it 'is the way of ensuring that the church assimilates such new elements as will help bring it that bit closer to the fullness of catholicity, and unity, which is the goal for it in the plan of God.' The phrase 'their own treasures' is understood by Bediako to mean the totality of religious and cultural history and traditions of a people. He states: 'Through "adaptation", the church participates in the *assimilation vitale* of new and fresh elements and insights provided by different cultures' (1999:355).

What Bediako is proposing is that Paul's acknowledgement of the many gods in Athens and the existence of an altar to an unknown god was an endorsement of the religious heritage of the Athenians. And when Paul stated, 'Now what you worship as something unknown I am going to proclaim to you', he was providing what was lacking in their religious worship and thus fulfilling their 'deepest religious and spiritual aspirations.'

Rev. John Stott (1921-2011) was an Anglican cleric, worldwide Evangelical leader, and prolific writer. In his commentary *The Message of Acts*, Rev. Stott (1990:284) addresses Paul's statement to the Athenians and gives a more biblical interpretation to it and in so doing, he dismisses the idea of 'adaptation' whether it be in the Graeco-Roman or African tradition:

> How then shall we interpret his statement that 'what' they were worshipping 'as something unknown' he was about to proclaim to them? Was he thereby acknowledging the authenticity of their pagan worship, and should we regard with equal charity the cultures of non-Christian religions? For example, is Raymond Panikkar justified, in *The Unknown Christ of Hinduism*, in writing: 'In the footsteps of St. Paul, we believe that we may speak not only of the unknown God of the Greeks but also of the hidden Christ of Hinduism'? Is he further justified in concluding that 'the good and bona fide Hindu is saved by Christ and not by Hinduism, but it is through the sacraments of Hinduism, through the message of morality and the good life, through the mysterion that comes down to him through Hinduism, that Christ saves the Hindu normally'?

The question Stott asks in this quote has to do with acknowledging authenticity in pagan worship and whether there is salvific sufficiency in pre-Christian religions that, when properly interpreted, point to Christ as the source of salvation. His answer is: 'No, this popular reconstruction cannot be maintained.' What Paul addressed was the Athenians' open acknowledgement of their ignorance and it was ignorance rather than worship of many gods that was the issue (1990:285). More importantly, that ignorance was not innocent, as Bediako would suggest, but as Stott (1990:287) states:

> Now he declares such ignorance to be culpable. For God has never 'left himself without testimony' (14:17). On the contrary, he has revealed himself through the natural order, but human beings 'suppress the truth by their wickedness'. *In the past God*

overlooked such ignorance. It is not that he did not notice it, nor that he acquiesced in it as excusable, but that in his forbearing mercy he did not visit upon it the judgement it deserved. *But now he commands all people everywhere to repent.* Why? Because of the certainty of the coming judgement.

The coming judgement (bad news) creates the need for who Christ is and what he did (good news). Of the three pre-Christian religious systems considered by Bediako (Jewish, Graeco-Roman, African) only the Jewish religion has the roots of Christianity. Its whole sacrificial system pointed toward Christ. From Genesis 3:15 through the prophets, the Jewish Scriptures spoke of a coming Messiah who would take God's judgement in our place. That Messiah is Christ.

The second point of Bediako's position to be addressed is the adaptation (or redemption) of African Traditional Religion to Christianity. He is adamant in both books quoted herein that Christianity is a 'Western' religion that came to Africa with Western theology and a European worldview and European cultural baggage. Thus the need for 'African' Theology and his goal for African Theology is to present 'a viable heritage of indigenous Christian tradition' (1995:62) in the African culture and traditional religion, what he calls 'an African Theology of synthesis' (1999:437). He further maintains that it can be done with 'only a minimal "paradigm-shift" as we pass from the spiritual universe of primal religions into the spiritual environment of the Christian faith' (1995:96). However, this is not a biblical position when contrasted with 2 Corinthians 5:17: 'Therefore, if anyone is in Christ, he is a new creation; the old has gone, the new has come!', where a radical paradigm-shift is indicated.

For a foreign religion to have an indigenous heritage is a contradiction in terms and again illustrates the African cultural way of resolving interpersonal relationships and conflicts as stated in chapter 2 (thesis→antithesis →synthesis). Dr. Bediako illustrates this by the success of newer independent 'spiritual' churches in Africa which 'appear to be attempting to work out their salvation in Christ within the traditional religious milieu' (1995:68).

Probably the best illustration of Bediako's theology of synthesis is his theology of ancestors. *Christianity in Africa* contains a chapter titled 'Christian Religion and the African World-view' with the subtitle 'Will Ancestors Survive?' Bediako (1995:212) states: 'The thesis of this chapter is that the place and significance of ancestors in the African primal world-view actually offers opportunities for "filling out" some dimensions of the spiritual experience and historical consciousness which are inherent in the Christian religion.' He goes on to state (1995:217) 'Christ, by virtue of his incarnation, death, resurrection, and ascension into the realm of spirit-power, can rightly be designated, in African terms, an Ancestor, indeed Supreme Ancestor.' This equating of Christ with ancestors fails to differentiate the essential difference between Christ as God-Man and African ancestors as mere human beings and the fact that Christ's resurrection was bodily while ancestors are believed to exist only as spirits.

He goes on to incorporate the phrase 'communion of the saints' into his theology of ancestors upon the presumption that the saving activity of God was not absent in times prior to the proclamation and acceptance of the Gospel in Africa. He states: 'If the God of African pre-Christian tradition has turned out to be the God of the Christians, then it is to be expected that He has not left himself without testimony in the past' (1995:224). Bediako has made an interesting parallel between the departed saints of the Old and New Testament and African ancestors and between the idea of God in African experience and the Christian God. But is it biblical?

Kwame Bediako has used his writings to state a case for the continuity of religious belief and experiences as one moves from African Traditional Religion to Christianity with Christianity 'filling in' what was lacking in the pre-Christian religious heritage of Africa. For him conversion means completion and it applies to African culture as well as African religion. Both can be redefined in Christian terms.

His position is reflected in what he calls 'an important statement' that he quotes from E W Fasholé-Luke (1999:427): 'the quest for African Christian theologies which has been vigorously pursued in the last decade amounts to attempting to make clear the fact that conversion to Christianity must be coupled with cultural continuity.'

In 1978, John Stott published a book titled *Christian Counter-Culture*. It was re-released later as part of The Bible Speaks Today commentary series under the title *The Message of The Sermon on the Mount: Christian Counter-Culture*. Perhaps some quotes from Rev. Stott's book will serve as biblical counter-points to Dr. Bediako's position of cultural continuity in conversion.

> It [The Sermon on the Mount] is the nearest thing to a manifesto that he [Jesus] ever uttered, for it is his own description of what he wanted his followers to be and to do. To my mind no two words sum up its intention better, or indicate more clearly its

challenge to the modern world, than the expression 'Christian counter-culture'. (1978:15)

For too often what they see in the church is not counter-culture but conformism, not a new society which embodies their ideals but another version of the old society which they have renounced, not life but death. (1978:16)

For insofar as the church is conformed to the world, and the two communities appear to the onlooker to be merely two versions of the same thing, the church is contradicting its true identity. . . .

For the essential theme of the whole Bible from beginning to end is that God's historical purpose is to call out a people for himself; that this people is a 'holy' people, set apart from the world to belong to him and to obey him; and that its vocation is to be true to its identity, that is, to be 'holy' or 'different' in all its outlook and behaviour. (1978:17)

And what do they [Christians] look like? Different! Jesus emphasized that his true followers, the citizens of God's kingdom, were to be entirely different from others. They were not to take their cue from the people around them, but from him, and so prove to be genuine children of their heavenly Father. To me the key text of the Sermon on the Mount is 6:8: 'Do not be like them.' (1978:18)

Thus the followers of Jesus are to be different—different from both the nominal church and the secular world, different from both the religious and the irreligious. (1978:19)

Jesus means refusing to be in tune with the world or to accommodate oneself to its standard. (1978:55)

Our Christian calling is to imitate not the world, but the Father. And it is by this imitation of him that the Christian counter-culture becomes visible. (1978:124)

In dealing with Matthew 7:13–14, Stott states: 'What is immediately striking about these verses is the absolute nature of the choice before us' (1978:193). The choices are laid out as one being the antithesis of the other. There are two gates: wide and small; two roads: broad and narrow; two destinations: destruction and life; and two crowds: many and few. Speaking of the small gate and narrow road that leads to life he states: 'Further, in order to enter it we must leave everything behind—sin, selfish ambition, covetousness, even if necessary family and friends. For no-one can follow Christ who has not first denied himself' (1978:195).

The two roads flow through African culture as it does through all others. The African middle road of consensus is not an option. As Stott writes, 'there is no middle way' (1978:196).

In chapter 2 of this work I showed the African way of resolving relational conflicts between people. It was described as thesis→antithesis→synthesis (or consensus). Bediako has proposed to use this model to resolve conflicts in religious relations between Christianity and African Traditional Religion. However, by proposing a continuity, one could even say, an extreme continuity, his model would be thesis→antithesis→synthesis→syncretism. As Stott puts it: 'The culture of the world and the counter-culture of Christ are at loggerheads with each other' (1978:56). They do not mix and there can be no synthesis. The idea of being at loggerheads indicates a conflict having reached an impasse, with no obvious resolution. This does not sound like a 'minimal paradigm-shift' would resolve the issue.

The redemption of the African culture is not an option to the African Christian. He is called to be salt and light in it, not to be of it. When the church is like the culture it is irrelevant. As Stott (1978:63) writes:

> The Sermon is built on the assumption that Christians *are* different, and it issues a call to us to *be* different. Probably the greatest tragedy of the church throughout its long and chequered history has been its constant tendency to conform to the prevailing culture instead of developing a Christian counter-culture.

The third part of Bediako's position to be addressed regards the use of redefinition of terms in his adaptation of African Traditional Religion to Christianity. In his book *Christianity in Africa*, he makes extensive use of the term 'vernacular'. He begins by using the term in its proper and normal usage referring to local language. In speaking of what happened on the day of Pentecost as recorded in Acts 2 he states (1995:60): '[It] gives an important biblical and theological warrant for taking seriously the vernacular languages in which people hear the wonders of God.' He goes on to state (1995:62): 'There is probably no more important single explanation for the massive presence of Christianity on the African continent than the availability of the Scriptures in many African languages.'

In a section titled 'The Value of a Vernacular Heritage in African Christianity' he uses the vernacular language to put Christian spin on the religious heritage of Africa. He writes (1995:61):

> Accordingly, in the African Christianity of the post-missionary era, the extent to what a church can be said to possess a viable heritage of Christian tradition in its indigenous language is the extent of that church's ability to offer an adequate interpretation of reality and a satisfying intellectual framework for African life.

He goes on to state that the existence of vernacular Bibles aids hearers to 'make their own response to it and on their own terms' (1995:62). The response and terms that are their own stem from what Bediako calls their 'vernacular heritage' which includes their traditional religion and world-view (1995:68). He is saying that since it is a good thing to translate Christian Scripture into the vernacular language, therefore, it must be a good thing to translate the Christian faith into the vernacular traditional religion and worldview. That this goes beyond contextualization to syncretism is evident in his redefinition of the vernacular use of 'God'.

In *Christianity in Africa* in a section titled 'The African World and the Problem of Unresolved Multiplicity' Bediako states that African Christian scholars 'have done less than full justice to the complexity of the African primal world' (1995:97). It was seen earlier that his theology of ancestors included them in his multiplicity of Divinity. In this longer quote he goes on to give his redefinition of God as the Transcendent:

> Keen to show the relationship of continuity between the pre-Christian religions and Christian belief, they have stressed, particularly and rightly so, the continuity of God. This must be reckoned an important achievement by African theology and is validated by the fact that in virtually every Christian community in Africa, the Christian name for God is usually a divine name hallowed in the pre-Christian religious tradition for the Supreme God. By stressing the centrality and uniqueness of God in African tradition, African theology has, however, left the wider spirit world of African primal religions—divinities, ancestors, natural forces—unaccounted for. In other words, it has answered to only part of what has been described as the 'unity and multiplicity of Divinity; in African primal religion, which I would prefer to call the unity and multiplicity of the Transcendent.

His use of the term 'the Transcendent' for the African Christian under-standing of a multiplicity of spirits and forces in Divinity (i.e. the *vital force* that postulates the AWV) making up God differs considerably from the bibli-cal revelation of a triune Godhead of Father, Son and Holy Spirit, not as a unity of a multiplicity of these different Gods, but One God. The Godhead is not indigenous to any culture as the Godhead existed before the world began and so can only be injected (or incarnated) into it. While the concept of a Supreme God may be a point of continuity between pre-Christian African religion and Christianity, the God that is concerned in each context is quite different.

In thinking about the scholarly writings of Dr. Bediako engaged with in this section a comment comes to mind. Other than language, food, clothes and houses, everything else in the Christian's culture must be submitted to the authority of Scripture. Dr. Bediako makes very little use of Scripture in his theology for Africa. There is no mention of sin, judgement, heaven or hell which are basic to Christian theology but which have been shown to be in conflict with the African worldview.

Going back to the quote of John Mbiti on page 1 of chapter 1, it was stated that traditional religion defines the African and to give up that religion 'means to give up their identity and the support and security that is embodied in it.' The safe way for Dr. Bediako is for an African to become a Christian without having to change religions. That can only be done if he can find roots of Christianity in the pre-Christian religious heritage of Africa.

No doubt the issue of continuity or discontinuity needs to be studied more by African theologians. It would be helpful and more biblical if the emphasis was on contextualization rather than synthesis. A better approach to ATR is needed.

Continuity/Discontinuity

It is Gehman's opinion that total discontinuity does not represent the view-point of Christianity. He posits a dialectical approach to ATR recognizing that in certain respects there is a radical *discontinuity* with ATR and in other respects there is remarkable *continuity* with ATR (Gehman 2005:399). Neither is total as shown by the areas of conflict and conformity previously presented in this chapter.

Points of Continuity

Gehman (2005:399) gives three points of continuity between ATR and Christianity.

(1) *Christian faith is a fulfilment of the African's desires.* He writes: 'Because of human nature, man has an inner hunger and thirst that cannot be met apart from a personal faith and trust in God through Christ.' Quoting Kato, Gehman writes: 'Christ is the fulfilment of the Old Testament and of the deep spiritual needs of the human hearts, not the fulfilment of African Traditional Religion or any other non-Christian religion.' Bediako was correct in saying that the African is looking for fulfilment in his traditional religion, but he stopped short of saying that fulfilment can only be found in Christ apart from religion.

(2) *African culture manifests a continuity with many elements of Hebrew culture.* The similarities in cultural practices and religious beliefs should appeal to Africans. The Hebrew religion and culture included rituals, taboos, sacrifices, spirit possession, polygamy, bride price and many other elements that Africans can identify with.

(3) *ATR provides valuable points of contact.* All of the areas of conformity between the BWV and the AWV provide points of contact between the two religions behind the worldviews. Belief in a Supreme Being and life after death is bridge enough between them to form a meaningful dialogue.

Points of Discontinuity

Four points of discontinuity are suggested by Gehman (2005:400):

(1) *ATR does not lead people to Jesus Christ.* In Christianity, the purpose of the incarnation of Jesus Christ was to save people from their sins. ATR does not recognize the need for salvation from sin.

(2) *ATR represents degeneration from true faith, not a development that leads to true faith.* The biblical support for this is found in Romans 1:18–32. Byang Kato (1985:32) illustrates this point:

> The various ethnic African groups have their traditional religions as an answer to the reality of their existence. The primary question being raised today is that of the nature of these religions in relation to Christianity. The Apostle Paul categorically points out that the worship of pagan gods is a distortion of God's revelation in nature (Romans 1:18–23). Whatever rationalization we may try to make, the worship of gods in Africa is idolatry.

(3) *ATR differs radically from the Christian gospel in its teachings.* Gehman (2005:401) points out: 'The former is a man-centred religion, while the later is God-centred. Sin in ATR is against traditions of society and the ancestors, while sin in the Bible is rebellion against God and transgression of his law.' With the concept of sin being different, the view of salvation is different, thus differentiating the reason and manner God deals with humanity.

(4) *Converts from ATR stress discontinuity, not continuity.* It was Dr. Gehman's experience, and my own experience as well, that those Africans who truly made the transition from ATR to Christianity felt like they had made a transition from darkness to light. Their home lives changed radically as relationships changed from being based on a hierarchical social order to being based on love.

There are two issues involved in the continuity/discontinuity debate. One involves evangelism and bridges from the African traditional culture and religion to conversion to the Christian Gospel. The other involves discipleship or praxis; how to live as a Christian after conversion. Gehman's writings deal primarily with conversion, and he has suggested a continuity/discontinuity model. Bediako and Stott have taken opposite sides of the debate in regards to living as a Christian in one's culture. Does a convert live as an African Christian as Bediako would propose or as a Christian African as Stott would propose.

The traditional African worldview cannot be accommodated in total as Bediako proposes, but perhaps neither does it need to be rejected in total as some might conclude, thus leaving room for the continuity/discontinuity model. There are some aspects of the African worldview and culture that conflict with the biblical worldview. Those aspects have been identified earlier in this chapter and need to be addressed in the process of making disciples in Africa.

The change from one religion to another is a life-changing event. Changing from ATR to Christianity brings changes in this life and the next. Identifying the areas of conflict and conformity in the worldviews of each religion and understanding the concepts of continuity and discontinuity will help one make the transition more definitive. The next chapter will address certain areas of belief and practice deemed necessary for one to hold in order to make the transition complete.

6

Conclusions and Recommendations

The focus of the research in this work has been on the belief systems of Christianity and African Traditional Religion as defined in terms of their respective worldviews. Areas of conformity and conflict in beliefs have been identified pointing toward the thesis that where the African Christian's beliefs differ from the biblical worldview there is a failure in praxis rendering the Christian religion to be ineffectual in the lives of those Africans who claim to have converted to Christianity. While the conversion process is not the subject area of this work, some thoughts on the process of religious conversion may be beneficial.

Religious Conversion

Psychologists have done intensive but inconclusive studies on the psychology of religious conversion. Most recognize its disruptive nature. Professor of Psychology Lewis Rambo (1998) writes: 'the issue of conversion is a very controversial topic, because quite often it does in fact disrupt people's lives. It does disrupt families . . . it is a disorientation, a disruption, and something that has caused a lot of complications in many people's lives.' Seventeenth century scientist, mathematician and philosopher Blaise Pascal recognized this disorientation in his own conversion to Christianity which gave him a totally new view of himself and everything else. He noted that the extraordinary illumination produced fear, anxiety and disturbed the repose he found in former objects of his delight; he no longer enjoyed them with tranquillity.

The disorientation Rambo and Pascal refer to makes people uncomfortable and for that reason many people will not consider religious conversion. Rambo goes on to state: 'When we step back a bit from the issue of what is a proper way of understanding conversion, we see that most people do not convert. At least the studies I've seen of sociologists in the United States and Europe show that most people remain in the religion into which they were born.' There is no reason to believe that what is true in the United States and Europe is not also true in Africa, for all humans share the religious nature. The concern of this work is that even though 65 per cent of sub-Saharan Africa has professed a conversion from ATR to Christianity, many, or even most of them, are still orientated toward the traditional religion into which they were born. Christopher Ejizu (2006) writes: 'Religious conversion is such a complex and fluid matter. Particularly in Africa, with the tremendous resilience and adaptability of the indigenous religions, the persistence of vital beliefs among many converts to Christianity or Islam, it is extremely difficult to be categorical about the state of religious conversion of the majority of people.'

There is not agreement among psychologists and sociologists as to whether one's beliefs or behaviour is the first to change in religious conversion. Psychologist Rambo (1998) writes:

> Many social scientists are saying that, in many cases, it is belief that follows practice, and not practice that follows belief. There is always a debate about the sequence, but I think one could argue that, in many groups, learning to behave in certain ways, and to affiliate in certain ways, often takes priority over some sort of belief system. The belief system is often something that people acquire much later, at least in its more sophisticated terms.

Psychology Professor Henry Newton Malony (1998) takes the view of sociologists: 'Initially, let it be admitted that while we are primarily considering the issue of religious conversion, conversion is a more general term that applies to all changes that involve a transformation of opinions from one belief to another.'

Malony puts forth the Lofton and Stark problem-solving model and states: 'However, I am firmly convinced that the psychological sequence proposed in this model is foundational for religious conversion wherever it occurs.' He explains the model: 'Their two-fold sequence begins with the experience of disequilibrium, a personal strain and stress, and continues with contextualizing that experience within a group situation', thus resulting in conversion.

Rambo (1998) brings up the issue of expectations: 'I begin with the assumption that conversion is what a group says it is. . . . What does a particular group say conversion is? What are the expectations of people's experiences? What behaviours or rituals must they enact?' He continues: 'One of the rather striking things we find is that expectations vary from group to group. Some groups expect the conversion process be largely cognitive and intellectual. In some groups, they expect it to be largely emotional and passionate. In others, it involves much more doing particular things, and acting the rituals.'

In this work Christianity is the target religion, so the expectations Christianity has on the sequence of belief and practice will be examined. Professor Donald Bloesch (2006) writes: 'Conversion is both an event and a process. . . . Again conversion is both personal and social. While it basically connotes a change in our relationship with God, it indicates at the same time an alternation in our attitudes toward our fellow human beings. Conversion is a spiritual event with far reaching social implications.' The event Bloesch talked about begins with a change of belief and the process and social implications is how the change of beliefs shows in changes of behaviour and praxis. Dr. Brian Allison speaks of Christian conversion as a radical change of belief and behaviour. Allison (2000) cites a verse from the Christian Scriptures to illustrate his point: 'They tell how you turned to God from idols to serve the living and true God' (1 Th 1:9b). He concludes: 'And so, the actual demonstration and proof of the acceptance of, and belief in, the Gospel is a radical change of lifestyle, this, conversion—a turning from idols to God.'

John Mbiti (1969:5) states the African view: 'What people do is motivated by what they believe, and what they believe springs from what they do and experience. So then, belief and action in African traditional society cannot be separated: they belong to a single whole.' It is also the position taken in this work that belief and action cannot be separated. Until belief and practice conform to Christian doctrine and praxis the conversion process from ATR to Christianity is not final and the potential converts cannot yet be called Christians. *The idea here is not perfection in Christian praxis, but the revelatory nature of behaviour in times of crisis as signifying the ultimate and final controlling beliefs.* As stated previously in this work, in times of crisis many converts to Christianity revert to ATR for relief signifying they do not believe in the promises and power of Christianity for greater relief. Belief ultimately determines practice.

None of the authors quoted above mentioned the function of the Holy Spirit in the process of conversion to Christianity. The Holy Spirit convicts people of sin and gives them a felt need for salvation. That is the beginning of the conversion process. Believing the Gospel of God's salvation brings about a change in one's spiritual nature by the power of the Holy Spirit. Then the process of 'working out your own salvation' begins. That is where discipleship comes in and where I pray this work can help converts live with a biblical worldview.

Paths of Divergence in Worldview Beliefs

Beginning with conformity of belief in a Supreme Being, God, and in this God being the origin of man and the universe by his creative acts, the worldviews of Christianity and ATR diverge with conflicting beliefs in many areas. The paths of divergence are seen as follows.

God in Relation to Man and the Universe

Attributes of God

Both worldviews hold to the existence of God as a common starting point and both worldviews see many of God's attributes as being the same. The BWV sees God as a personal being who communicates to man and who can be known on a personal level by man. What man can sense the most about God are his love and his holiness. When man is in right relationship with God, his love is the dominant perception. When, because of sin, man is not in right relationship with God, his holiness is the dominant perception making man feel unworthy or ashamed. In the AWV God is remote and cannot be known as a personal being. He is perceived as being good because he has provided life and everything needed to live it, but he is not perceived as being loving. God is perceived as being holy in the technical sense of 'set apart for divine service' but not in the sense of being unable to tolerate anything morally impure. The Christian convert should see God as loving and holy in the biblical sense.

God as Father

It has already been stated that African ontology is firmly anthropocentric, and thus makes man look at God and nature from the point of man's relationship with them. Since the source of ATR is African, the God of ATR reflects the image of African man as evidenced in their many expressions attributing human nature to God. This is most evident in the way ATR views God as a father to Africans. They look to him, not only as their Creator, but also as their provider who is there to help in time of need. This reflects the African child's view of his father. His father created him and provides for him and if the child needs help he can go to his father. Otherwise the mother and siblings do the interacting with the child. As long as the child's needs are met and he does not have any major problems, he has no interaction with his father. In Mbiti's book *Concepts of God in Africa* he does not even mention the fatherhood of God. Magesa (1997:45) mentions other relations attributed to God besides Father, as Mother, Grandparent, Elder and Great Ancestor. These reflect the African view of the hierarchy of authority and power with the elders or ancestors having more authority over a child than the father does. The BWV sets God in authority over the father with the father having authority over the child. The result being the child's relationship to his father is the most important in his life and it sets the model for the Christian relationship with God. He is pictured in the Bible as the Christian's Heavenly Father. In addressing his followers, Jesus stated that if earthly fathers, 'though being evil, give good gifts to their children, how much more will your father in heaven give good gifts to those who ask him' (Mt 7:11). God is described as a father to the fatherless (Ps 68:5). That Christians are called the children of God is a sign of God's great love (1 Jn 3:1). In the BWV man that is rightly related to God is able to know him not only as his creator but also as his kind, loving Father. Christian converts should hold that view.

Evil

The existence of evil in a universe created by a good God gives rise to what the philosophy of religion calls 'theodicy' or the problem of evil. The 'problem of evil' is stated as follows: If God is perfectly good and omnipotent, how can it be that evil exists? If God is good he should *want* to prevent evil. If God is omnipotent, he would be *able* to do so. If God is both of these things then why is there evil? In the AWV evil comes about as God's punishment for some act by an individual or the community. There is no belief in natural evil. Events such as floods, epidemics or wars are generally seen as the activity of God or other spirit beings. In the BWV evil is a result of man's disobedience to God (sin) resulting in a degeneration in the nature of man and the created universe (Gn 3:14–19). Natural evil happens because created things atrophy and malfunction or collapse. Moral evil happens because unregenerate man is evil by nature and is incapable of not doing evil. However, in the BWV God can cause all evil acts to work for good to his children (Rm 8:28). The Christian convert should hold the view that evil may not have a supernatural cause and that even though it is bad, evil can serve a good purpose.

God's Relationship to the Universe

God's continuing relationship to the universe is called divine providence. One of the most fundamental African beliefs about God is that he supplies the needs of his creatures. In the AWV God's providential care of his creatures is shown through the provision of sunshine, rain, fertility, health and plenty for humans, animals and fields. This is what some call 'general providence' which occurs through the fixed laws of nature. Christianity added to 'general providence' the idea of 'special providence' specifically related to each individual being. The BWV adds to the AWV the idea of God's providence governing the personal events of one's life as well as the things that happen in nature. Moreland and Craig (2003:56) state: 'The biblical worldview involves a very strong conception of divine sovereignty over the world and human affairs, even as it presupposes human freedom and responsibility.' Providence comes from the Latin *providere* (to foresee) and the corresponding Greek word is *pronoia* (forethought). Forethought indicates an end result desired and foresight indicates a plan for attaining that end. The BWV holds that everything that happens to an individual is God's providence in governing the affairs of one's life to accomplish God's purpose and plan for that life. That should be the view of the Christian convert.

Man in Relationship to God and the Universe

Nature of Man

(1) Ontological nature. Both the BWV and the AWV hold that man has a material and immaterial part to his being. The material part is his physical body. The immaterial part is made up of his spirit and/or soul. In the AWV the spirit (also called soul) of man represents the vital or life force animating the physical body. Man has no control over it. In the BWV the immaterial part of man is comprised of spirit, understood as the breath of life, and soul, understood as the mind, will and emotions or what gives man his personality. Mind, will and emotions are things that man can control, giving rise to his moral nature.

(2) Moral nature. In the BWV man can control his mind, will and emotions meaning that he can know what is right and moral and will to do it. Man is morally responsible. Because of the sin of the first man, the BWV holds that all of his progeny have a nature bent toward immorality. In the AWV the moral nature of man is neutral. He can commit an immoral act but that does not make him immoral by nature.

The Christian convert needs to believe in the tri-partite nature of man and that he has responsibility for his own soul. He also needs to understand that man is born with a sin nature which separates him from God until that nature is changed.

Man's Relationship to God

(1) God as Father of man.

It was stated previously that God relates to man as a father. In the BWV that relationship is reciprocal as man relates to God as his Father. God is seen as a personal source of provision, security and love. Man can know God as Father because of the intimate spiritual relationship (Rm 8:15–16) and because of the sense of self-worth man receives from the relationship. In the BWV man's worth was shown in God's sacrifice to save him from eternal separation from him. The BWV has the lowest and highest view of man, seeing him as a reprobate sinner separated from God but even in that condition worth more than God's own Son who was sacrificed for man's sins. The AWV holds that God is the Father of all people because God is the creator of mankind. The traditional African relates to God more as Creator than as Father, putting the relationship on a more impersonal level.

(2) Approaching God.

A. Worship. Both the BWV and the AWV hold that God is to be worshipped. In the BWV God is to be worshipped because of who he is and for what he has already done in saving man from eternal damnation. The biblical view of worship is bowing before a holy God asking nothing in return. In ATR worship is usually mixed with prayers of petition and sacrifices offered to ancestral spirits.

B. Sacrifice. In the BWV the sacrifices of animals required by God before the atonement of Christ are no longer needed. Christians are to present themselves to God as living sacrifices (Rm 12:1), living to please God rather than themselves. In the AWV sacrifices to God are still needed in order to restore the balance in nature that has been disturbed through the displeasure of the spirit beings. In the BWV God is to be approached with nothing but a humble heart submitted to him. In the AWV God is to be approached with a material offering with the hopes of getting something in return.

C. Intermediaries. In the BWV Jesus Christ, who himself is God, is the only mediator between God and man (1 Tm 2:5). The Bible depicts him as sitting at the right hand of God making intercession for Christians (Rm 8:34).

The BWV holds that God has given Christians the authority to approach him directly (Heb 4:16) because of their relationship to Jesus Christ.

According to Harry Sawyerr, in the AWV, approaching God is modelled after the African communal system. Sawyerr (1970:7) explains:

> In relation to this, we have to bear in mind that, in African community, there is a clear practice of rule by kings or chiefs, and that these chiefs are not easily approachable and are therefore only reached through intermediaries. For all practical purposes, the chief is distant from ordinary men. He is addressed only through the intermediary and, in turn, he addresses his petitioners only through the intermediaries. Even when the chief is present, a petitioner would request the intermediary to pass his plea to the chief. . . . The chief is however, the one person to whom any of his subjects may run in times of danger and under whose protection they may find a safe sanctuary.

Even at the family level it is the custom among some African societies for the children to speak to their fathers through their mothers or older brothers and sisters.

In the AWV, God is the chief and the ancestors perform the function of intermediary between God and man. Intermediaries are needed because of God's position in the universe and because of his remoteness from the people. The African convert to Christianity should know God as Father and let that be his model as father to his own children.

Man's Relationship to the Universe

According to the Bible man is made in the image and likeness of God and is told to fill the earth and rule over it. The biblical view and the African view of man's relationship to the universe is expressed by Daniel Fountain (1996:324):

> Two Hebrew words in Genesis 1:28, *radah* and *kabash*, are translated as 'have dominion over' and 'subdue' or 'rule over.' In other words, God told man to take charge of nature and control it. . . .
>
> But Genesis does not exist in tribal African tradition. Studying nature, taking charge of it, improving it, and preventing disasters are concepts absent in African culture. Taking charge of our environment is hard work, much too hard without a thorough conviction that it is important and possible. This conviction comes only from a transformation at the very centre of beliefs,

values, and worldview, a paradigm shift from the African view of nature to the biblical one.

In the BWV man is to take dominion over nature. In the AWV man is to live in harmony with nature, not upsetting the way things are in nature if at all possible.

An African convert to Christianity needs to believe that God really is a loving Father directly approachable, requiring no sacrifice or the use of any intermediary. This God reached down to man through Jesus Christ and because of what Christ did, man can know God who loves him and wants to communicate to him on a personal level. The African convert also needs to see the created world as being here for the benefit of man; for man to use, but not abuse, as he lives on the earth.

The Universe and Reality

Nature of the External World

Magesa (1997:39) states: 'In the conception of African Religion, the universe is a composite of divine, spirit, human, animate and inanimate elements, hierarchically perceived, but directly related, and always interacting with each other.' In the AWV all of these elements are infused with a vital force that must be acknowledged. The BWV does not hold to the existence of vital force in the external world.

The AWV holds to an interconnectedness of man with nature on a metaphysical level. Alyward Shorter (2002) explains:

African ethnic religions are typically 'religions of nature'. That does not mean that they are 'nature religions', in which natural phenomena are objects of worship. It means that created nature offers both an explanation of the divine and at the same time the means of contact with divine reality. In African religion, the physical environment is not only sacred, but it is also an organic universe. In other words, nature is biologically continuous with humanity, and it connects human beings with the world of spirit.

The BWV does not hold to this organic connection in which nature is biologically continuous with humanity.

Reality

The BWV sees reality as being objective though divided between the material and the immaterial. In creation there is a hierarchy of order beginning with

God flowing downward to angels, man and the rest of creation. In biblical ontology the spirit world consists of God's Holy Spirit, good angels who obey God in ministering to humans and fallen angels who rebelled against God and now obey Satan in attacking humans. In the BWV spirits can be around but not in inanimate objects. The AWV holds that the world is awash with spirits with all things having their own spirit dimension. These are spirits, as well as spirit beings such as the living-dead, the ancestor spirits. As far as rank, the ancestor spirits are the highest being able to make contact with God. The African convert to Christianity needs to view the reality of the spirit world with the biblical worldview which holds that God created and controls all spirits so that man does not need to be afraid of them.

How Reality Can be Known

The BWV holds that reality can be known because God has revealed knowledge about it through his general or natural revelation and his special revelation as recorded in the Bible. One can perceive reality through the senses and then measure that perception against what God has revealed about it. In the AWV reality can be known by what is perceived and by what the tradition of the elders and ancestors says about it. In analysing the ontology, epistemology, and ethics inherent in African proverbs, Gerald Wanjohi (1996) writes: 'By far the majority of Gikuyu proverbs on the origin of knowledge belong to empiricism. They emphasize experience as a condition for knowledge. Obviously, this is possible only through the senses.' The Christian convert needs to believe that man's senses are not perfect and man's ability to interpret what is perceived by the senses is imperfect and therefore, he needs to look to God and his Word as the only true source of knowledge about reality.

Concept of Time

The BWV holds that time is the chronological succession of events one experiences in life. The direction of time is one-dimensional, moving forward to other events that have not yet happened. The AWV holds that time is a rhythmic cycle of events moving backward carrying the individual toward the ultimate state of impersonal spirit. The Christian convert should view time as moving forward toward a glorious future as an eternal being.

Meaning of History

In the BWV history tells of origins (Genesis 1–11) and origins reveal purpose. Biblical history reveals the origin of man and the universe and answers the 'why' of man's existence. Beyond Genesis 11, biblical history records God's dealing with mankind in the process of generation→degeneration→regeneration and the ultimate establishment of the kingdom of God. History has a beginning and an end. In the AWV history is the accumulation of remembered people and events. When no one is alive that remembers a person or event it disappears from history. History had a beginning but will not end. The Christian convert should view history as God's story of his dealing with mankind and recognize his own part in that story.

Reality and Morality

Basis of Morality

In the BWV a proper view of morality flows from a proper view of reality. Biblical reality recognizes the existence of a holy, moral and righteous God who created man and gave him moral rules to live by. These rules are recorded in the Bible and are regarded as absolute standards of morality. The reality of man's moral nature makes him accountable to God. Violating God's moral standard causes separation in man's relationship with God. In the AWV man's relationship with his community sets the moral standards. Peace and harmony in the community is the moral imperative. Anything that disrupts that is considered by the African to be immoral. Moral standards are not absolute but are determined by resultant consequences. African converts to Christianity need to see the reality of moral standards coming from God and not man or tradition, and the reality of his ultimate accountability to God based on those standards.

Policing of Morality

In the area of morals the BWV holds that God is not only the law-giver (making acts of immorality to be against him), but he is also the law-enforcer and judge. All people will eventually appear before him to give an account (Rm 14:12). The AWV holds that any immoral act is against the community or society and therefore must be punished by the corporate community of both the living and the dead. The punishment deserved is determined by the ancestors and is either inflicted directly or communicated to the community leaders to be carried out. Converts to Christianity must see their accountability to God who can punish body and soul and obey him rather than seeing their accountability as being to their community which can only punish the body.

Morality and Relationships

Moral Basis of Relationships

In the AWV the moral basis of relationships is defined by peace and harmony in the community. To report a thief to the police would be wrong if the thief was someone important and his arrest would cause a problem in the community. Even the theft act itself is not immoral until it is made public and brings shame on the community. Someone can steal and lie about it and still remain moral until it is found out. For the African, relationships are the most important thing, but they are not based upon truth or trust. They are based upon culturally defined expectations of maintaining relationships. If telling the truth would mean a breach in relationships, whatever the truth is doesn't matter; the sin would be in the telling of it. In the BWV man's primary relationship is with God and man's relationship with God is morally determined. Because God's moral laws include how man is to relate to his fellowman, to violate one of his laws against another man is the same as violating it against God. To lie to your neighbour is just as immoral as lying to God. The African convert to Christianity needs to see his moral responsibility to God as the basis of his relationships with other people, rather than looking to cultural expectations.

Love in Relationships

The concept of love in relationships is almost totally absent in Africa. Finding a book on ATR that even mentions love is a rare find. My observation from living in Africa is confirmed by Mbiti (1970:30):

> In their daily lives, Africans do not talk much about love, and this is something perhaps too deep to be discussed in words. A person shows his love for another more through action than words. In the same way, it is rare to hear or find people talking about the love of God. They, however, assume that God loves them and shows his love through concrete acts and blessings. We do not have many examples in which people talk about the love of God.

Love in relation to God and to other people is assumed or imputed, but not acknowledged verbally by Africans, probably because it would be perceived as making one vulnerable to another. If love is not acknowledged why would it even be assumed in African relationships? The answer is found in the BWV concerning the nature of man. The biblical view states that because God knows people's deepest emotional needs, he has made a general provision to meet those needs through marriage and family. Every human being in the world wants to be loved and appreciated by someone else. If love is not professed, love will be assumed because love is needed. In the AWV love in relationships is not professed but assumed. In the BWV love is professed and celebrated as the basis of relationships. Love is God's nature (1 Jn 4:8) and since man is made in the image of God, the need to give and receive love is in man's nature. An African convert to Christianity needs to acknowledge the basis of love in relationships to God and man.

Husband-Wife Relationship

In the BWV no human relationship is as important as the marriage relationship between husband and wife. As mentioned above, God made provision to meet man's deepest needs through marriage and family. For the child those needs are to be met by the parents. For the adult those needs are to be met in the spouse. God is love (1 Jn 4:8) and he has given us the gift of love, communication and emotional security in marriage. Marriage is important because it meets deep human needs. God knew that, and established marriage as the first human institution. Soon after the first man was created a wife was created for him (Gn 2:18).

There is another reason the BWV holds that marriage is the most important human relationship. The BWV is the worldview of Christianity and in Christianity the marriage relationship between husband and wife is a human picture of the spiritual relationship between Jesus Christ and his church. Ephesians 5:22–33 in the Christian Bible explains how and why the human relationship depicts that spiritual relationship. The wife represents the church and the husband represents Christ. The duty of the wife is to submit to the husband (Eph 5:22). The duty of the husband is to love his wife (Eph 5:25): 'Husbands, love your wives, just as Christ loved the church and gave himself up for her.' The biblical view of marriage begins with the husband leaving his father and mother and cleaving to his wife (Gn 2:24) and that relationship being lived out as the wife submits to the husband and the husband gives himself sacrificially to the wife.

In the AWV marriage does not exist to meet the deepest human needs or to serve any religious purpose other than the religious implication of fertility. For the African, marriage is a function of utility and an obligation. Marriage in Africa is considered normal, natural and fully expected. Everyone is expected to marry after initiation as his sacred duty to his family and clan in order to raise children and carry on his name and family. In the African view, marriage is looked upon as a sacred duty and failure to get married and produce offspring is seen as stopping the flow of life through the individual, and hence, the diminishing of mankind upon the earth. It is regarded as committing a major offence in the eyes of society and people will be against him.

The way marriage partners are chosen reflects duty, as opposed to love, as being the motivation for marriage. Customs vary with some parents choosing a marriage partner for their child before it is born; other parents make the choice when the child is ready for marriage and some societies let the young people themselves decide whom to marry. Whatever the custom, a choice must be made so that the marriage duty can be met. After they have married and produced children the marriage obligations are met and the obligation as parents takes prominence. The African convert to Christianity must view marriage as a sacred union with natural and supernatural manifestations. In the Christian marriage one's spouse is the most important person and worthy of highest honour whether or not children are produced.

In examining the differing views of the BWV and AWV regarding morality and relationships another issue pertaining to the husband-wife relationship needs to be addressed. In the BWV the husband has a moral obligation (because God commanded it) to feed and care for his wife (Eph 4:28–29). The man is the one God commanded to work for his and his wife's food. When man sinned, part of the curse pronounced by God was addressed directly to him: 'Cursed is the ground because of you; through painful toil you will eat of it all the days of your life. It will produce thorns and thistles for you and you will eat the plants of the fields. By the sweat of your brow you will eat your food until you return to the ground' (Gn 3:17–19a). Because of his sin, the man was commanded to produce his own food from start to finish (before he sinned, he only had to pluck what he wanted to eat as it was already produced) and the production would be made very difficult for him. His sin brought corruption upon himself and creation as the ground would henceforth produce corrupt things.

According to the customs and traditions of the AWV, the woman carries the responsibility to not only cook the food for her husband, but also to produce it. The woman has to deal with the thorns and thistles and produce food by the sweat of her brow. African men have, in effect, reversed the curse of Genesis 3 and have put it upon the woman. The African man that converts to Christianity needs to understand what has happened and assume his rightful place of provider for his wife and family.

Relationships and Eternity

The two worldviews under consideration continue to diverge along a path of morality in relationships to the connection between relationships and eternity. Both worldviews hold that how one meets his moral obligations in relationships while living determines one's state in eternity. They diverge in their beliefs about who one's moral obligation is to and what one's state in eternity will be.

Relating to God

In the BWV one's relationship with God while living determines where he will spend eternity. One that is rightly related to God, or 'saved' at death, will spend eternity with God in heaven. One who is not rightly related to God at the time of death will spend eternity in hell, or eternal torment. Being rightly related to God is defined as believing and obeying the Christian Gospel. In the AWV one's relationship to God while living affects only his contemporary existence and has no eternal consequences. Worship, sacrifice and offerings are given to God as petitions for things desired while living. One's destiny is already fixed so that all the African needs God for is this life.

Relating to Man

The BWV holds that one's relationship with others is a reflection of one's relationship to God. If a person is rightly related to God, obeying his com-mands, he will treat others as he wants to be treated and he will love others as he loves himself (Mt 22:39). Beyond that, he will follow Christ's example and love others with a self-sacrificial love (Jn 13:34). He relates to people in this way because he is grateful for what God has done for him and not for some future benefit in this life or the next. In the AWV one's relationship with oth-ers has a bearing on how he will be remembered after his death and how he is remembered will determine how long he will exist in the *Sasa* period. The *Sasa* period is the duration of time after death that one lives in the memory of his progenies and exists as a living-dead, or ancestor. The African knows that how he treats others in this life will determine how he is remembered. If he is remembered well he will be spoken of well from one generation to the next and as long as he is remembered and spoken of his personality will continue to exist. The African convert to Christianity needs to see his relationship with God as being determinative for eternity and his relationship with God needs to be reflected in his relationships with others, which is not determinative for eternity.

Eternity—Where?

Genesis 1–11 contains the genesis of the biblical worldview concerning life, death, and life after death for all humanity. Man's life is depicted as being a result of God's creative act (Gn 1:27), with man being created (male and female) in such a way that he can procreate after his own kind (Gn 1:28). Man being made in the image and likeness of God was created to live eternally with God. Death, always being a possibility, became a reality when man sinned by disobeying God (Gn 2:17). Death is depicted as being spiritual (man's spirit separated from, or dead to, God's Spirit) (Gn 3:8) and physical (Gn 3:19). Life after death is depicted in God's approaching man and providing a covering for his sin affecting reconciliation (Gn 3:9, 21) and setting aside spiritual death, but not physical death (Gn 3:22). The seed for the Christian view of life after death is contained in the *Protevangelium* in Genesis 3:15. The customs and traditions passed down from the ancestors and elders are embedded in ATR and form the basis for the African view of life, death and life after death.

Death

In the BWV death is both spiritual and physical. Spiritual death means that man's spirit is not in communion with God's Spirit because of man's sin nature. The BWV holds that to be the state of everyone at birth. Physical death occurs when man's spirit or soul separates from the physical body because the mechanical part of the physical body has quit functioning. The BWV holds that as long as man's physical body is living, spiritual death is not a permanent condition. Man can choose to be reconciled to God spiritually by believing the Christian Gospel.

In the AWV death is a process that begins when the physical body stops functioning. People in all African communities believe there is a spiritual part of a person which continues to live on after the physical body dies. While a person is living he has a vital force that animates him to fulfil his purpose of transmitting and maintaining life. A person dies when the vital force leaves his body. In the African view, when one can no longer maintain or transmit life he is dead.

There are several paradoxes in the African view of death. The dead person is perceived as being cut off from humanity, and yet, there must be continuing contact between the living and the dead. The grave is symbolic of the separation between the dead and the living but by turning it into a shrine it converts it into a place of contact between the two. The African has since accepted death as part of the natural rhythm of life; and yet, paradoxically, every human death is thought to have external causes, making it both natural and unnatural. Death is perceived as a change of status (from lower to higher), marking entrance into a new and deeper relationship with living human beings and with the whole universe. That is why to become an ancestor is the goal of African people. More rituals are performed at death than during any other rite of passage because death is seen as a portent of extreme danger. All other transactions are during life; but death ushers a human being into the unseen world of the departed ancestors. The danger is present because death is perceived to always be caused by external forces. The danger gives rise to a fear of death.

The African converting from ATR to Christianity should believe that the African's ambivalent feelings toward death are not biblical. Death should be viewed in terms of a change in location of the spiritual personality from a physical body on earth to the spiritual presence of God (2 Cor 5:8) and not something to be feared (1 Cor 15:55).

State of Being in Eternity

The BWV holds that after death the person remains in a conscious state of spiritual being, retaining their own personal identity throughout all eternity. Death may be felt in the form of physical pain in the body but will not mark a metaphysical change in the personality of the person. The person will continue to exist forever. In the AWV, death is recognized as the point when the spirit separates from the body, but the spirit is still distinguishable by more or less the same features as it had when the person lived. However, in the African view this state where the spirit is distinguishable is not permanent for all eternity, but is only for the duration of time the person is part of the ancestors, or the living dead, after which time the spirit loses its personal distinction and joins the world of impersonal spirits. The African convert to Christianity should believe that after death his personal consciousness will exist for all eternity.

The Living-dead

The BWV does not hold to a concept of the living-dead or ancestors, as believed in ATR and forbids consulting the dead (Dt 18:10–13). The beliefs held by the AWV are in opposition to the BWV. John Mbiti coined the term 'living-dead' referring to the African belief that after death, personalities are retained, social and political statuses are maintained, and in many ways the hereafter is a carbon copy of the present life. Africans both acknowledge and deny the separation of death. A person dies and yet continues to live: he is a living-dead.

The belief in the living-dead, or ancestors, is dealt with by every writer on ATR. Ancestor veneration is a very important part of the total complex of African culture and may be regarded as the cement which holds African societies together. While most African theologians would disagree with the use of the word 'veneration', all acknowledge the role of ancestors in African society. Professor Jack Partain (1986) describes the role of ancestors: 'Deceased ancestors remain close by, as part of the family, sharing meals and maintaining an interest in family affairs—just as before death. Yet they are thought to have advanced mystical power, which enables them to communicate easily with both the family and God. Thus they are considered indispensable intermediaries.' Partain goes on to describe the authority attributed to the ancestors: 'Moreover, the ancestors sanction society's customs, norms and ethics. Without them, Africans are left without moral guidelines or motivation, and society is powerless to enforce ethics.' When the last person who knew him dies, the living dead loses his personal identity and immortality and is now considered dead, as far as humans are concerned. This completes the dying process in the AWV. The convert from ATR to Christianity must recognize the belief in the living-dead to be contrary to the BWV regarding life after death and renounce it.

Reality of Heaven and Hell

In the BWV heaven and hell are real places of final destiny for the souls of human beings. In a physical sense heaven is described in the Bible as being upward from the earth (Gn 1:8, 11:4) and is designated as the dwelling place of God (Gn 28:17; Rv 12:7–8). In Christianity, the term heaven is used to represent the final abode of the saved, or the righteous, signifying those who died in right relationship with God. They will dwell with him forever. The biblical view of hell is of a place of eternal punishment for the unrighteous, or those who died not in right relationship with God (Mt 23:33). In the AWV heaven is considered to be the dwelling place of God and is believed to be above the earth, or in the sky. There is no belief that humans could ever go there. The AWV holds no belief in hell or any such place like it. African converts to Christianity should embrace the concept of a final destiny in either heaven or hell in their worldview.

Final Judgement

The BWV holds to the concept of a final judgement which is understood to be the ultimate and lasting separation of good and evil at the terminus of human history. The exact time of the judgement has been set by God (Ac 17:31), but has not been revealed to mankind (Mt 24:36). The AWV does not include the concept of a final judgement. The majority of Africans do not look for any form of judgement or reward in the hereafter. African Christians must believe in and live this life with a view toward a final judgement.

Eternity—Where?

This question deals with whether or not one can now know for sure where they will spend eternity. In the BWV there is assurance of salvation from spending eternity in hell as punishment for sin and rebellion against God. Salvation from that destiny comes by believing, in faith, the Christian Gospel (Heb 10:22). One can know for sure that their final destiny is heaven rather than hell because God will give that assurance (Rm 8:16; 1 Jn 5:10). Since there is no belief in a heaven or a hell as one's final destiny, the AWV holds that one's eternity will be spent in the spirit world which is here on earth. Death is seen as an ontological change from physical/spiritual to only spiritual, but not a removal from the earth. Mbiti (1975a:116) gives a psychological basis for that belief: 'As a whole these ideas paint the hereafter in features, colours and descriptions which are very much like those of the present life. This is to be expected since, if the hereafter was terribly different from the present life, people would find it disturbing to their imagination and would feel that they would become strangers in that world when they die. This would make them resent death more.' Converts from ATR to Christianity need to know that they will spend eternity in a place far better than this life and that is assured because of their relationship to God through Christ.

Effects of Holding Both Worldviews on the Christian Church in Africa

Missionary/educator Richard Gehman (2005:6) writes: 'a careful look at the African landscape reveals that the deep-seated traditional worldview is held simultaneously by those who embrace either Christian or western thought.' In writing about the ways African Traditional Religions and Christianity inter-act, Lamin Sanneh (1983:242) states: 'One underlying assumption in all these questions, is the continuing vitality of African religions both as influences in the ordinary perception of Christians and as a force in the organizational aspects of Christianity.' Both Christianity and Islam seeking to win converts from ATR face this issue. Quoting Bolaji Idowu, Gehman (2005:12) writes:

> While, as we have said, every African may wish to be regarded as connected with one or the other of the two 'fashionable' religions, most are at heart still attached to their own indigenous beliefs. It is now becoming clear to the most optimistic of Christian evangelists that the main problem of the church in Africa today is the divided loyalties of most of her members between Christianity with its Western categories and practices on the one hand, and the traditional religion on the other. It is well known that in strictly personal matters relating to the passage of life and the crises of life, African Traditional Religion is regarded as the final succour by most Africans.

Magesa (1997:7) calls this divided loyalty 'the "duality" of African Christians' way of life' meaning they often seek their comfort in their traditional religious systems. This is echoed by Osadolor Imasogie (1983:14): 'The superficiality of the African Christian's commitment is evidenced by the fact that when he is faced with problems and uncertainties he often reverts to traditional religious practices.'

As stated in chapter 1, the accepting of a new religion without discarding the beliefs of the old religious system is called syncretism. Charles Kraft (1999:390) gives the affect of syncretism on Christianity: 'the mixing of Christian assumptions with those worldview assumptions that are incompatible with Christianity so that the result is not biblical Christianity.' Syncretism is seen to be a driving force in African religion and culture as Africa embraces globalization. Byang Kato (1985:25) expounds the incentives for syncretism in culture and Christianity:

> Incentives for syncretism in Africa are not hard to find. The incentives for universalism (the idea that all will be saved in the end) are the same for syncretism, since only a thin line separates the two ideologies. The reasons for growing syncretistic tendencies in Africa may be summed up briefly.

> (i) The prevailing wind of religious relativism in the older churches of the West is being carried abroad by the liberal missionaries in person and through literature.

(ii) The crying need for universal solidarity in the world fosters religious respect one for the other.

(iii) Political awareness in Africa carries with it a search for ideological identity. Some theologians seek to find this identity in African Traditional Religions.

(iv) Emotional concerns for the ancestors who died before the advent of Christianity force some theologians to call for recognition of the religious practices of pre-Christian idol worshippers.

(v) Cultural revolution promotes a return to the traditional socio-religio-cultural way of life in Africa. Since it is hard to separate culture from religion, the tendency is to make them identical and cling to idolatrous practices as being an authentic African way of life.

(vi) Inadequate biblical teaching has left the average Christian with an inability in 'rightly handling the Word of truth.' Syncretistic or neo-orthodox teachers bring their views, and even Christian leaders fail to discern what is right according to the teaching of God's Word.

(vii) The African loves to get along with everybody. He is, therefore, not inclined to offend his neighbour by letting him know what the Bible says about non-Christian religions. That is why liberal ecumenism is thriving in Africa.

(viii) Liberal Christianity has done a thorough job in picking up key brains from the Third World and grooming them in liberal schools in the Western world.

(ix) The study of comparative religions, without affirmation of the uniqueness of Christianity, has helped produce theologians of syncretistic persuasion.

(x) The legitimate desire to make Christianity truly African has not been matched with the discernment not to tamper with the inspired, inerrant content of the revealed Word of God.

With the incentives for syncretism being so prevalent in Africa today, making converts from ATR to Christianity who are totally converted in belief and practice is hard to accomplish and hard to measure. It is hard to measure because the foundational core beliefs are not manifested until times of crisis and some individual Christian's crises are handled in secret, out of the view of the Christian community. As stated in chapter 1, 65 per cent of sub-Saharans profess to be Christians. If that were truly the case, African culture would have a definite Christian reflection as psychologists tell us that people cannot live in conflict with their core beliefs very long without some kind of breakdown. However, in Africa the core beliefs are remaining traditional. Christopher Ejizu (2006) states: 'The traditional world-view, including a strong belief in the dynamic presence and activities of spirit beings and cosmic forces in people's lives and belief in reincarnation, persists among most Africans.'

African culture is slowly shedding its colonial influences and reverting back to its traditional ways. Some churches in Africa are accommodating that trend. Some African Independent Churches, including the Aladura and Cherubim and Seraphim, have incorporated into their doctrines and practices the presence and influence of ancestral spirits and other spirit beings, divination, belief in magic and the practice of traditional religious rituals. If the Christian church in Africa is following the same trend as culture it will render itself culturally irrelevant. For Christianity to change Africans, and thereby impact Africa, a new approach is needed.

Recommendations to the Church in Africa

The traditional approach to the problem of syncretism in African Christianity is to teach correct or orthodox doctrine. The belief is that lack of knowledge of Christian doctrine and beliefs is the reason African Christians hold on to some conflicting traditional religious beliefs and behaviour. Many books have been written by African and Christian missionary theologians about the doctrines that need to be taught in African churches. See Gehman (1999, 2005), Imasogie (1983), Kato (1985), Mbiti (1986), O'Donovan (1996), Olsen (1972) and Pobee (1979) as examples. The approach taken by these and other authors is stated by Gehman (2005:xi): 'Thus the viewpoint contained in this book is more than a generally Christian viewpoint [worldview], as noble as that may be. Rather, it is intended to expound relevant biblical teaching and apply it to the issues in our study.' Those authors who incorporate worldview into their books do so from the perspective of theology and its affect on one's worldview. Imasogi (1983:12) writes: 'The observed lack of total commitment of the average African Christian to Christ is due to the lack of "fit" between Christian theology and African life.' It is my view that Christian theology will never 'fit' into African life because Christian theology is strange doctrine to the African worldview.

My recommended approach to the problem of syncretism in the African church is through philosophy rather than theology. It is based upon teaching worldview rather than doctrine. Worldview is the universal, and doctrine makes up the particulars. Teaching doctrine that does not assimilate into one's worldview will ultimately be rejected and will not bring about change in praxis. In this case, a new doctrine is like a pebble in the shoe. It will make a person walk differently for a while, but because it is not comfortable, eventually the pebble will be removed and things will return to the comfortable normal. What is needed in an African convert to Christianity is a change in worldview to one that can assimilate Christian doctrines as they are learned. The current approach is to teach the particulars expecting the universal to change. In my opinion, the equation needs to be reversed. My recommended approach is to teach the universal—the biblical worldview—and the Christian particulars will fall into place.

The teaching of the biblical worldview in African churches should be from a pragmatic approach, teaching the practical rather than the ideological aspects of it. It has been my observation that ATR and the worldview it demands will not get Africans what they really want in this life or the next. With the advent of modern technologies Africans desire the convenience and status of owning automobiles, mobile phones and computers, but the traditional beliefs making up their worldview prevent them from accumulating the funds needed to buy them. As stated earlier in this work, sustaining the harmony or balance among beings in the community is the most important ethical responsibility for Africans, and it forms the basis of any individual's moral character. On the individual level that balance is maintained by sharing what you have. To save money is considered hoarding, which constitutes greed, and in the words of Magesa (1997:62): 'Greed constitutes the most grievous wrongs' with greed being the antonym of hospitality and sociability. For those holding the African worldview based upon traditional beliefs, improving one's life is virtually impossible and they are frustrated.

Likewise, ATR and the worldview it demands will not get Africans what they desire for the next life. Their desire is that at death they join the ancestors and remain one as long as possible. But if they really analysed the African view of ancestors they would see that the living fear them, honour them out of obligation and blame them when calamities befall them. Humanly speaking, other than the power ancestors are perceived to have, that does not seem to be a very rewarding state of being. In speaking of the deficiency of the African worldview Mbiti (1969:127) writes: 'So long as their concept of time is two dimensional, with a *Sasa* and a *Zamani*, African peoples cannot entertain a glorious "hope" to which mankind may be destined.' Mbiti (1969:128) goes on to state: 'Yet behind these fleeting glimpses of the original state and bliss of man, whether they are rich or shadowy, there lie the tantalizing and unattained gift of the resurrection, the loss of human immortality and the monster of death. Here African religions and philosophy must admit defeat: they have supplied no solution.' For the Christian convert the biblical worldview does offer solutions to man's deepest needs and fears, offering peace, prosperity of soul and security for this life and the next.

The church in Africa consists of those who already profess to be Christians. What the church needs is a strategy, not to evangelize or proselytize, but a strategy to de-syncretize the beliefs and practices of its members. The strategy I propose follows.

Teach Genesis 1–11

Genesis 1–11 contains the foundational teachings of the biblical worldview. It presents God and his dealings with mankind which makes up the theme of human history. Every event that happens on earth fits in with that theme somehow. It explains the way the universe was originally and why things are the way they are now. It tells why there is sin in the world and why mankind is separated from the physical presence of God. It also introduces God's plan to restore that separation. Emphasis needs to be placed on the last event recorded in Genesis 11 where Abram was called by God to leave his family and his culture and to trust God for his future. Abram's call is the African's call and he set the example they should follow. For all the reasons stated throughout this book, I recommend teaching the church in Africa the contents of Genesis 1–11. A suggested outline for incorporating the Christian view into the teaching on Genesis 1–11 would be the one presented in chapter 3.

Teach the Philosophical Elements of the Biblical Worldview

Philosophy helps people form rationally justified beliefs about all aspects of life and reality including origins, or beginnings, and an end. My recommended approach would be to teach the biblical answers to the philosophical questions as delineated in chapter 3. The questions are repeated here.

Is there a Supreme Being, and if so, what is it like?

What is the origin and nature of man?

What is reality and what is ultimate reality?

What is truth?

What is the origin and nature of the universe?

What is God's relationship with the universe?

What is the meaning of time?

Do laws and causality govern the universe absolutely?

Why do man and the universe exist and do they have a final end?

Does evil have a purpose?

Who or what determines what is moral and immoral?

How do we know what is right?

What is man's relationship to the natural environment?

Is there aesthetic value to religious experience?

What is the meaning of history?

Is history cyclical or linear in progression?

What can we know and how can we know it?

What justifies a belief?

In order for the claim of superiority over the African worldview to be justified, the biblical worldview must answer the above questions in a way that does not violate the laws of logic or the criteria for accepting or rejecting truth claims as given in chapter 2. The answers given to the above philosophical questions in chapter 3 can be used and when compared to the answers based on the African worldview given in chapter 4, the path of divergence in worldviews as presented earlier in this chapter can clearly be shown.

Teach a Clear Presentation of the Gospel

The Gospel is simply defined as the message of salvation offered by God to all. Those who believe it are saved. The whole story explaining man's need for salvation is included in Genesis 1–11. The *protevangelium*, encapsulated in Genesis 3:15 as a seed containing the whole Gospel story of God's plan of salvation for mankind through the Seed of the woman, Jesus Christ, needs to be taught in language, signs and symbols that Africans can understand. A clear presentation of the Gospel should also include the costs one should be prepared to pay both socially and personally in self-sacrifice. If believed, a clear presentation of the Gospel should put one in the state of disequilibrium talked about earlier in this chapter as being necessary to the conversion process, and cause disorientation and disruption in one's life. At this point they believe something that conflicts with one or more basic core beliefs they hold as part of their worldview and it causes them personal stress. This stress will be relieved as their worldview changes to concur with God's worldview. Everything from beginning to end is explained and all fear of the unknown is gone.

Teach Expectations

Rambo's assertion that conversion is what a group says it is applies here. A convert to Christianity needs to be taught what he can expect to happen to him and what the Christian community expects from him. Initially, the convert should expect his becoming a Christian to resolve the sense of disequilibrium and disorientation he felt when believing the Gospel as he comprehends more of what being a Christian means. The convert should expect to understand things differently and expect to do things differently than before his conversion. Christian conversion is the putting of Christ on the throne of a person's life and allowing him to control every aspect of it. The Christian expectation is that believing the Gospel demotes man from being ruler to being subject, and behaviour should change accordingly. Christianity expects belief to precede and determine praxis. How Christian beliefs are worked out in praxis may be culturally determined as long as it remains biblical.

Teach the Need for the Conversion Experience

Many people converting from ATR to Christianity see it only as a matter of change in behaviour and maybe some beliefs. Following the Islamic model, they believe that if they say and do certain things they have adopted a new religion. Even the concept of conversion is absent from the African worldview. However, conversion is required as understood in Christianity. The Christian understanding of conversion is a change in attitude or belief about God, sin and Christ that will bring a person into right relationship with God. Jesus Christ explains the concept in Acts 26:18: 'to open their eyes and turn them from darkness to light, and from the power of Satan to God, so that they may receive forgiveness of sins and a place among those who are sanctified by faith in me.' In the Christian view a convert's understanding of the Gospel should show the need for conversion and the actuality of the conversion experience should bring peace to his soul.

Teach Praxis

A convert needs to understand how his new worldview should be put into practice. My recommended approach is to teach Christian living following the path of divergence between the biblical worldview and the African world-view as presented earlier in this chapter. Areas where the worldview beliefs conflict reflect areas of behaviour that need to be changed. Beginning with conformity of views in a Supreme Being or God, the two worldviews diverge along the path of God's relationship to man, man's relationship to God, the nature of man, man's relationship to nature, reality, morality, relationships and preparation for eternity. The need to converge the African Christian's personal beliefs in these areas to the biblical worldview is vital to the success of the Christian church in Africa. The African Christian must believe and behave like a biblical Christian.

Teach the Religious Dimensions of Worldview

The religious dimensions of worldview should be incorporated into teaching the biblical worldview of Christianity. The writings of Ninian Smart and others as presented in chapter 2 could be most helpful in formulating the teaching of content and practice of religious dimensions. Smart gives six dimensions of religion in worldview specifying that beliefs are formed by the doctrinal, mythical and ethical dimensions, with those beliefs experienced and practiced in the ritual, experiential and social dimensions. The comparison of the religious dimensions of Christianity and ATR as given in chapter 5 could serve as a useful starting point for producing teaching material in this area. Religion becomes reality in these six dimensions and teachings should be culture-specific to render belief and practice biblical and relevant.

Conclusion

This work has addressed the religions of ATR and Christianity in Africa from the standpoint of worldview beliefs. It is hoped that this work can be useful to the Christian church in Africa in teaching the biblical worldview to its members in order to address the problem of syncretism. Unless trained differently, when Africans become Christians they try to interpret the Scriptures through the filter of their own worldview. That results in their Christian praxis being more traditional African than Christian. As Van Rheenen (1991:89) points out: '**Christian conversion without worldview change in reality is syncretism**' (emphasis mine). From the Christian religion standpoint the worldview one holds has eternal consequences. The African man's eternity will not depend upon how he sees himself as an African but how God sees him in relation to the realities of sin and salvation as first presented in Genesis 1–11 and elucidated in the New Testament of the Christian Bible. The biblical worldview holds that the church is God's instrument on earth to teach the African man the realities of life and death according to Genesis 1–11 and the promised salvation through faith in the atoning work of Jesus Christ according to the New Testament. The two worldviews, African and Christian, will not converge unless the church is true to its mission.

Bibliography

Achebe, C 1958. *Things Fall Apart*. Nairobi: Heinemann Educational Books, LTD.

Addo, P E A 2002. *The Loss of African Traditional Religion in Contemporary Africa*. Available from: http://www.afrikaworld.net/afrel/lossrelg.htm [Accessed 19 July 2006].

Aganaba, S 2002. *Dealing With Spirits of the Dead*. Serre Kunda, The Gambia: Daysprings Publications.

Akrong, A 2005. *An Introduction to African Traditional Religions*. Available from: http://www.africawithin.com/religion/intr_to_atr.htm [Accessed 28 November 2005].

Albert, E M et al. 1988. *Great Traditions in Ethics*, 6th ed. Belmont, CA: Wadsworth Publishing Company.

Allen, C J (ed) 1969. *Genesis-Exodus. The Broadman Bible Commentary*. Nashville, TN: Broadman Press.

Allison, B 2000. *Christian Conversion*. Available from: http://www.inplainsite.org/html/christian_conversion.htm [Accessed 2 September 2006].

Ames, E A 1910. *The Psychology of Religious Experience*. Boston, MA: Houghton Mifflin Company.

Anderson, B W 1963. *The Beginning of History*. New York: Abingdon Press.

Atkinson, D 1990. *The Message of Genesis 1-11*. Leicester, England: InterVarsity Press.

Audi, R (ed) 1995. *The Cambridge Dictionary of Philosophy*. Cambridge: Cambridge University Press.

Axelsen, D 1979. 'Philosophical Justifications for Contemporary African Social and Political Values and Strategies' in Wright, R A (ed). *African Philosophy: An Introduction*, 2nd ed, 183-198. Washington, DC: University Press of America.

Ayoade, J A A 1979. 'Time in Yoruba Thought' in Wright, R A (ed), *African Philosophy: An Introduction*, 2nd ed, 71-89. Washington, DC: University Press of America.

Bancroft, E H 1976. *Christian Theology: Systematic and Biblical*. 2nd ed. Grand Rapids, MI: Academie Books, Zondervan Publishing House.

Barrett, D B (ed) 1982. *World Christian Encyclopedia*. Nariobi: Oxford University Press.

Barton, P 2004. Ancient Africans in Recent America. *New Africa* No 433, 38-39.

Bediako, K 1995. *Christianity in Africa: The Renewal of a Non-Western Religion*. Edinburgh, UK: Edinburgh University Press Ltd.

_____ 1999. *Theology and Identity: The Impact of Culture upon Christian Thought in the Second Century and in Modern Africa*. Oxford, UK: Regnum Books International.

Bhattacharya, N and Eckblad, T 1997. Towards a Biblical Worldview: Reflections of a South Asian and a North American. *The International Journal of Frontier Missions*, 14(2), 87.

Blackburn, S 1994. *The Oxford Dictionary of Philosophy*. Oxford: Oxford University Press.

Bloesch, D G 1984. s v 'Sin'. *Evangelical Dictionary of Theology*.

_____ 2006. *Conversion*. Available from: http://mb-soft.com/believe/text/conversion.htm [Accessed 4 September 2006].

Bohannah, P 1964. *Africa and Africans*. Garden City, NJ: The Natural History Press.

Brown, L M (ed) 2004. *African Philosophy: New and Traditional Perspectives*. NY: Oxford University Press.

Buswell Jr, J O 1967a. s v 'Revelation'. *The Zondervan Pictorial Bible Dictionary*.

_____ 1967b. s v 'Truth'. *The Zondervan Pictorial Bible Dictionary*.

Carnell, E J 1952. *A Philosophy of the Christian Religion*. Grand Rapids, MI: Wm. B. Eerdman's Publishing Co.

Carr, D 1995. s v 'philosophy of history'. *The Cambridge Dictionary of Philosophy*.

Clark, K J et al. 2004. *101 Key Terms in Philosophy and Their Importance for Theology*. Louisville, KY: Westminister John Knox Press.

Cochrane, C C 1984. *The Gospel According to Genesis*. Grand Rapids, MI: William B. Eerdmans Publishing Company.

Conteh, P S 2007. *An Introduction to the Religion of the Limba of Sierra Leone*. Pretoria: Unisa Press.

Davidson, B 1966. *African Kingdoms*. New York: Time Incorporated.

_____ 1991. *African Civilization Revisited*. Trenton, NJ: Africa World Press.

Davidson, R 1973. *Genesis 1-11*. Cambridge: Cambridge University Press.

Davis, J D 1924. *A Dictionary of the Bible*, Fourth Revised Edition. Grand Rapids, MI: Baker Book House.

Devine, E and Braganti N L 1995. *A Traveler's Guide to African Customs and Manners*. New York: St. Martins Press.

Dewitt, R 2004. *Worldviews: An Introduction to the History and Philosophy of Science*. Oxford: Blackwell Publishers.

Diop, C A 1974. *The African Origin of Civilization: Myth or Reality*. Chicago: Lawrence Hill Books.

Dyrness, W 1979. *Themes in Old Testament Theology*. Downers Grove, IL: InterVarsity Press.

Dzobo, N K 2006. *Knowledge and Truth: Ewe and Akan Conceptions*. Available from: http://www.africacultureonline.com/forums/showthread.php?t=9663 [Accessed 28 July 2006].

Earle, R 1984. s v 'Fear'. *Evangelical Dictionary of Theology*.

Eboussi-Boulaga, F 2000. 'The Topic of Change' in Karp, I and Masolo, D A (eds), *African Philosophy as Cultural Inquiry*, 187-214. Bloomington, IN: Indiana University Press.

Edwards, P (ed) 1967. *The Encyclopedia of Philosophy* (Eight Volumns). New York: Macmillan Publishing Co., Inc.

Ejizu, C I 2006. *Conversion in African Traditional Religion*. Available from: http://afgen.com/conversion.html [Accessed 1 September 2006].

Elwell, W A (ed) 1984. *Evangelical Dictionary of Theology*. Grand Rapids, MI: Baker Books.

Erickson, M J 2001. *The Concise Dictionary of Christian Theology*, Revised Edition. Wheaton, IL: Crossways Books.

Evans, C S 2002. *Pocket Dictionary of Apologetics & Philosophy of Religion*. Downers Grove, IL: InterVarsity Press.

Feagin, S L 1995. s v 'aesthetics'. *The Cambridge Dictionary of Philosophy*.

Feinberg, P D 1984. s v 'Bible, Inerrancy and Infallibility of'. *Evangelical Dictionary of Theology*.

Ferch, A J 1985. *In the Beginning*. Washington, DC: Review and Herald Publishing Association.

Finegan, J 1962. *In the Beginning*. New York: Harper & Brothers.

Forbes, G 1995. s v 'reality'. *The Cambridge Dictionary of Philosophy*.

Forde, D (ed) 1954. *African Worlds: Studies in the Cosmological Ideas and Social Values of African Peoples*. London: Oxford University Press.

Foullah, L A 2002. *Current Social Issues in Sierra Leone*. Freetown: Mount Aureol Publishers.

Fountain, D E 1996. Why Africa's Transformation Waits in *Evangelical Missions Quarterly* Vol 32 No 3, 320-324.

Gehman, R J 1999. *Who Are the Living-Dead?* Nariobi: Evangel Publishing House.

_____ 2005. *African Traditional Religion in Biblical Perspective*, Revised Edition. Nariobi: East Africa Educational Publishers.

Geisler, N 1976. *Christian Apologetics.* Peabody, MA: Prince Press.

Geisler, N and Brocchino, P 2001. *Unshakable Foundations.* Minneapolis, MN: Bethany House.

Geisler, N and Feinberg, P D 1980. *Introduction to Philosophy.* Grand Rapids, MI: Baker Book House.

Gittins, A J 1987. *Mende Religion: Aspects of Belief and Thought in Sierra Leone.* Nettetal: Steyler Verlag-Wort und Werk.

Guthrie, D 1981. *New Testament Theology.* Leicester, UK: InterVarsity Press.

Gyekye, K 1997. *Tradition and Modernity: Philosophical Reflections on the African Experience.* New York: Oxford University Press.

Hallen, B 2003. Ethical Knowledge in an African Philosophy in *Florida Philosophical Review*, vol III. Issue 1, Summer 2003, 81-90. Available from: http://www.cas.ucf.edu/philosophy/fpr/journals/volumn3/issue1/hallen5.pdf [Accessed 23 November 2005].

Halley, H H 1965. *Halley's Bible Handbook.* Grand Rapids: Zondervan Publishing House.

Hargreaves, J 1998. *A Guide to Genesis.* London: SPCK Publishing.

Harlow, R E 1968. *Start of the Race: Studies in Genesis.* Toronto: Everyday Publications.

Harris, M 1977. *Cannibals and Kings: The Origin of Cultures.* New York: Vantage Books.

Hiebert, P G 1983. *Cultural Anthropology.* Grand Rapids, MI: Baker Book House.

_____ 1985. *Anthropological Insights for Missionaries.* Grand Rapids, MI: Baker Book House.

_____ 1997. Conversion and Worldview Transformation. *The International Journal of Frontier Missions*, 14(2), 83-86.

Henderson, G [s a]. *Studies in Genesis.* Edinburgh, Scotland: B. McCall Barbour.

Henry, C F H 1984. s v 'Eternity'. *Evangelical Dictionary of Theology.*

Hesselgrave, D J 1984. *Counseling Cross-Culturally.* Grand Rapids, MI: Baker Book House.

_____ 1997. Worldview, Scripture and Missionary Communication. *International Journal of Frontier Missions*, 14(2), 79.

Hick, J 1973. *Philosophy of Religion*. Englewood Cliffs, NJ: Prentice-Hall, Inc.

Hobbs, H H 1975. *The Origin of All Things*. Waco, TX: Word Books.

Hordern, N 2004. Humans Are Not the Sole Intelligent, Thinking Beings On Earth. *New Africa*, No. 434, 56-58.

Horwich, P 1995. s v 'truth'. *The Cambridge Dictionary of Philosophy*.

Hountondji, P J 1996. *African Philosophy*, 2nd ed. Bloomington, IN: Indiana University Press.

Hughes, P E 1984. s v 'Myth'. *Evangelical Dictionary of Theology*.

Imasogie, O 1983. *Guidelines for Christian Theology in Africa*. Ibadan, Nigeria: University Press Limited.

Inch, M A 1984. s v 'Ethics'. *Evangelical Dictionary of Theology*.

Inyang, J 2005, *Hegel's Idea of the Absolute and African Philosophy*. Available from: http://www.frasouzu.com/Seminar%20Papers/Hegel%20 The%Absolute%20and%20African%20Philosophy.htm [Accessed 23 November 2005].

Jahn, J 1989. *Muntu: African Culture and the Western World*. New York: Grove Press.

Johnson, A G 1995. *The Blackwell Dictionary of Sociology*. Cambridge, MA: Blackwell Publishers, Inc.

Johnstone, P and Mandryk, J 2001. *Operation World, 21st Century Edition*. Waynesboro, GA: Paternoster USA.

Kamalu, C 1990. *Foundations of African Thought: A Worldview Grounded in the African Heritage of Religion, Philosophy, Science and Art*. London: Karnak House.

Karp, I and Masolo, D A (eds) 2000. *African Philosophy as Cultural Inquiry*. Bloomington, IN: Indiana University Press.

Kato, B H 1985. *Biblical Christianity in Africa*. Achimota, Ghana: African Christian Press.

Katter, R L 1967. *The History of Creation and Origin of the Species*. Minneapolis, MN: Theotes Logos Research, Inc.

Kaunda, K D 1966. *A Humanist in Africa*. Nashville, TN: Abingdon Press.

Kenyatta, J 1965. *Facing Mt. Kenya*. New York: Vintage Books.

Kidner, D 1967. *Genesis*. London: The Tyndale Press.

King, N Q 1970. *Religions of Africa*. New York: Harper & Row.

Kraft, C H 1999. 'Culture, Worldview and Contextualization', in Winter, R D and Hawthorne, S C (eds). *Perspectives on the World Christian Movement*, 3rd ed, 384–391. Pasadena, CA: William Carey Library.

Krige, J D and Krige, E J 1954. 'The Lovedu of the Transvaal' in Forde, D (ed), *African worlds: Studies in the Cosmological Ideas and Social Values of African Peoples*, 55-82. London: Oxford University Press.

Kurian, G T (ed), 2001. *Nelson's New Christian Dictionary*. Nashville, TN: Thomas Nelson Publishers.

Lacey, A R 1986. *A Dictionary of Philosophy*. London: Routledge.

Lamb, D 1987. *The Africans*. New York: Vintage Books.

Lemos, N M 1995. s v 'value theory'. *The Cambridge Dictionary of Philosophy*.

Lewis, G R 1984. s v 'God, Attributes of'. *Evangelical Dictionary of Theology*.

Lewis, R G 1991. *The Social Structure of the Pokot and Its Implications for Church Planting: A New Paradigm for Strategic African Missions*. D.Miss diss., Biola University.

Lockyer Sr, H L (ed) 1986. *Nelson's Illustrated Bible Dictionary*. Nashville, TN: Thomas Nelson Publishers.

Logan, W M 1957. *In the Beginning God: The Meaning of Genesis 1-11*. Richmond, VA: John Knox Press.

Loveless, W 1973. *What A Beginning?* Washington, DC: Review and Herald Publishing.

Macionis, J J 1989. *Sociology*, 2nd ed. Englewood Cliffs, NJ: Prentice-Hall, Inc.

Mackintosh, C H 1972. *Genesis to Deuteronomy*. Neptune, NJ: Loizeaux Brothers.

Magesa, L 1997. *African Religion: The Moral Traditions of Abundant Life*. Marynoll, NY: Orbis Books.

Makinde, M A 2005. *Whither Philosophy in Africa*. Available from: http://www.bu. edu/wcp/Papers/Afri/AfriMaki.htm [Accessed 23 November 2005].

Malony, H M 1998. *The Psychology of Religious Conversion*. Available from: http:// www.religiousfreedom.com/Conference/japan/Malony.htm [Accessed 30 August 2006].

Mandryk, J 2010. *Operation World, Seventh Edition*. Colorado Springs, CO: Biblica Publishing.

Maranz, D E 2001. *African Friends and Money Matters*. Dallas: SIL International and International Museum of Culture.

Masolo, D A 1994. *African Philosophy in Search of Identity*. Bloomington, IN: Indiana University Press.

_____ 2006. African Sage Philosophy in *The Stanford Encyclopedia of Philosophy* (Spring 2006 Edition). Available from: http://plato.stanford.edu/entries/african-sage/ [Accessed 28 July 2006].

Mbiti, J S 1969. *African Religions and Philosophy*. Garden City, NJ: Anchor Books.

_____ 1970. *Concepts of God in Africa*. London: SPCK.

_____ 1975a. *Introduction to African Religion*. Oxford: Heinemann International.

_____ 1975b. *The Prayers of African Religion*. Marynoll, NY: Orbis Books.

_____ 1986. *Bible and Theology in African Christianity*. Nairobi: Oxford University Press.

_____ 2006. *General Manifestations of African Religiosity*. Available from: www.afrikaworld.netafrel/mbiti.htm [Accessed 19 July 2006].

McFall, E A 1970. *Approaching the Nuer of Africa Through the Old Testament*. South Pasadena, CA: William Carey Library.

Meldau, F J 1969. *A Bird's-Eye View of the Bible*. Lincoln, NE: Back to the Bible Publications.

Middelmann, U 1974. *Pro-existence*. Downers Grove: InterVarsity Press.

Miller, D L 2001. *Discipling Nations, The Power of Truth to Transform Cultures*, 2nd ed. Seattle, WA: YWAM Publishing.

Minkus, H K 1979. 'Causal Theory in Akwapim Akan Philosophy' in Wight, R A (ed), *African Philosophy: An Introduction*, 2nd ed, 91-132. Washington, DC: University Press of America.

Moreland, J P and Craig W L 2003. *Philosophical Foundations for a Christian Worldview*. Downers Grove, IL: InterVarsity Press.

Moreau, S 1986. A Critique of John Mbiti's Understanding of the African Concept of Time in *East Africa Journal of Evangelical Theology*, Vol 5.2, 36-48.

Morris, H M 1976. *The Genesis Record*. Grand Rapids, MI: Baker Book House.

Mudimbe, V Y 1988. *Invention of Africa: Gnosis, Philosophy, and the Order of Knowledge*. Bloomington, IN: Indiana University Press.

_____ 1994. *The Idea of Africa (African Systems of Thought)*. Bloomington, IN: Indiana University Press.

Naugle, D K 2002. *Worldview: The History of a Concept.* Cambridge, UK: William B. Eerdmans.

New Shorter Oxford English Dictionary, 4th ed 1993. Oxford: Clarendon Press.

Nielsen, N C et al. 1988. *Religions of the World.* New York: St. Martin's Press.

Noebel, D A 1991. *Understanding the Times.* Manitou Springs, CO: Summit Press.

Noll, M A 1984. s v 'Confessions of Faith'. *Evangelical Dictionary of Theology.*

Nyamiti, C 2006. *Ancestor Veneration in Africa.* Available from: http:// www. afrikaworld.net/afrel/nyamiti.htm [Accessed 19 July 2006].

O'Donovan, W 1996. *Biblical Christianity in Africa Perspective.* Carlise, UK: Paternoster Press.

Ogunade, R 2003. *The Future of the Science Religion Dialogue in Africa* in Metanexux Views 2003.01.28. Available from: http://www.metanexus. net/metanexus_online/show_article2.asp?id=7827 [Accessed 22 July 2006].

Olela, H 1979. 'The African Foundations of Philosophy' in Wright, R A (ed). *African Philosophy: An Introduction.* Washington, DC: University Press of America.

Olsen, H 1972. *African Myths About Christianity.* Kijambe, Kenya: African Inland Church Publications.

Opoku, K A 1978. *West African Traditional Religion.* Accra, Ghana: FEP International Private Limited.

Orr, J 1948. *Christian View of God and the World as Centring in the Incarnation.* Grand Rapids, MI: Wm. B. Eerdmans Publishing Company.

Osterhaven, M E 1984. s v 'Lord's Supper, Views of'. *Evangelical Dictionary of Theology.*

Packer, J I 1984a. s v 'Faith'. *Evangelical Dictionary of Theology.*

_____ 1984b. s v 'Regeneration'. *Evangelical Dictionary of Theology.*

Parratt, J 1996. *A Guide to Doing Theology.* London: SPCK.

Parrinder. E G 1969. *Africa's Three Religions.* London: Sheldon Press.

_____ 1974. *African Traditional Religion*, 3rd ed. London: Sheldon Press.

Partain, J 1986. *Christians and Their Ancestors: A Dilemma of African Theology.* Availlable from: http://www.religion-online.org/showarticle. asp?title=1078 [Accessed 7 December 2005].

Pember, G H 1876. *Earth's Earliest Ages.* Grand Rapids, MI: Kregel Publications.

Phillips, J 1980. *Exploring Genesis.* Chicago, IL: Moody Press.

Phillips, W G and Brown, W E 1991. *Making Sense of Your World*. Chicago, IL: Moody Press.

Pink, A W 1950. *Gleanings in Genesis*. Chicago: Moody Press.

Pobee, J S 1979. *Toward an African Theology*. Nashville, TN: Abingdon.

Porcella, B 1967. s v 'Evil'. *The Zondervan Pictoral Bible Dictionary*.

Priest Jr, D 1990. *Doing Theology with the Maasai*. Pasadena, CA: William Carey Library.

Public Affairs Television 1996. *Talking About Genesis: A Resource Guide*. New York: Doubleday.

Purtill, R 1995. s v 'principle of contradiction'. *The Cambridge Dictionary of Philosophy*.

Rambo, L 1998. *The Psychology of Religious Conversion*. Available from: http://www.religiousfreedon.com/conference/Germany/rambo.htm [Accessed 30 August 2006].

Reese, W L 1980. *Dictionary of Philosophy and Religion*. Atlantic Heights, NJ: Humanities Press, Inc.

Richardson, A 1953. *Genesis 1-11*. London: SCM Press LTD.

Richmond, Y and Gestrin P 1998. *Into Africa: Intercultural Insights*. Yarmouth, ME: Intercultural Press, Inc.

Ritchie, I 2006. *Creation in African Thought*. Available from: http://www3.sympatico.ca/ian.ritchie/ATSC.Chapter3.htm [Accessed 17 July 2006].

Roberts, W D (ed) 1985. *Africa: A Season of Hope*. Ventura, CA: Regal Books.

Routley, E 1962. *Beginning the Old Testament*. Philadelphia: Muhlenberg Press.

Sahakian, W S and Sahakian, M L 1966. *Ideas of the Great Philosophers*. New York: Barnes & Noble Books.

Sanneh, L 1983. *West African Christianity: The Religious Impact*. Maryknoll, NY: Orbis Books.

Sawyerr, H 1970. *God: Ancestor or Creator: Aspects of Traditional Belief in Ghana, Nigeria, and Sierra Leone*. London: Longman Group Ltd.

Schaeffer, F A 1972a. *Genesis in Space and Time*. Downers Grove, IL: InterVarsity Press.

_____ 1972b. *He Is There and He Is Not Silent*. Wheaton: Tyndale House Publishers.

_____ 1982. *The God Who is There*, in vol 1 of *The Complete Works of Francis A. Schaeffer*. Westchester, IL: Crossway Books.

Schultz, S J 1990. *The Old Testament Speaks*, 4th ed. San Francisco: Harper & Row.

Shelley, B L 1995. *Church History in Plain Language*, Updated 2nd Edition. Dallas: TX: Word Publishing.

Shorter, A 2002. *Incultration of African Traditional Religious Values in Christianity—How Far?* Available from: http://www.afrikaworld.net/afrel/shorter.htm [Accessed 12 November 2002].

Sire, J W 1997. *The Universe Next Door: A Basic Worldview Catalog*, 3rd ed. Downers Grove, IL: InterVarsity Press.

Smart, N 1983. *Worldviews: Crosscultural Explorations of Human Beliefs*. New York: Charles Scribner's Sons.

Sow, A I et al. 1979. *Introduction to African Culture*. Paris: UNESCO.

Stott, J 1978. *The Message of The Sermon on the Mount: Christian counter-culture*. Nottingham, UK: InterVarsity Press.

_____ 1990. *The Message of Acts: To the ends of the earth*. Leicester, UK: InterVarsity Press.

Taiwo, O 2005, *Exorcising Hegel's Ghost: Africa's Challenge to Philosophy*. Available from: http://www.africa.ufl.edu/asq/v1/4/2.htm [Accessed 23 November 2005].

Tempels, P 1959. *Bantu Philosophy*. Paris: Presence Africaine.

Tenney, M C (ed) 1967. *The Zondervan Pictorial Bible Dictionary*. Grand Rapids, MI: Zondervan Publishing House.

The International Observatory on End of Life Care 2006. *Ethical Issues in Uganda*. Available from:http://www.eolc-observatory.net/global_analysis/uganda_ethical_issues.htm [Accessed 17 July 2006].

Theological Advisory Group 1994. *A Biblical Approach to Marriage and Family in Afric*a. Machakos,Kenya: Scott Theological College.

Thomas, W H G 1946. *Genesis*. Grand Rapids, MI: Wm. B. Eerdmans Publishing Co.

Thorpe, S A 1991. *African Traditional Religions*. Pretoria: University of South Africa.

Turnbull, C M 1962. *The Lonely African*. New York: Simon & Schuster.

van Dyk, P J 2001. *A Brief History of Creation*. Pretoria: Unisa Press.

Van Rheenen, G 1991. *Communicating Christ in Animistic Contexts*. Psasdena, CA: William Carey Library.

_____ 1996. *Missions: Biblical Foundations and Contemporary Strategies*. Grand Rapids, MI: Zondervan Publishing House.

Veith, G E 1994. *Guide to Contemporary Culture*. Leicester, UK: Crossway Books.

Vine, W E 1981. *Vine's Expository Dictionary of Old and New Testament Words*, NT Vol 3. Old Tappan, NJ: Fleming H. Ravell Company.

Wagner, G 1954. 'The Abaluyia of Kavirondo' in Forde, D (ed), *African Worlds: Studies in the Cosmological and Social Values of African Peoples*, 27-54. London: Oxford University Press.

Walsh, B J and Middleton, R J 1984. *The Transforming Vision*. Downers Grove, IL: InterVarsity Press.

Wanjohi, G J 1996. 'The Ontology, Epistemology, and Ethics Inherent in Proverbs: The Case of the Gikuyu' from Nussbaum, S (ed): African Proverbs, CD Rom, Colorado Springs, CO: Global Mapping International.

Weerstra, H M 1997a. Worldview, World Religion, and Missions. *International Journal of Frontier Missions*, 14(1), 1.

_____ 1997b. Christian Worldview Development. *International Journal of Frontier Missions*, 14(1), 3-11.

_____ 1997c. Worldview, Missions and Theology. *International Journal of Frontier Missions*, 14(2) 49.

_____ 1997d. Christian Worldview Development: Part II. *International Journal of Frontier Missions*, 14(2) 51-62.

Wesley, J 1872. *The Works of John Wesley*, Vol V. Grand Rapids, MI: Zondervan Publishing House.

Wiersbe, W W 1998. *Be Basic*. Colorado Springs, CO: Chariot Victor Publishing.

Wilcock, M 1979. *The Message of Luke*. Leicester,UK: InterVarsity Press.

Wilkes, P (ed) 1981. *Christianity Challenges the University*. Downers Grove, IL: InterVarsity Press.

Wiredu, K 2004. 'Truth and an African Language' in Brown, L M (ed), *African Philosophy: New and traditional Perspectives*. New York: Oxford University Press.

Wood, L J 1975. *Genesis: A Study Guide*. Grand Rapids, MI: Zondervan Publishing House.

Woodson, L 1974. *The Beginning*. Wheaton, IL: Victor Books.

Woodward, K L 2001. 'The Changing Face of the Church'. *Newsweek International Edition*, April 16, 2001, 42-48.

Wright, R A (ed) 1979. *African Philosophy: An Introduction*, 2nd ed. Washington, DC: University Press of America.

Young, W C 1954. *A Christian Approach to Philosophy*. Grand Rapids: Baker Book House.

Zamani, K 2004. 'No Matter Where You Come From, So Long as You Are Black, You Are an African.' *New Africa* No. 433, 30-36.

Langham Partnership is working to strengthen the church in the majority world. We provide doctoral scholarships for future principals and teachers at majority world seminaries and for those who will take up strategic positions of leadership in the church. We send carefully chosen evangelical books, as gifts or at low cost, to church pastors and to teachers at Bible colleges, and we foster the writing and publishing of Christian literature in many regional languages. We also run training workshops and produce materials to raise the standard of biblical preaching and teaching, and work to develop preaching networks locally. For further information see www.langham.org or email global@langham.org

Lightning Source UK Ltd.
Milton Keynes UK
UKHW021845160120
357092UK00008B/273